LAW REPORTING IN BRITAIN

EDITED BY

CHANTAL STEBBINGS

THE HAMBLEDON PRESS
LONDON AND RIO GRANDE

Published by the Hambledon Press 1995
102 Gloucester Avenue, London NW1 8HX (UK)
P.O. Box 162, Rio Grande, Ohio 45674 (USA)

ISBN 1 85285 129 5

A description of this book is available from
the British Library and from the Library of Congress

Typeset by The Midlands Book Typesetting Company
Printed on acid-free paper and bound in
Great Britain by Cambridge University Press.

Po 00162

Contents

Preface

This volume is a collection of most of the principal papers delivered at the 11th British Legal History Conference, held in July 1993 at the University of Exeter, U.K. The theme of the conference, which is reflected in this volume, was *Law Reporting*, and the volume accurately represents a coherent historical study of various aspects of the history of law reporting in Britain. The conference adhered closely to this theme; all the papers there presented dealt with some aspect of law reporting, and were selected to cover as many different aspects of the theme as possible, both in content and in chronology, while retaining academic rigour. While this volume is limited to essays on the subject of law reporting which are either entirely British in content, or have a significant British element, the conference received contributions from many eminent legal historians of both the Common Law and the Civil Law traditions. Presentations were heard from South Africa, New Zealand, Canada and the USA. Many of the papers presented but not included in this volume will appear in due course in other publications.

While there is, as the conference made clear, much current and scholarly research into the subject of law reporting, with its intimate involvement in the doctrine of judicial precedent, books dedicated to the subject are few, and most research is found in diverse legal journals. This volume seeks to address this issue and, while of course not comprehensive, does purport to cover at least one aspect of each of the principal areas of the subject. John Baker and David Seipp address the reporting of criminal cases, while Michael Macnair discusses the reporting of Chancery cases and William Gordon and Alain Wijffels explore the civilians in Britain. Modern legal history is not neglected, being the subject of the essays by Steve Hedley and Raymond Cocks. The chronological development of law reporting is discussed by Paul Brand, David Ibbetson and Hamilton Bryson, while James Oldham reflects on manuscript law reports. Indeed, as a whole, the essays reflect the long and continuous development of law in Britain, covering a period of some 600 years of law reporting.

I would like to extend my warmest thanks to all those who participated in the Conference, speakers and delegates, to make it such an enjoyable and, I hope, fulfilling occasion. It was held in that atmosphere of stimulating and friendly scholarship which is characteristic of legal historians, with old friends and colleagues reunited, debates resumed. I would also like to take this opportunity to thank the University of Exeter for hosting the conference, and to thank warmly the *Journal of Legal History*, Oxford University Press, Cambridge University Press, the Society of Public Teachers of Law and the University of Exeter for their generous, and much appreciated, financial support. We all eagerly await the next conference to be held in Durham in 1995.

Chantal Stebbings

Exeter, June 1994

List of Contributors

Professor John H. Baker	St Catharine's College, Cambridge
Dr Paul Brand	Institute of Historical Research, London
Professor W. Hamilton Bryson	School of Law, University of Richmond, Virginia, USA
Professor Raymond Cocks	University of Keele
Professor William M. Gordon	School of Law, University of Glasgow
Steve Hedley	Christ's College, Cambridge
Dr David J. Ibbetson	Magdalen College, Oxford
Dr Michael Macnair	Law Division, Southampton Institute of Higher Education
Professor James Oldham	Georgetown University Law Center, Washington DC, USA
Professor David J. Seipp	Boston University School of Law, Boston, USA
Professor Alain Wijffels	Faculty of Law, University of Leiden, Netherlands

The British Legal History Conference

The first British Legal History Conference was held in 1972 in Aberystwyth, on the initiative of Professor Daffyd Jenkins. Since then there have been meetings at London/Cambridge (1974 and 1975), Edinburgh (1977), Birmingham (1979), Bristol (1981), Norwich (1983), Canterbury (1985), Cardiff (1987), Glasgow (1989) and Oxford (1991). The Conference has become established as a leading forum for the discussion of all aspects of the history of law.

Proceedings of the Conference have been published as follows:

Legal History Studies 1972, ed. D. Jenkins (University of Wales Press, Cardiff, 1975)

Legal Record and the Historian, ed. J.H. Baker (Royal Historical Society, London, 1978)

Law, Litigants and the Legal Profession, ed. E.W. Ives and A.H. Manchester (Royal Historical Society, London, 1983)

Customs, Courts and Counsel, ed. A. Kiralfy, M. Slatter and R. Virgoe, in *Journal of Legal History*, 5 (1984), and as a separate volume (Frank Cass, London, 1985)

The Political Context of Law, ed. Richard Eales and David Sullivan (The Hambledon Press, London, 1987)

Legal Record and Historical Reality, ed. Thomas G. Watkin (The Hambledon Press, London and Ronceverte, WV, 1989)

Legal History in the Making, ed. W.M. Gordon and T.D. Fergus (The Hambledon Press, London and Rio Grande, OH, 1991)

The Life of the Law, ed. Peter Birks (The Hambledon Press, London and Rio Grande, OH, 1993)

1

The Beginnings of English Law Reporting

Paul Brand

The first English law reports were compiled during the final years of the reign of Henry III. By the early 1290s the first collections of reports of cases heard during particular terms in the Common Bench and of cases heard during particular eyre sessions were being compiled. The practice of law reporting had become well established by the end of the reign of Edward I.

Reports from this earliest stage of English law reporting survive in at least forty-six different MSS. Comparatively little of their content is as yet available in print. Some reports belonging to this period were printed, albeit in severely truncated form, in Sir Anthony Fitzherbert's *La Graunde Abridgement* of 1514–16. During the great age of Year Book publishing printers found a ready market for Year Books of the reign of Edward III but fought shy of printing earlier reports. Year Books of the reign of Edward II were eventually put into print in 1678. A further two centuries were to elapse before publication of the reports of the reign of Edward I began.

Between 1863 and 1879 Alfred John Horwood edited five volumes of reports belonging to the reign of Edward I as part of the Rolls Series. Horwood's work made a substantial body of reports available in print in what are reasonably accurate and intelligent texts. There were two main defects in his work. Horwood took all his reports from just four MSS and did not make full use even of those MSS.[1] He was, moreover, quite uncritical in accepting the ascriptions of cases to particular courts and dates given in the subheadings of his manuscripts. He made no attempt to check whether or not these were accurate or even to ascertain to how much of the succeeding text they applied. The only sure way of doing this is by finding the plea-roll enrolments which correspond to the reports, a practice pioneered by his successor Pike in his Rolls Series edition of *Y.B. 12 & 13 Edward III* in 1885. It should still have been clear to Horwood, if only from the names of the justices mentioned in the reports, that some

---

[1] When two or more of his manuscripts reported the same case he did not attempt to collate the different versions found in the various manuscripts. He did not even print the wholly independent reports of the same case which they sometimes contained.

of the reports he printed and assigned to particular courts and dates could not have come from them.[2]

Horwood edited no reports of a date earlier than 1292.[3] He was certainly aware that at least one of his four MSS contained earlier reports.[4] All four of the MSS he used in fact contain earlier reports.[5] No such reports found their way into print until 1952 when W.H. Dunham Jr published two collections of reports, copies of enrolments and notes drawn mainly from two different MSS now in the British Library and dating from the final years of the reign of Henry III and the first six years of the reign of Edward I as part of a Selden Society volume.[6]

The reports of the period prior to 1307 currently available in print are thus drawn in the main from just six out of the forty-six surviving MSS known to contain such reports and many, and perhaps a majority, of the reports of the same period even in those six MSS remain as yet unpublished. I have been working for some years on the entire corpus of pre-1307 reports and have made substantial progress in transcribing and identifying the reports which they contain. Volumes I and II of *The Earliest English Law Reports*, which will contain all the reports which can be identified as being of Common Bench cases and of a date earlier than 1290, should appear as a Selden Society volume in 1995. I want here to look at the wider corpus of surviving pre-1307 reports and to attempt to find answers to a series of related questions. I will try to establish when law reporting began and what form the earliest surviving reports took; when the practice of making collections of termly law reports and reports of cases heard in particular eyres first developed and why; the relationship between chronologically arranged collections and other collections arranged on a topical basis; who compiled reports and for what purposes; and to what uses reports were put.

---

[2] Many of the reports Horwood assigned to the 1293–94 Middlesex eyre contain the names of justices who did not sit in that eyre. Some even contain the names of justices who had died or were out of office by the time that eyre was held: see e.g. *YB 21 & 22 Edward I*, pp. 429–33 (case heard before Saham, one of the justices disgraced in 1290), 483–85 (case heard before Gisleham, a justice of the Common Bench who died early in 1293).

[3] This is not entirely true. The earliest reports he knew he was editing belonged to that year. Among the reports he printed as belonging to the 1294 Middlesex eyre, however, there are individual Common Bench reports from various terms in 1290 (*YB 21 & 22 Edward I* at pp. 399–407, 433–45) and a whole section of reports from Michaelmas term 1291 (*YB 21 & 22 Edward I* at pp. 477–605). There is also a report which must be from the 1280s at *YB 21 & 22 Edward I*, pp. 429–33 and two further reports from the 1280s among the reports Horwood printed as belonging to the 1302 Cornwall eyre (*YB 30 & 31 Edward I*, pp. 279–85).

[4] *YB 20 & 21 Edward I*, p. xv.

[5] The other three MSS have earlier reports in those sections where the reports are arranged topically rather than chronologically. Horwood noted the existence of these sections but made no attempt to identify or edit their contents.

[6] *Casus Placitorum and Reports of Cases in the King's Courts, 1272–1278* (69 Selden Soc.).

Over 300 cases heard prior to 1290 are the subject of surviving reports. There are reports of just over 140 Common Bench cases and of a slightly larger number of General Eyre cases. Most of the latter come from the 'northern' eyre circuit of 1278–88. There are also two reports of cases in the Exchequer of the Jews, around fifty reports of assizes heard before a variety of justices and a number of reports which cannot as yet be identified as coming from any particular court.

The earliest English law report so far identified comes from Michaelmas term 1268. It is of a case brought by writ of entry in the Common Bench. The serjeants and justices involved are not named,[7] and the report records their interchange in the form of indirectly reported speech ascribed to the parties concerned, just like a plea roll enrolment.[8] The language of the report is Latin but it is not the smooth Latin of the clerks who made the plea roll enrolments. The reporter also preserves much more of the unsuccessful arguments subsequently discarded by the parties than was normal in enrolments. This is the first in a sequence of five entries relating to specific cases heard in the Common Bench in Michaelmas term 1268 which was copied, probably by mistake, into a fifteenth century MS now in the Huntington Library in California.[9] None of the other entries is a law report in quite the same sense, though at least one other entry does record (albeit in indirect speech) some of the dialogue between the parties.[10] From not much later comes a short section of notes and reports copied into Cambridge University Library MS Dd.7.14.[11] It contains eleven entries. Some are certainly case-derived. A majority merely summarise a single point of law. Three do, however, give us (although in Latin and in indirect, reported speech) some of the dialogue between parties to litigation which resemble, but are done with rather more skill than, the 1268 report. One can probably be identified as the report of a case heard in the 1269 Northamptonshire eyre.[12] Another is a report of a case heard in the Common Bench in Hilary term 1272.[13] A third refers to the opinion of Richard of Middleton, probably an opinion given while he was acting as the senior justice of an eyre circuit in 1268–69 on a circuit which included Northamptonshire.

---

[7] Only the heading identifies the case as having been heard in the fifty-second regnal year (of Henry III) before Martin of Littlebury.

[8] This will be 1268.1 in vol. I of *The Earliest English Law Reports*. All other such references are likewise to reports to be published in that volume or vol. II of *The Earliest English Law Reports*.

[9] San Marino, CA, Huntington Library, MS HM 19920, fos 40r–42r.

[10] 1268.4.

[11] At fos 358r–359r.

[12] This is the report at the bottom of fol. 358v and top of 359r. It only uses first names but the count used and the facts of the case are sufficiently distinctive to show that it is the same case as that of which only the initial count was copied into CUL, MS LI.4.18, fol. 189v (which gives the full names of the parties and the place concerned).

[13] 1272.1.

The latest example of this type of early report so far found is of a case of 1287. It was always comparatively uncommon.[14] A second type of early report takes the form of French dialogue in direct speech ascribed to the parties involved (rather than to the serjeants who actually spoke for them) and to wholly anonymous justices. The first undoubted example is of a case heard in the 1272 Lincolnshire eyre,[15] and reports of this kind remain not uncommon throughout the period down to 1290.[16] There are also a number of reports of generally similar form but with the speaker of a single speech identified as a particular serjeant or justice.[17]

The third main type of early report resembles the second in giving in direct speech at least part of what was said in court but also identifies at least some, though generally not all, of the lawyers, judges and clerks who are participants in the case. The earliest identified report of this kind (the classic form of Year Book report) comes from a collection of reports mainly of the 1280s in Cambridge University Library MS Dd.7.14.[18] It is a report of a Common Bench case heard in Michaelmas term 1270.[19] The same collection also includes a similar report of a second case from the 1272 Lincolnshire eyre.[20] Three other unidentified reports of the same kind probably dating from before 1273 are printed by Dunham in *Casus placitorum*.[21] Reports of this kind are by far the most common type of report even in this early period of law reporting. The vast majority are in French. A small minority are in Latin.[22]

Most of the thirty-nine MSS which contain pre-1290 reports contain no more than a handful of such reports. Only five MSS contain more

---

[14] For other Common Bench examples see 1273.1; 1276.2 (ii); 1276.7 (ii) (with one passage of direct speech); pre-1279.2 (ii); pre-1279.3 (i); pre-1279.4; 1283.4; 1283.5 (ii); 1287.4 (i); 1287.7 (iii); 1278-89.23. For a report of similar form but in French see 1284.15.

[15] *Casus placitorum*, Collection I, no. 9 (at pp. 65–67). It is not identified by Dunham but is a report of the case enrolled on JUST 1/483, m. 40d.

[16] For examples of reports of Common Bench cases of this type see 1274.1; 1274.2; 1275.2; 1275.4; 1275.5 (i), (ii); 1277.3; 1277.5; pre-1279.1; pre-1279.3 (ii); 1279.3; 1283.3; 1285.5 (i); 1278-89.17 (ii). Of these 1275.5 (i), 1277.5 and 1278-89.17 (ii) also have preliminary explanations of the relevant facts; 1279.3 has a single speech ascribed to 'le contur Willem'.

[17] For examples of Common Bench reports of this kind see 1276.4 (single speech ascribed to Alan of Walkingham); 1277.1 (single speech ascribed to Master Roger of Seaton); 1283.5 (i) (single speech ascribed to William of Bereford); 1283.9 (judgment ascribed to Brompton); 1284.5 (single speech ascribed to Bocking); 1288.3 (single speech ascribed to Thomas Weyland); 1278–89.7 (judgment ascribed to Weyland).

[18] At fos 369v–394v.

[19] 1270.2.

[20] As fos 370v–371r. The case reported is one enrolled on JUST 1/483, m. 30. There is a related (but inferior) version of the same report in BL, MS. Add. 5925 at fol. 58r.

[21] *Casus placitorum*, Collection I, nos 18, 21–22 (pp. 77–78, 79–81).

[22] For examples of Common Bench reports of this kind in Latin see 1283.1; 1283.6 (ii).

than thirty. In three of these five the pre-1290 reports are found in topical collections which also include a much larger number of reports of a later date. These collections cannot have been put together before the early fourteenth century. Most of the reports in Lincoln's Inn MS Miscellaneous 87, for example, are of cases heard in the Common Bench during the chief justiceship of John of Mettingham (1290–1301) and the latest cases are from the 1302 Cornish eyre.[23] In the two remaining MSS, which contain the largest number of such reports, the pre-1290 reports form part of miscellaneous collections from the 1270s and 1280s arranged in no particular chronological order. The pre-1290 reports in British Library, MS Royal 10.A.V. all come from a single section of the MS.[24] The Common Bench reports are mainly of cases heard during 1283 and 1284.[25] The eyre reports are mainly of cases heard in the 1284 Leicestershire eyre and the 1285 Warwickshire and Northamptonshire eyres. The *incipit* and *explicit* of this section suggest that the collection was copied into the MS some time after Hengham had become chief justice of the Common Bench (in Michaelmas term 1301) and by or for someone who did not know that these were old reports being passed off as new ones. It was, however, probably put together originally in or shortly after 1286, the date of the last identified material which it contains. Cambridge University Library, MS Dd.7.14, however, is our richest source of pre-1290 reports. It contains forty-eight pre-1290 Common Bench reports and sixty-nine pre-1290 eyre reports. Most come from two specific sections of the MS. The strengths of the first of these sections[26] are very similar to those of BL, MS Royal 10.A.V. Although there is some grouping of cases from particular periods or even particular eyres,[27] the overall arrangement is not chronological. There is some 1290 material in this section but it looks as though it may be a later addition to a collection originally put together in or shortly after 1286. The second substantial section is more varied,[28] but its largest single identifiable element consists of thirteen reports of cases heard during the 1289 Wiltshire eyre.[29] Again there is no obvious sign of either a chronological or a topical arrangement of cases. A single reporter may have been responsible for most of the reports in both sections.

Legal historians interested in the beginning of law reporting have, not surprisingly, looked for the precursors of these early reports. They have focussed special attention on two educational works compiled in

[23] The other similar MSS are BL, MSS Add. 5925 and 35116.

[24] At fos 91v–118v. It also contains notes and copies of enrolments.

[25] There are also reports of cases of 1277, 1281 and 1286.

[26] At fos 369v–394v.

[27] There is a sequence of eight Common Bench cases all from 1283–4 at fos 373v–375r and a sequence of eight cases all from the 1284 Leicestershire eyre at fos 380r–382v.

[28] At fos 396v–409v.

[29] Reports of cases identifiable as coming from this eyre are at fos 400v, 400v–401r, 402r (two), 405v–406r, 406r–v, 408r (two), 403r (two), 408v (two), 409r–v.

or shortly before 1260.[30] *Casus placitorum*, the earlier of the two, is a miscellaneous collection of legal notes which survives in a number of different manuscripts. These share much common material but differ widely from each other. A small number of the notes in the *Casus* do seem to be directly derived from real cases and have something of the exchange of arguments or allegations which are the basic and most fundamental characteristic of the Year Book report. A few ascribe the eventual judgement to a particular named justice. One even records more than one point raised in pleading in a particular case. However, such notes only form a small proportion of the *Casus* and none of the 'reports' amount to more than a few lines of text. Nor are any of the arguments reported in the form of direct speech or ascribed to particular serjeants. A few of these notes can then be seen as distant precursors of our early reports (and more particularly of the two variant early forms of law report). They seem, however, to represent a significantly earlier stage in the process of evolution of the report.

Where we do get what sounds like real courtroom dialogue is in *Brevia placitata*. John Baker has recently suggested that this dialogue may not be, as Maitland thought, more or less imaginary but that it may be 'based on real cases, albeit with the details removed'.[31] This is an attractive hypothesis but one difficult to test in the absence of that identifying detail.[32] Some of the factual situations presupposed in the cases were so commonplace that it is difficult to believe that the dialogue needed to be taken from any specific case.[33] Others look more plausibly special but raise other difficulties. Are we really to believe in a case brought by the writ of right *de racionabili parte* in which it was alleged that the defendant was a bastard born before the marriage of his parents and the *bishop* was instructed to enquire into this point?[34] This would only be plausible if the compiler was using his knowledge of a case heard before 1236, not in any case heard after that date.[35] There are also difficulties about accepting as genuine the long *ne vexes* case with its intricate argument about the obligation of suit of court found in at least seven of the MSS of *Brevia placitata* (and which, if genuine, must date from before the legislation on suit of court

[30] The relevant literature is reviewed by John Baker in 'Records, Reports and the Origins of Case-Law in England', in Baker (ed.), *Judicial Records, Law Reports and the Growth of Case Law* (Berlin, 1989), pp. 15–46 at p. 18.

[31] Ibid., p. 18.

[32] There is also a further difficulty. The compilers of *Brevia Placitata* are most likely to have drawn on cases heard during the second half of the 1250s. Most of the plea rolls for that period do not survive.

[33] For examples see the passages of dialogue which follow the writ of dower *unde nichil habet: Brevia placitata*, pp. 5–6, 45–46; the writ of *precipe in capite: Brevia placitata*, pp. 53–54, 163–64.

[34] *Brevia placitata*, pp. 7–8, 48–49, 159–60.

[35] Thorne, *Bracton*, iii, pp. xiv–xvii.

of 1259).[36] This supposes that the socage wardship of an infant would be granted by a lord's court to a paternal uncle who was already in possession of the other share of the inheritance, in breach of a long-standing and apparently generally observed rule that socage wardships be held only by relatives who could not inherit the land concerned. The dialogue in *Brevia placitata* was clearly written by someone well-acquainted with the verbal formulas used in the courts and in its dialogue we can probably hear the voices of the professional lawyers and justices of the 1250s, but I am not convinced that all or even any of the dialogue represents even edited versions of actual courtroom discussions.

Some early law reports were themselves also certainly used to teach law. The earliest identified law report (of a Common Bench case of Michaelmas term 1268) has at the end what seems to be a teacher's comment on the case. The fifth note in this same sequence, after giving the general principle illustrated and established by the case, goes on to point out the rule which the case shows. It seems likely that these reports and notes were being used in teaching not long after the cases were heard. They now survive only in a fifteenth-century MS but in none of the three entries where there is a reference to the regnal year when the case was heard (the fifty-second regnal year of King Henry III) is the king concerned specified.[37] This indicates that the original text was compiled before the end of Henry's reign. Nor was it just the earliest surviving reports that were used for this purpose. A substantial minority of pre-1290 reports have at some point (often at the beginning) a *casus* (a statement of facts relevant to the case) which is most likely to have been the work of a teacher trying to explain the case to his students.[38] We are also clearly hearing a later teacher in a comment intruded into the middle of a report of a replevin case of 1285 and in two notes at the end of the same report.[39]

Some pre-1290 law reports were, then, used for educational purposes. This does not prove that all the reports of this period were compiled with educational purposes in mind. Serjeants involved in litigation might well have found it helpful to possess some kind of *aide-memoire* of what had been said in court, particularly if the litigation itself took place over several days. There is at least one reference from the 1280s to one of the serjeants possessing a clerk who might have kept such a record.[40] Clients might well have expected their attorneys to tell them what had been said in court by their serjeants, by their opponents and by the justices. Those same

---

[36] *Brevia placitata*, pp. 133–36, 219–21.

[37] 1268.1; 1268.2; 1268.5.

[38] For examples see 1275.5 (i); 1277.5; 1283.9; 1283.10; 1284.4 (i); 1287.3 (i); 1288.2; 1278–89.17 (ii); 1278–89.21 (i).

[39] 1285.5 (i).

[40] CP 40/50, m. 53d (deed delivered to Henry Warner, the clerk of Alexander of Coventry).

attorneys might also be called upon to avow or disavow what had been
said by 'their' serjeants. This meant they needed to follow what was said in
court.[41] They also had the requisite opportunity.[42] An attorney involved in
the litigation seems by far the most likely author for a report which follows
a case from the 1285 Northamptonshire eyre into the Common Bench the
following year.[43] The same is also true of a report which covers in detail
both what happened in a Common Bench case in 1287 and the subsequent
and related King's Bench error proceedings three years later.[44]

Nor was it just the lawyers involved in the case who might need their own
record. The clerks of the court who were to prepare the official enrolled
(and generally highly compressed) version of what had been said must
have needed to make their own rough first draft of the enrolment. Some
of these rough drafts, and even some of the drafts produced in subsequent
intermediate stages, may well have found their way into circulation among
these early reports. This would explain some of the Latin reports which
are in indirect speech but do not have the polish of the related plea roll
enrolments.[45] A particularly strong case can be made for a Latin report of
a *quare impedit* case of 1283. This is difficult to follow because the reporter
has failed to notice and fully record the intervention and involvement of
a third, rival claimant to the same advowson. Exactly the same problem
arises (and for exactly the same reason) in the plea roll enrolment of the
same case.[46] There were other reasons for clerks associated with the court
to keep their own record of what had been said. A substantial proportion of
early reports are of cases adjourned for judgement. When this happened
the justices may simply have relied on the plea roll enrolment in their
subsequent private discussion of the point at issue or they may have relied
on the memories of the justices involved in the hearing. A third possibility
is that what they actually used was an unofficial record of what had been
said made for them by their clerks. Some of our reports may have had
their origins in such unofficial reports.

When cases were adjourned for judgment justices also sometimes consulted
the justices of other courts before giving judgment.[47] Some of our reports
may have had their origin in reports of cases sent to those other justices for

---

[41] P. Brand, *The Origins of the English Legal Profession*, (Oxford, 1992) pp. 98–100.

[42] Ibid., p. 87.

[43] 1286.3 (ii). A different set of serjeants were used by the litigants in the Common
Bench. The author of this report also knew the reasons for the eventual non-suit of the
plaintiff. See also 1275.4 and 1275.5 where the authors of the reports knew both what
had been said in pleading in the 1275 Worcestershire eyre and of the eventual judgment
given in the cases concerned in the Common Bench.

[44] 1287.3 (i) (though at least one serjeant (Higham) was present at both stages).

[45] For what look like possible examples see 1276.2 (i) (an incomplete report); 1276.7
(ii); pre-1279.2 (ii); pre-1279.3 (i); 1287.7 (iii).

[46] 1283.1.

[47] P. Brand, *The Making of the Common Law*, (London, 1992) pp. 393–98.

their advice. One plausible example is a French report of a case heard in
the 1284 Leicestershire eyre. This gets the names of the parties completely
correct and notes the adjournment of the case for judgment. At the end it
has a brief and authoritative note in Latin which looks like a response to
a request for advice on the point at issue:

> 'I say that the [verdict of the] inquisition which was taken should not prejudice
> John junior since they were not parties to a plea because the king was seised
> of the manor at the time.'[48]

Reports from the second half of Edward I's reign are almost ten times as
numerous as those for the period prior to 1290. It is also from shortly after
1290 that there come the first surviving collections of reports belonging
to particular Common Bench terms or particular sessions of the General
Eyre.

Collections of eyre reports specifically ascribed to particular eyres survive
for each of the eyres on the 'southern' eyre circuit of 1292–94, for the
1299 Cambridgeshire and Isle of Ely eyres and for the 1302 Cornish
eyre. Most exist in only a single MS, although there are four surviving
MSS of the 1302 Cornish eyre. Horwood edited most of these collections
but did not know of the reports of the 1293–94 Kent eyre,[49] or of the
1299 Cambridgeshire and Isle of Ely eyre.[50]

The earliest surviving collection of Common Bench reports from a
particular term belong to Michaelmas term 1291. Horwood edited these
as part of the enormous collection of reports he wrongly ascribed to the
1294 Middlesex eyres.[51] Horwood also edited Common Bench reports for
Hilary term 1292 and for Easter and Trinity terms 1293.[52] During the
first half of the 1290s, however, there also existed an alternative form
of chronological collection, one which mixed together reports from two
consecutive terms. Among the reports printed by Horwood as belonging
to Easter term 1293 are two such collections: one of reports belonging to
Hilary and Easter terms in 1292[53] and another of reports belonging to
Trinity and Michaelmas terms of the same year.[54] There is another and
quite different sequence of reports mainly from these last two terms in BL,

---

[48] CUL, MS Dd.7.14, fos 381r–v.

[49] BL, MS Add. 37657, fos 67v–79v.

[50] BL MS Stowe 386, fos 99r–108v.

[51] The sequence is printed at pp. 453–605 of *YB 21 & 22 Edward I*. It is interrupted by
at least one report from the following Hilary term (*YB 21 & 22 Edward I*, p. 495) and by a
report from Easter term 1293 (ibid., p. 577–87). There is another report from Michaelmas
term 1291 at *YB 21 & 22 Edward I*, pp. 419–27.

[52] *YB 20 & 21 Edward I*, pp. 297–369; *YB 21 & 22 Edward I*, pp. 3–297.

[53] *YB 21 & 22 Edward I*, pp. 47–95.

[54] *YB 21 & 22 Edward I*, pp. 95–151.

MS Additional 31826,[55] and a similar collection of reports from Easter and Trinity terms 1295 in BL, MS Additional 37657.[56]

After this initial flowering of the termly or bi-termly report form, there is a gap in the surviving termly collections until Michaelmas term 1298. Four different collections of reports survive for this term.[57] There is then a further short interval without such collections until Michaelmas term 1299. From then until the end of the reign of Edward I there survives a continuous flow of termly law reports. For most terms there is more than one surviving collection. Indeed, for Michaelmas term 1302, there are as many as six different collections.[58] Horwood printed reports for some, though not all, of these terms but he only used three of the eight MSS now known to contain chronological collections from this period. There is thus an urgent need for a new edition of even those Year Books which Horwood did edit, as well as for a scholarly text of the reports of those terms for which reports survive but which Horwood's edition omitted.

The beginning of these strictly chronological collections coincides with a noticeable increase in the number of reports surviving from any one term or eyre. For no Common Bench term prior to 1290 have I been able to find more than seven reported cases,[59] and there is only one eyre session prior to 1290 (the 1285 Northamptonshire eyre) for which there survive as many as thirty-three reported cases.[60] It seems possible that chronological collections started to be made and to circulate simply because more cases from any one term or any one eyre session were being reported. This may in turn reflect the fact that the courts themselves were now for the first time providing special facilities for reporting. The first known reference to the 'crib', an enclosure set aside for the use of the apprentices, comes in a petition from the apprentices to the king dating from early in the reign of Edward II. This specifically describes the purpose of the 'crib' as being 'for the education of [the petitioners]' and asks permission to set up a second 'crib' on the other side of the court. There is no hint that the existing 'crib' has only recently been erected and the fact that the body of apprentices had clearly outgrown the first 'crib' suggests that it had probably been established some years earlier, when the body of apprentices present in

---

55 At fos 54v–60v.

56 At fos 99r–106v.

57 BL, MSS Add. 31826, fos 152r–154r; 37657, fos 111r–113r; IT MS Misc. 1, fos 1r–2v; CUL, MS Ee.6.18, fos 9r–10r.

58 Horwood printed reports for this term from LI, MS Hale 188 (*YB 30 & 31 Edward I*), pp. 3–71. There are also reports for this term in BL, MS Add. 37657 at fos 186v–192r; BL, MS Stowe 386 at fos 157r–168v; LI MS Misc. 738 at fos 31r–v, 29r–v, 33r–35r (the original order); BL, MS Add. 31826 at fos 170v–183v; CUL, MS Ee.6.18, fos 70r–75r (?).

59 Seven cases heard in Trinity term 1284 are reported. No one MS contains more than three reports.

60 No one MS contains more than twenty of these reports.

the court had been substantially smaller.[61] Perhaps it dates back to *c.* 1290. We may thus owe the beginning of the chronological collections to the provision by the court of somewhere set aside for the reporters where they could do their work.

The law reports of this period also survive in collections organised not on a chronological but on a topical basis, by form of action or related types of form of action. These collections are the main source for reports of those 'missing' terms of the 1290s for which no chronological collections survive.[62] They also contain important variant texts, indeed sometimes quite different versions, or reports of cases also found in the chronological collections. Some MSS consist wholly of topical collections of reports of this kind.[63] Others contain a mixture of chronological and topical collections. Lincoln's Inn, MS Miscellaneous 738, for example, has a first section (at fos 1–52) which contains chronologically arranged reports and a second section (at fos 53r–122r) which contains mainly topically arranged sections.[64] As with other topically arranged sections the main ingredient is reports from the Common Bench from the period when John of Mettingham was chief justice of the court (1290–1301) but there is at least one report of a case heard as late as Michaelmas term 1305. This report is not duplicated in the chronological collection ascribed to that term and there is other evidence to suggest that some preliminary work had been done on the cases in the chronological sections in preparation for their rearrangement within the topical sections. It is unlikely to be coincidence that the sequence of reports for Easter term 1305 has a run of eleven consecutive replevin or related cases (at fos 39r–v); still less likely that mere chance so arranged it that within the section of reports for Michaelmas term 1305 there are sequences of nine consecutive replevin reports, followed by seven consecutive debt reports, followed by four consecutive dower reports, followed by six consecutive entry reports and then three consecutive account reports (at fos 39v–41v). Clearly the process of rearranging reports into topical sections was left unfinished. What we have is a collection frozen at a particular point in the rearranging

[61] SC 8/189, no. 9409, printed by Turner in *YBB 3 & 4 Edward II*, p. xlii. For another early reference to the 'crib' see *YB 2 & 3 Edward II*, ed. F.W. Maitland (19 Selden Soc., 1904), pp. xv–xvi.

[62] Reports have been identified in these collections from every Common Bench term after 1289 other than Trinity term 1298. This was the first term after the Common Bench moved from Westminster to York and the plea roll for the term indicates that much less business than usual was transacted during it.

[63] These include the two closely related BL, MSS Add. 35116 and Harley 25; BL, MS Harley 2183 and LI, MS Hale 174. BL, MS. Additional 32088 is similarly arranged but its reports are abridgements and not full reports. The reports in BL, MSS Harley 493A and 493B (originally a single MS) are also arranged topically but are interspersed among related material drawn from registers of writs and instructional treatises.

[64] There are, however, also miscellaneous sequences of reports and copies of enrolments at fos 94v–96r, 100r–v, 102v–105v, 107r–v, 115r, 121r–122v.

process. Something similar can also be observed in another Lincoln's Inn
MS, Miscellaneous 87. None of the topical collections is earlier than the
first decade of the fourteenth century. It seems probable, therefore, that
this form of arrangement only became fashionable a decade or so later
than the beginning of the strictly chronological reports. Our evidence
also suggests that the topical collections were themselves created through
a process of rearranging what were originally chronologically arranged
reports. This in turn suggests that where the only surviving reports of
particular cases and particular terms come from these topical collections
they bear mute witness to the existence of lost chronological collections for
the terms concerned.

The reports compiled during this period were certainly used, like their
predecessors, for the teaching of law. This is clearly true of the earliest
termly collection of reports we now have, from Michaelmas term 1291,
which has several examples of the explanatory *casus* or statement of
relevant facts,[65] incorporates a number of explanatory comments and
notes on points established or illustrated by the cases;[66] it even has
one general piece of rather bland advice for those preparing to speak
in court.[67] The collection of reports from Hilary term 1292 printed by
Horwood provides even clearer evidence. It incorporates a number of
notes which (while possibly inspired by a case heard during that term) in
their current form are clearly the words of a teacher talking to a class.[68]
If I am right about the connexion between the beginning of the termly
or two-termly collections of reports and the establishment of a 'crib' for
apprentices,[69] then it seems likely that many of our reports were also
compiled for educational purposes: perhaps both for the self-education
of the 'reporters' and for their future use in teaching other learners around
the courts at Westminster or in York.

But even after 1290 this may not explain the origins of all our reports.
One of the lawyers involved in the litigation seems the most likely source
for a report of an annuity case which not merely records what was said in
the Common Bench in Hilary term 1292, and the jury verdict delivered
the following Michaelmas term, but also notes what was said before the
king's council by Chief Justice Mettingham and counsel for both sides at
the Easter or Michaelmas Parliament of 1293 and the terms of the eventual
settlement.[70] It is also most likely that it was one of the lawyers involved
who knew what had been said in preliminary meetings of the serjeants
employed by one of the litigants in three cases reported in 1304 and

[65] *YB 21 & 22 Edward I*, pp. 493, 531, 535, 559, 571.

[66] E.g. *YB 21 & 22 Edward I*, p. 489 (feoffatus fuit de serviciis et hoc est notabile ut patet in fine).

[67] *YB 21 & 22 Edward I*, p. 567.

[68] *YB 20 & 21 Edward I*, pp. 301–3, 303, 303–5, 319–21.

[69] Above, pp. 10–11.

[70] BL, MS Add. 35116, fos 267r–v (report of case enrolled on CP 40/92, m. 95).

1306.[71] There was in any case an overlap between the lawyers involved in litigation and the apprentices of the court, for apprentices did on occasion act as attorneys.[72]

Nor is it implausible that some of the post-1290 reports are the work of clerks associated with the justices of the court. A number certainly look like by-products of the drafting process. Take for example a Latin 'report' of a Michaelmas 1290 replevin case: it gives the avowry and much of the subsequent argument in the case in language almost identical to that of the plea roll but omits the initial count and also records an additional argument made by the plaintiff in answer to the avowry. It concludes with a judgment specifically ascribed to Chief Justice Mettingham. Its language is very close to that of the anonymous judgment recorded on the plea roll, but it omits the second part of the justification for the judgment recorded on the plea roll.[73] Another report of the same case ascribes the judgment given in court to one of the junior justices, Robert of Hartforth.[74] The first report perhaps comes from a clerk associated with Chief Justice Mettingham and may show him drafting a judgment which was eventually given (though in a modified form) by one of his junior colleagues. It also seems most likely to have been a clerk who knew that when a *nisi prius* verdict was returned into the Common Bench in Michaelmas term 1304 Howard J. (before whom the verdict was given) was questioned about it by Hengham, who thought the jury needed to be reexamined on a particular point. The reporter also knew that Bereford did not think this was necessary. It seems unlikely that any of this took place in open court.[75]

There are references in both published and unpublished reports of the reign of Edward I to the need for uniformity in the law, as applied in different cases, and to the judges' awareness that the decision they made in one particular case might determine the law applied in similar cases in the future. In a Common Bench report of 1287, for example, we find Bereford addressing the court as a serjeant and saying, 'Sir, I have seen the same adjudged before you yourselves in this court and there should be but one law for all men of the kingdom'. Chief Justice Weyland responded, 'You are certainly wrong. If that be so tell us between which parties'.[76] We also find counsel and justices referring to specific cases and the decisions made in them as relevant to, if not determining, the case now under discussion. Thus in a 1296 case we see Serjeant Higham saying 'in answer to what you have said that he cannot join in the litigation because he has not been prayed in aid and is not a party to the plea we tell you

[71] Brand, *Origins of the English Legal Profession*, p. 96.
[72] Ibid., pp. 113–16.
[73] BL, MS Harley 25, fos 4v–5r (= BL, MS Add. 35116, fos 150r–v).
[74] BL, MS Add. 31826, fos 362r–v.
[75] BL, MS Add. 31826, fol. 345r.
[76] 1287.7 (ii).

that he can join in as you yourselves saw when John of Breckles and his wife Sara joined with their tenant in demesne to disclaim holding of Sir Robert Veel'.[77] Counsel's knowledge of past decisions seems not to come from reading law reports. Past cases are normally referred to as having been 'heard' or 'seen'. 'Seeing' seems to refer to being physically present in court and 'seeing' legal proceedings rather than 'reading' a report of them. The written word was only clearly relevant in those cases where the judges decided to look for past precedents by looking through old plea rolls. However, even in those cases where the reference is to 'hearing' or 'seeing' cases, it is not certain that we are not dealing with a misleadingly metaphorical phrase. There is no reason why serjeants and justices should not already have been refreshing their memories of past cases by looking at reports that they or others had made. They may thus already have been 'seeing' and 'hearing' some of these cases in exactly the same way as we do now. The real challenge, however, for us is to 'see' these cases and 'hear' their participants with something of the same understanding of the surrounding legal context that these early readers possessed.

---

[77] BL, MS Egerton 2811, fol. 157r.

2

Crime in the Year Books

David J. Seipp

'The miserable history of crime in England can be shortly told. Nothing worth-while was created. There is no achievement to trace.'[1] With those words, Professor Milsom opened his chapter on 'Crime' in the first edition of his *Historical Foundations of the Common Law*. In thirteen preceding chapters, Professor Milsom explained the intricate development of substantive doctrines of property, contract and tort. In the last chapter, he said that he found nothing to explain, because nothing was developed. The reason was simple. Criminal proceedings did not permit the elaborate give-and-take of tentative special pleading between serjeants and justices, the driving force of doctrinal development in other branches of law. In the final words of the chapter and of the book: 'Crime has never been the business of lawyers.'[2]

Milsom's second edition moderated the opening sentences a bit, but he retained the major point. Criminal cases lacked 'the kind of discussion by which law develops as an intellectual system'. This was primarily because, before the eighteenth century, 'the lawyer was not even allowed to play any real part; and if he had been, few defendants could have paid him'.[3] There is just one Year Book case cited in Milsom's chapter on criminal law. The report, from 1469, states that indicted defendants were not

---

[1] S.F.C. Milsom, *Historical Foundations of the Common Law*, (1st edn, London, 1969), p. 353. I thank John Baker, Paul Brand, Carol F. Lee, David Millon, Aviam Soifer, and participants in the Eighth British Legal History Conference for their helpful suggestions. I thank Philip Jones and Scott Matasar for their excellent research assistance.

References are to the Vulgate (1678–80) edition of the Year Books unless otherwise indicated as RS (Rolls Series), SS (Selden Society), Ames (Ames Foundation), B & M (Baker & Milsom, Sources of English Legal History), Rogers (Ralph V. Rogers, privately printed, 1948), St. Tr. (State Trials), Stath. (Statham's Abridgment), Fitzh. (Fitzherbert's Abridgment) or Brooke (Brooke's Grand Abridgment). Dates are calculated by historical year beginning 1 January.

[2] Ibid., at p. 374. The point that absence of defence counsel stunted the development of criminal law is made in earlier works. William Holdsworth, *A History of English Law* (5th edn, London, 1942), iii, p. 616.

[3] S.F.C. Milsom, *Historical Foundations of the Common Law*, (2nd edn, London, 1981), p. 403. Milsom's second edition states: 'There are only administrative achievements to trace.'

permitted to retain counsel except to argue points of law. 'But', Milsom added, 'hardly ever would a prisoner know there was anything to say about that.'[4] Milsom's view is borne out in the writings of many other current English legal historians.[5]

One therefore would expect to find very few Year Book reports of criminal pleas.[6] One would expect to find neither serjeants nor apprentices pleading for the defendant or for the prosecution in the Year Books. One would expect to find no lawyers hearkening back to earlier Year Book cases or elaborating complex procedural and substantive doctrines of criminal law. One would be wrong.

My reading of the Year Books suggests that medieval English lawyers believed that criminal law was very much a part of their business. They reported interesting points of law in criminal cases, just as they did in other cases. Lawyers wrote, copied and recopied these reports because they regularly pleaded and argued on behalf of criminal defendants throughout the fourteenth and fifteenth centuries.

I find 810 reports and notes about criminal proceedings in the printed Year Books covering the period from 1300 to 1500. By criminal proceedings I mean felonies prosecuted either by appeal (a private prosecution) or by indictment. This number excludes the reports of eyres — these would add another 485 reports of criminal proceedings from four eyres between 1300 and 1330. I exclude the eyres because these reports are concentrated in a relatively few manuscripts, all edited and printed in modern times.[7] So I have 810 mentions of criminal proceedings interspersed among approximately 18,000 total cases in the Year Books over this whole period. That is just over 4½ per cent — one report about criminal proceedings for every twenty-one reports about wholly civil matters. The proportion

---

[4] Ibid., at p. 413 (citing Pasch. 9 Edw. 4, pl. 4, fol. 2 (1469); in the first edition of *Historical Foundations*, pp. 361, 427 (first note to page 361).

[5] E.g., J.H. Baker, *An Introduction to English Legal History*, (3rd edn, London, 1990), p. 570 ('the absence of pleading and of special pleaders from the criminal courts'); J.H. Baker, *The Order of Serjeants at Law* (London, 1984), p. 11 ('The royal judges ... prohibited counsel to prisoners accused of felony'); J.M. Kaye, 'Introduction', in *Placita Corone* (London, 1966), p. xxiii ('professional advocates ... were largely excluded from taking part in such [indictment] proceedings'); Robert C. Palmer, 'The Origins of the Legal Profession', *Irish Jurist*, 11 (1976), p. 130 ('a person under indictment could not have counsel, ... [even] before coming into court'); Edward Powell, *Kingship, Law and Society: Criminal Justice in the Reign of Henry V* (Oxford, 1989), p. 78 ('Persons accused of felony were not allowed defence counsel [at trial]').

[6] Year Books, as we know, were reported by lawyers (probably apprentices) in order to preserve information useful to their careers. See, e.g., A.W.B. Simpson, 'The Source and Function of the Later Year Books', *Law Quarterly Review*, 87 (1971), pp. 95–98; E.W. Ives, 'The Origins of the Later Year Books', in Dafydd Jenkins (ed.), *Legal History Studies 1972* (Cardiff, 1975), p. 138.

[7] Cornwall eyre, 30 & 31 Edw. 1, RS 497–545 (1302); Kent eyre, 6–7 Edw. 2, 24 SS 57–156 (1313–1314); London eyre, 14 Edw. 2, 85 SS 40–104 (1321); Northampton eyre, 3–4 Edw. 3, 98 SS 151–241 (1329–1330).

increases sharply from one per twenty-eight in the fourteenth century to one per fourteen in the more sparsely reported fifteenth century. I estimate that the whole of the reported criminal proceedings are roughly comparable to the number of reported cases on each one of the most important civil writs, such as trespass and debt. This total goes a long way toward contradicting the view of legal historians who suppose, as Professor Plucknett wrote many years ago, that 'the Year Books contain but very scanty references' to the subject of criminal law;[8] and that 'our criminal law did not secure the sustained attention of the legal expert' in the fourteenth and fifteenth centuries.[9]

I have four points to make about these reports. First, I will examine and reject two reasons why lawyers with no professional interest in criminal law might have reported these cases anyway — their entertainment value and their news value. Secondly, I will explore the role that lawyers played as advocates for and against criminal defendants in these reports. Thirdly, I will give a very brief overview of the substantive criminal law and criminal procedure explained in the reports. Finally, I will link these reports of criminal law to the English lawyers' vision of the whole of their intellectual domain — the whole of the common law.

1. Entertainment Value and News Value

Skeptics would offer two possible reasons why young lawyers who had no professional role to play in criminal proceedings might have written and copied these reports anyway — their entertainment value and their news value. These hypotheses do not explain the great majority of the reports of criminal cases.

I am the first to admit that criminal cases are entertaining. They are now and probably were then, for the same reasons. For example, the reports from 1300 to 1500 tell us about seventy-seven hangings (some of more than one defendant) with another twenty-seven hangings about to happen when the report ends. In addition, five defendants are drawn and hanged; four are burned alive; three are beheaded; three are hanged, drawn and quartered; and one is hanged, beheaded, drawn and quartered. Thirteen defendants stood mute and suffered the *peine forte et dure* for refusing to

---

[8] Theodore F.T. Plucknett, 'A Commentary on the Indictments', in Bertha Haven Putnam, *Proceedings before the Justices of the Peace in the Fourteenth and Fifteenth Centuries* (London, 1938), p. cl. See Bertha Haven Putnam, *The Place in Legal History of Sir William Shareshull* (Cambridge, 1950), p. 127 ('relatively few reports of criminal cases in the year books'). Plucknett and Putnam excepted the *Liber Assiasrum* from their remarks, but this contributes only 174 of my 810 cases, many of which were also reported in the ordinary Year Books of Edward III and in the early Abridgments.

[9] Putnam, *Proceedings before the Justices of the Peace*, p. cxlix.

plead. One died in trial by battle. There is a certain morbid, juvenile thrill in envisioning this mounting accumulation of public executions.

Among the various felonies, homicide is now and probably was then the most captivating topic for lawyer and layperson alike. Homicide accounts for 202 of the 481 felonies mentioned specifically in these reports. There are more homicides than the total number of robberies, larcenies, mayhems, rapes, burglaries and arsons combined. Barbara Hanawalt's researches in the fourteenth-century gaol delivery rolls tell us that homicide was much less frequently prosecuted than crimes against property.[10] Thus lawyers disproportionately reported homicide cases in their Year Books.

But only about thirty-five cases, in my considered judgment, have real entertainment value beyond the mere mention of a killing or of a hanging. Gory detail is supplied for the killings and maimings in six cases.[11] In six reports, lawyers exercised their imaginations to come up with what seem to be their favourite hypothetical cases: servants killing their masters and, even more popular, wives enlisting their lovers to kill their husbands.[12] In two cases, coroners had to dig up the bodies of buried murder victims in order to frame new indictments.[13]

Real drama is achieved when the Year Books report the life-and-death dialogue between justices and criminal defendants. 'What have you to say why you shall not be put to death?' How many of us could answer that? Not surprisingly, the justices got the best lines. In 1464, Chief Justice Danby told a defendant that 'you will be the cause of your own death', to the grave peril of his soul, if he kept insisting that God, Our Lady, and the Holy Church would be his judge.[14] In 1388, Chief Justice Tresilian told an outlaw who walked into court with dubious grounds for reversing his outlawry that 'I would not be in your situation for £100'.[15] Justice Willoughby told a defendant in 1330: 'Say something else, or we will say

[10] Barbara Hanawalt, *Crime and Conflict in English Communities* (Cambridge, Mass., 1979), pp. 61, 97–98, 118; Barbara Hanawalt, *Crime in East Anglia in the Fourteenth Century* (Norwich, 1976), pp. 9–10. See also Philippa C. Maddern, *Violence and Social Order: East Anglia, 1422–1442* (Oxford, 1992), pp. 28, 50.

[11] 22 Edw. 3, Lib. Ass. pl. 71, fol. 101; Fitzh. Corone 180, Brooke Corone 88 (1348); 40 Edw. 3, Lib. Ass. pl. 25, fol. 245; Fitzh Corone 216; Brooke Corone 118 (1366); Mich. 44 Edw. 3, pl. 55, fol. 44; Lib. Ass. pl. 17, fol. 287; Fitzh. Corone 94; Brooke Corone 12 & 14 (1370); Mich. 9 Hen. 6, 51 SS 48, 50 (1430); Pasch. [6] Hen. 7, pl. 1, fol. 41; Fitzh. Corone 63 (1491); Mich. 13 Hen. 7, pl. 17, fol. 10 (1497).

[12] Pasch. 15 Edw. 2, fol. 463; Fitzh. Corone 383; Brooke Corone 214 (1322), also in Pasch. 16 Edw. 2, 31 SS xxix–xxx & n. 1 (1323); 33 Edw. 3, Lib. Ass. pl. 7, fol. 200; Fitzh. Corone 210; Brooke Corone 116 (1359); Mich. 9 Hen. 5, pl. 15, Rogers 20 (1421); Mich. 28 Hen. 6, Stath. Corone 54, fol. 57b; Fitzh. Corone 458 (1449); Pasch. 18 Edw. 4, pl. 3, fol. 1 (1478); Mich. 1 Ric. 3, pl. 5, fol. 4; Fitzh. Corone 46 (1483).

[13] Mich. 21 Edw. 4, pl. 55, fol. 70, 71; Brooke Corone 166 (1481); Mich. 2 Ric. 3, pl. 5, fol. 2; 64 SS 74; Brooke Corone 172 (1484).

[14] Pasch. 4 Edw. 4, pl. 18, fol. 11, 12; Fitzh. Corone 27 (1464). Other dialogues are in 27 Edw. 3, Lib. Ass. pl. 42, fol. 138 (1353) and [Hil.] 19 Hen. 6, pl. 2, fol. 1, 2 (1441).

[15] Pasch. 11 Ric. 2, pl. 29, Ames 278 (1388).

enough.'[16] In 1340, the tables were turned, and the defendant was Chief Justice Willoughby. He and his counsel wrangled unsuccessfully to evade bribery charges on hyper-technical pleas until he finally threw himself on the king's mercy, leading Lord Wake to remark that this was the wisest plea that Willoughby ever pleaded.[17]

Even more vivid are two dialogues that took place on the field of battle. In each case, the defendant was on his back, and the chief justice told him that his choices were to keep fighting from there or to be hanged.[18] Three prosecutions ended in dramatic courtroom revelations. In one, justices heard a captured outlaw change his story and immediately ordered his execution.[19] In another, justices caught a plaintiff and a defendant colluding in a false appeal in order to save the defendant from an indictment.[20] In a third, the murdered husband turned up alive in court, and so the defendant went free.[21] In three provocative reports, women who were pregnant when they were sentenced to death were allowed to remain in prison until they gave birth, but when two turned up pregnant again at the next session of court, they were out of luck.[22] For those who like happier endings, one jury gave a verdict of pious perjury,[23] three convicted felons were rescued on their way to the gallows,[24] one was pardoned at the last moment,[25] and one survived his hanging.[26]

Mystery looms in a report of 1406. Serjeant Tyrwhit asked a justice to suppose that he (the justice) witnessed a killing and then presided over the trial of a defendant he knew to be innocent. Tyrwhit concluded that the justice could not upset a jury's verdict of guilty, but at best could only delay the hanging and try to intervene with the king to obtain a pardon.[27] In three reports, the situation was reversed; justices berated

[16] Hil. 4 Edw. 3, pl. 21, fol. 9; Lib. Ass. pl. 1, fol. 6; Fitzh. Corone 144 (1330).

[17] Mich. 14 Edw. 3, pl. 109, RS 259 (1340).

[18] Pasch. 10 Hen. 5, pl. 3, Rogers 54 (1422); Mich. 19 Hen. 6, pl. 74, fol. 35; Fitzh. Corone 6, Brooke Corone 46 (1440).

[19] Trin. 19 Edw. 3, pl. 19, RS 175; Fitzh. Corone 123 (1345).

[20] 37 Edw. 3, Lib. Ass. pl. 9, fol. 217 (1363). Another revelation from a view of mayhem is in Pasch. 8 Hen. 4, pl. 1, fol. 21; Stath. Corone 51; Fitzh. Corone 74 & 458 (1407).

[21] Hil. 8 Hen. 4, pl. 2, fol. 17 (1407).

[22] 12 Edw. 3, Lib. Ass. pl. 11, fol. 34; Fitzh. Corone 168; Brooke Corone 72 (1338); Trin. 22 Edw. 3, Stath. Corone 78, fol. 58b; Fitzh. Corone 253 (1348); 23 Edw. 3, Lib. Ass. pl. 2, fol. 107; Fitzh. Corone 130 & 188; Brooke Corone 97 (1349), also reported in Pasch. 25 Edw. 3, pl. 30, fol. 85 (1351).

[23] 18 Edw. 3, Lib. Ass. pl. 14, fol. 59; Fitzh. Corone 177; Brooke Corone 84 (1344) (finding that a stolen sheep was worth less than twelve pence, with the result that the defendant was not hanged.)

[24] Trin. 19 Edw. 3, pl. 21, RS 177, 179 (1345); Hil. 1 Hen. 7, pl. 2, fol. 6; 64 SS 125; Fitzh. Corone 48 (1486); Mich. 6 Hen. 7, pl. 9, fol. 11, 12 (1490).

[25] Mich. 19 Hen. 6, pl. 103, fol. 47; Fitzh. Corone 8; Brooke Corone 47 (1440).

[26] Mich. 6 Edw. 4, pl. 11, fol. 4; Brooke Corone 146 (1466).

[27] Pasch. 7 Hen. 4, pl. 5, fol. 41 (1406).

juries for rendering verdicts of self-defence or outright acquittal.[28] Two other cases had other attractions. In the first, a man was sentenced to death in 1327. His crime was that he had forged the king's seal. So what did he do? He produced the king's charter of pardon and went free.[29] That is the only joke I have found among these Year Book cases. For my second example, the graphic details of an alleged rape prosecuted in the London Eyre of 1321 will go untranslated, but they found their way into twelve manuscripts of *Novae Narrationes*.[30] This is the only instance I have found of medieval law student pornography in the Year Book literature.

This concludes the entertainment portion of this essay. Another reason why lawyers with no professional interest in criminal cases might nevertheless report them in the Year Books is to record news about the great folk of the realm or about people the lawyers knew in their own community. The number of criminal cases that may have been reported for their newsworthy character seems to be even smaller than the number that appear to provide some entertainment. A rare exception to the norm is a report from 1464 about Edward IV's capture of some of the leading supporters of Henry VI.[31] The report mentions several beheadings, but no judicial proceedings. The Year Books give brief sidelong glimpses of six of the principal sources of disorder in the fourteenth and fifteenth centuries: William Wallace in 1305;[32] Hugh le Despenser (father and son) in 1326;[33] Sir John Oldcastle in 1417;[34] Jack Cade in 1450;[35] Thomas Fauconberge in 1471;[36] and Sir Humphrey Stafford in 1485.[37] Other notorious troublemakers such as Owen Glendower, Roger Mortimer, Wat Tyler and Harry Hotspur are missing entirely. Neither of the most notorious criminal gangs of the fourteenth century, the Folvilles and the Coterels, appears by name in the reports, although Robert Ledham, the leader of a large gang during the 1450s, does show up twice in a

---

[28] 43 Edw. 3, Lib. Ass. pl. 31, fol. 274; Fitzh. Corone 226; Brooke Corone 124 (1369); Mich. 7 Ric. 2, pl. 4, Ames 58, 59 (1383); Mich. 9 Hen. 5, pl. 23, Rogers 21 (1421).

[29] Trin. 1 Edw. 3, pl. 16, fol. 23 (1327).

[30] London eyre, 14 Edw. 2, 85 SS 87–90 (1321); *Novae Narrationes*, CX.23–26, at 80 SS 341–44.

[31] Pasch. 4 Edw. 4, pl. 40, fol. 19, 20 (1464).

[32] The report of his sentence appeared in Trin. 11 Edw. 3, RS 171 (1337). A lesser source of trouble, John de Mowbray, was tried in 1322 and mentioned in Pasch. 17 Edw. 2, fol. 540 (1324).

[33] A land dispute challenged sales by the Despensers after their return from exile in Trin. 15 Edw. 3, pl. 25, RS 229, 231 (1341).

[34] A reporter's note is appended to Pasch. 1 Hen. 5, pl. 8, fol. 5, 6; Brooke Corone 210 (1413).

[35] Hil. 35 Hen. 6, pl. 6, fol. 44, 45 (1457).

[36] Trin. 11 Edw. 4, pl. 8, fol. 4 (1471).

[37] Trin. 1 Hen. 7, pl. 1, fol. 25, 26; 64 SS 115; Fitzh. Corone 49; Brooke Corone 128 (1486).

confrontation with Justice William Paston's son John.[38] Only one of the twenty-three cases in the State Trials Series for the period 1300 to 1500 is mentioned in the Year Books, and that in a single sentence.[39]

A dozen reports concern members of the legal community. I have mentioned the prosecution of Chief Justice Willoughby.[40] Lawyers also noted a brawl in Westminster Hall,[41] the wounding of the chaplain of Gray's Inn,[42] and the killing of a serjeant's servant.[43] Three men struck jurors or threatened justices and immediately had their right hands cut off for their contempt of court.[44] But Chief Justice Tresilian's dramatic trial is not recorded in the Year Books. Nor are proceedings arising from the kidnapping of Justice Willoughby in 1322 or the murders of Justice Beler in 1326, Justice Seton in 1358,[45] Chief Justice Cavendish in 1381, and apprentice Nicholas Radford in 1455. As in the rest of the Year Books, names of the parties were usually not important to the reporters. Only 157 of the 810 criminal cases give any names for either defendants or plaintiffs.

All the cases that provide entertaining details or newsworthy names also imparted legal knowledge to their readers. For example, a Year Book report of 1484 tells us that a servant of Serjeant William Jenney was killed in Suffolk.[46] We learn that the coroner had to exhume the body of this servant in order to frame a new indictment 'on the view of the body'. We learn, with a growing awareness of the irony, that Serjeant Jenney himself showed the error in the original indictment for the suspected killer of his own servant. We also learn that an indictment is void if it describes the defendant as a 'vagabond', part of a developing doctrine about required and forbidden 'additions' to parties' names.[47] Entertaining aspects of these

[38] Mich. 37 Hen. 6, pl. 4, fol. 2, 3 (1458); Pasch. 37 Hen. 6, pl. 8, fol. 19, 20; Fitzh. Corone 23 & 24 (1459). See Norman Davis (ed.), *The Paston Letters* (Oxford, 1983), p. 39 & n. 1.

[39] Sir John Oldcastle's trial is in Hil. 1 Hen. 5, 1 St. Tr. 225 (1414), and is briefly mentioned in Pasch. 1 Hen. 5, pl. 8, fol. 5, 6; Brooke Corone 210 (1413).

[40] Mich. 14 Edw. 3, pl. 109, RS 259 (1340).

[41] Trin. 15 Edw. 3, pl. 47, RS 271, 273, 275 (1341).

[42] Mich. 2 Hen. 4, pl. 41, fol. 8 (1400).

[43] Mich. 2 Ric. 3, pl. 5, fol. 2; 64 SS 74; Brooke Corone 172 (1484).

[44] Mich. 19 Edw. 3, pl. 78, RS 453 (1345); Mich. 22 Edw. 3, pl. 26, fol. 13 (1348); 39 Edw. 3, Lib. Ass. pl. 1, fol. 231 (1365). A fourth was pardoned in 41 Edw. 3, Lib. Ass. pl. 25, fol. 256; Stath. Corone 128; Fitzh. Corone 280 (1367). Prison was the sentence in Hil. 32 Hen. 6, pl. 30, fol. 34 (1454).

[45] A hired killer stabbed Seton in 1358, and he died later of the wounds. Seton's prosecution of a woman for slander appears in 30 Edw. 3, Lib. Ass. pl. 19, fol. 177; Brooke Corone 115 (1356).

[46] Mich. 2 Ric. 3, pl. 5, fol. 2; 64 SS 74; Brooke Corone 172 (1484). The report states that the killing took place in 1480.

[47] The same point is made in Pasch. 22 Edw. 4, pl. 1, fol. 1 (1482). On the general point see Mich. 9 Hen. 4, pl. 11, fol. 3 (1407); Hil. 9 Edw. 4, pl. 1, fol. 48; Fitzh. Corone 33; Brooke Corone 56 (1470).

reports were merely an attractive accompaniment to necessary learning about how to get out of answering a criminal indictment.

In well over 700 of my 810 cases, the reporters stripped away any possibly entertaining or newsworthy details, and gave readers only the points of law at issue. In this respect, criminal cases in the Year Books closely resemble reports of common pleas. I conclude that criminal pleas and common pleas were reported for the same reasons. Some may advance a third hypothesis, that young lawyers with no immediate professional interest in criminal law might have reported these cases in expectation of becoming justices of the King's Bench or justices commissioned to take gaol deliveries years or decades later in their careers. That suggestion is contradicted by the cases themselves, as I will now explain.

2. Lawyers as Counsel for Defence and Prosecution

My second point is that lawyers practised regularly as counsel for criminal defendants and for the prosecution. *Any* number of reports in which lawyers pleaded on behalf of criminal defendants would be a surprise. While most reports are notes that name no members of the legal profession, and many others mention only justices, I find 172 cases, some from every decade between 1300 and 1500, in which lawyers spoke as counsel.

The Year Books name 119 different lawyers taking on this business. Fifty-one spoke in more than one case, and thirty-one spoke for more than one side — for the prosecution in some cases and for defendants in others.[48] This suggests that there was no specialisation into a defence bar or a prosecution bar in medieval England.[49] Serjeants dominated the discussion before 1350, but thereafter a roughly equal number of apprentices appear as counsel in criminal cases.

Lawyers spoke for the defence in 123 reports and for private prosecutors or the king in 109. I will focus on the 123 reports in which one or more lawyers spoke for the defendant. In three-quarters of these reports, the Year Book makes very clear that the lawyer appeared as formal counsel for the criminal defendant, explaining why 'we' should not be arraigned or pleading that 'we' were not guilty. In one-quarter, the lawyers might have spoken as interested bystanders present in court,[50] but I think it more likely that most of them were counsel retained by defendants.

---

[48] The most frequent criminal advocate, Thomas Kebell, also appears most frequently as a civil advocate in the Year Books. E.W. Ives, *The Common Lawyers of Pre-Reformation England* (Cambridge, 1983), pp. 3, 149.

[49] King's Serjeants frequently appeared on behalf of defendants.

[50] A report of Mich. 7 Edw. 4, pl. 11, fol. 16, 17 (1467) makes the point that anyone can inform the court that an indictment was insufficient or unrecorded. See Ives, *Common Lawyers of Pre-Reformation England*, p. 153.

To divide the cases in a different way, more than three-quarters of the reports in which lawyers spoke in favour of the defendant are identified as appeals. Legal historians have long accepted that defendants could retain counsel in appeals, but would not expect to find so many appeals in the Year Books. Of my grand total of 810 cases, 350 mention appeals and only 248 mention indictments, while the rest of the reports are silent on the mode of prosecution. Appeals thus loomed larger than indictments in the lawyers' professional learning. Again, the reports fail to mirror the gaol delivery rolls, in which indictments outnumbered appeals.[51] This is further confirmation that criminal appeals were by no means obsolete in the two centuries before 1500, a point that Christopher Whittick made some years ago.[52]

The more surprising Year Book reports are of indictments for felonies in which lawyers spoke on behalf of defendants. I have twenty-eight of these cases. Again, legal historians will concede that counsel could raise points of law for indicted defendants, but will insist that they could not do anything else. Let us see what they did. In eleven of the reports, defence counsel argued that the facts alleged in the indictment did not amount to a felony (for example, because the homicide victim had been an outlaw).[53] In five, they argued that the defendant had already been acquitted for the same offence (our plea of autrefois acquit or double jeopardy).[54] In another five cases, the lawyers contended that the indictment was defective for uncertainty (such as failure to specify one of two feasts of St Peter in the calendar) or some other error of form.[55] Elsewhere in these twenty-eight reports, lawyers performed many roles. One asked for

[51] John Bellamy, *Crime and Public Order in England in the Later Middle Ages* (London, 1973), p. 121.

[52] Christopher Whittick, 'The Role of the Criminal Appeal in the Fifteenth Century', in J.A. Guy & H.G. Beale (eds), *Law and Social Change in British History* (London, 1984), pp. 55–72.

[53] Hil. 2 Edw. 3, pl. 17, fol. 6; Lib. Ass. pl. 3, fol. 3; Fitzh. Corone 148; Brooke Corone 67 (1328); Mich. 18 Edw. 3, pl. 29, RS 101 (1344); Pasch. 21 Edw. 3, pl. 5, fol. 54; Lib. Ass. pl. 12, fol. 79 (1347); 27 Edw. 3, Lib. Ass. pl. 27, fol. 135 (1353); 30 Edw. 3, Lib. Ass. pl. 37, fol. 179 (1356); 42 Edw. 3, Lib. Ass. pl. 5, fol. 258; Fitzh. Corone 224 (1368); Trin. 7 Hen. 6, pl. 18, fol. 42, 43; Fitzh. Enditement 11; Brooke Corone 45 (1429); Trin. 9 Edw. 4, pl. 35, fol. 26; Fitzh. Enditement 18 (1469); Mich. 6 Hen. 7, pl. 9, fol. 11, 12 (1490); Trin. 10 Hen. 7, pl. 3, fol. 25 (1495), also reported in Trin. 10 Hen. 7, pl. 17, fol. 28 (1495).

[54] Pasch. 17 Edw. 2, fol. 543 (1324); Trin. 2 Edw. 3, pl. 14, fol. 26; Fitzh. Corone 150 & 283; Stath. Corone 121 (1328); 41 Edw. 3, Lib. Ass. pl. 9, fol. 253; Fitzh. Corone 220; Brooke Corone 120 (1367); Pasch. 4 Edw. 4, pl. 14, fol. 10; Fitzh. Corone 25; Brooke Corone 195 (1464); Pasch. 4 Hen. 7, pl. 1, fol. 5; Brooke Corone 139 (1489).

[55] Trin. 7 Hen. 6, pl. 18, fol. 42, 43; Fitzh. Enditement 11; Brooke Corone 45 (1429); Pasch. 8 Edw. 4, pl. 2, fol. 3; Fitzh. Enditement 16; Brooke Corone 149 (1468); Pasch. 22 Edw. 4, pl. 33, fol. 12, 13 (1482); Pasch. 3 Hen. 7, pl. 2, fol. 5; Fitzh. Enditement 22 (1488); Pasch. 6 Hen. 7, pl. 4, fol. 2 (1491).

a writ to get the defendant's body and the record before the King's Bench, one traversed the indictment, two pleaded charters of pardon, two pleaded not guilty, one asked for bail, and one simply begged favour to dismiss the defendant.[56] The number of cases is small, to be sure. Yet these instances show that defence counsel were not uniformly restricted to a narrow set of issues.

Nothing in these twenty-eight reports suggests that the defendant or the court had to identify an issue of law before the defence counsel could begin to speak, or that counsel had to be 'assigned' by the court. The Year Books speak of 'assigning' counsel to criminal defendants only in two very unusual proceedings of high crimes against high persons. Courts specially assigned counsel in 1340 for Chief Justice Willoughby, arraigned on corruption charges, and again in 1486 for the Yorkist leader Sir Humphrey Stafford, arraigned for treason.[57]

Where do we get the rule that became the later orthodoxy: 'persons accused of felony were not allowed defence counsel',[58] at least in indictments, and at least when points of law did not arise? As I have just shown, there is plenty of evidence of contrary experience throughout the Year Books, but we also have three mentions of this proposition between 1300 and 1500. A Latin report of a rape indictment, apparently from the Cornwall eyre of 1302, has the justice tell the defendant who brought a friend along: 'the law does not permit you to have counsel against the king where he sues ex officio'.[59] In 1406 Chief Justice Gascoigne told a defendant in the course of an appeal that if one were indicted at the king's suit one would not have counsel.[60] Finally a reporter's note at the end of a 1469 case, the single case cited by Milsom, states that the defendant in a felony indictment will not have counsel against the king unless there is a matter in law.[61] All three

---

[56] 41 Edw. 3, Lib. Ass. pl. 22, fol. 255; Brooke Corone 192 (1367); Hil. 6 Hen. 4, pl. 4, fol. 4 (1405); Hil. 11 Hen. 4, pl. 8, fol. 41; Stath. Corone 13 & 43; Fitzh. Corone 89 & Enditement 25; Brooke Corone 30 & 188 (1410); Hil. 32 Hen. 6, pl. 30, fol. 34 (1454); Pasch. 4 Edw. 4, pl. 14, fol. 10; Fitzh. Corone 25; Brooke Corone 195 (1464); Pasch. 22 Edw. 4, pl. 22, fol. 7, 8 (1482); Pasch. 4 Hen. 7, pl. 1, fol. 5; Brooke Corone 139 (1489). A report in 1352 noted that an indicted defendant showed his charter of pardon 'without counsel of law'. 26 Edw. 3, Lib. Ass. pl. 46, fol. 129 (1352).

[57] Mich. 14 Edw. 3, pl. 109, RS 259 (1340); Trin. 1 Hen. 7, pl. 1, fol. 25, 26; 64 SS 115; Fitzh. Corone 49 (1486). According to the chronicles reprinted in the State Trials, Parliament refused to assign counsel to Nicholas Brambre, Mayor of London, on trial for high crimes and misdemeanours in 1388. 11 Rich. 2, 1 St. Tr. 89 (1388).

[58] Powell, *Kingship, Law and Society*, p. 78 ('Persons accused of felony were not allowed defence counsel').

[59] Appendix II, Cornwall eyre, 30 or 31 Edw. 1, RS 528, 530 (1302) and 'Introduction' at p. xliv. If there was a broader rule that common persons could never have counsel in any case where the king was a party, it was short-lived. Baker, *Order of Serjeants*, p. 11.

[60] Hil. 7 Hen. 4, pl. 4, fol. 35, 36; Brooke Corone 20 (1406).

[61] Pasch. 9 Edw. 4, pl. 4, fol. 2; Fitzh. Corone 31; Brooke Corone 54 (1469). This is the case cited by Milsom, *Historical Foundations*, 2nd edn., p. 413.

reports make clear that defendants could have counsel in appeals without any restriction.

There were foreshadowings of some sort of practice forbidding counsel for criminal defendants before 1300. The early twelfth-century *Leges Henrici Primi* has a passage — as one might expect, a confused passage — stating that a person accused of one of the felonies should immediately deny the charge before seeking counsel with friends or advisers.[62] In the *Placita Corone*, composed in the 1270s, a justice bullied a defendant into pleading without benefit of counsel in an appeal.[63] By 1291, however, a pleader named Robert Duffhus lost part of his annuity when he failed to counsel his client defending an indictment for homicide.[64]

These early sources suggest that the practice of the royal courts was to insist that (1) one must appear personally to answer a criminal charge; (2) one must answer it alone and speak for oneself; and (3) one must answer it immediately, without delay for consultation with anyone else. 'What have you to say why you shall not be put to death?' The defendant's demeanour when personally denying the charge and choosing a mode of trial was an opportunity for the justices to form an initial impression of the defendant's guilt or innocence. If the defendant could interpose a delay to confer with counsel, the crucial psychological moment would be lost forever. A practice that merely avoided delays in answering the charge would have permitted lawyers to take active roles before and during the rest of the criminal proceeding, as the Year Books demonstrate they did between 1300 and 1500.

After 1500, a rule against counsel in indictments is justified at length in St German's *Doctor and Student*, more briefly in Smith's *De Republica Anglorum*, and more narrowly in Staunford's *Plees del Corone*.[65] On the other hand, a chief justice told ten new serjeants in 1521 that they would be consulted in two sorts of causes — 'bloody matters' of treason, murder and the like, and 'pecuniary causes' of land, debt and the like.[66] I suspect

[62] L.J. Downer (ed. & trans.), *Leges Henrici Primi* (Oxford, 1972), ch. 47, sec. 1 at pp. 156, 158 and note at p. 356.

[63] Kaye, *Placita Corone*, p. 17; *see* J.B. Post, 'Placita Corone', in Thomas G. Watkin (ed.), *Legal Record and Historical Reality* (London, 1989), p. 4.

[64] Paul Brand, *The Origins of the English Legal Profession* (Oxford, 1992), p. 102, citing CP 40/90, m. 107, also discussed in Palmer, 'Origins of the Legal Profession', *Irish Jurist*, 11 (1976), p. 130.

[65] Christopher St. German, *Doctor and Student*, 91 SS 284–86, and J.L. Barton, 'Introduction' at 91 SS liii; Thomas Smith, *De Republica Anglorum* (Cambridge, 1982), bk. 2, ch. 9, at pp. 90–91 (*c.* 1565); William Staunford, *Les Plees del Corone* (London, 1557), ch. 63, at fol. 151v.

[66] Baker, *Order of Serjeants*, p. 287. See the discussion of this passage in J.H. Baker, 'Introduction', in *The Reports of Sir John Spelman*, ii, 94 SS *299*.

that the rule forbidding counsel for criminal defendants really had effect only in the more repressive Tudor and Stuart regimes.[67]

3. Legal Content of the Cases

My third point relates to the legal content of these Year Book reports. Because lawyers created and copied these reports as part of their professional libraries, the Year Books give us a 'lawyers' eye view' of criminal proceedings. By the emphasis the reports give to some issues over others, we can tell what it was about criminal law that interested lawyers most.[68] I find that five broad topics occupied large, roughly equal shares of attention from the lawyers: (1) the definition of felonies; (2) the related double jeopardy and principal-accessary rules; (3) pleading in appeals and indictments; (4) alternatives to jury trial; and (5) financial consequences of criminal proceedings.

First, more than one hundred reports in the Year Books addressed the ordinary question of substantive criminal law: 'Do the facts alleged by the prosecution amount to a felony?' Lawyers laboured over these two centuries to define the contours of homicide, robbery, larceny, mayhem, rape, burglary, arson, high treason and petty treason, along with receiving felons, allowing felons to escape and breaking prison.[69] In many ways, the concept of intent became the touchstone of substantive criminal law doctrine. Lawyers focused on intent when they agreed that an attempt to murder or to rob was a felony,[70] when they executed children who

[67] See J.B. Post, 'The Admissibility of Defence Counsel in English Criminal Procedure', in Albert Kiralfy et al. (eds), *Custom, Courts and Counsel* (London, 1984), pp. 25–28 (1984); also in *Journal of Legal History*, 5 (1984), pp. 25–28. I am unsure whether sixteenth- and seventeenth-century English lawyers were imitating continental practice when they denied counsel to defendants in indictments. Sir John Davies, in his eulogy of the common law, wrote that no professor of the law of England had ever been known to defend any indicted felon, but added that 'the advocates and orators in other countries do'. John Davies, 'Preface Dedicatory', in *Les Reports des Cases & Matters en Ley* (1615), p. [16] (Irish Reports).

[68] Many of the Year Book reports of criminal cases permit the reader to draw conclusions about settled rules. One can learn an outcome in more than half (about 63 per cent) of the criminal prosecutions described in the reports (448 of 706). My impression is that a far higher proportion of civil pleas leave the legal outcome unresolved or ambiguous.

[69] This contradicts the impression left by James Fitzjames Stephen, *A History of the Criminal Law of England* (London, 1883), ii, pp. 202–3 (the 'immense majority' of Year Book cases 'relate to matters of practice long since obsolete').

[70] Pasch. 15 Edw. 2, fol. 463; Fitzh. Corone 383; Brooke Corone 214 (1322), also in Pasch. 16 Edw. 2, 31 SS xxix–xxx & n. 1 (1323); Trin. 9 Edw. 4, pl. 36, fol. 26, 27 (1469).

showed malice in the commission of crimes,[71] and refused to execute an insane killer,[72] and when they balked at calling homicide in self-defence a felony.[73] Generalisations are rare, but we do find one lawyer stating broadly in 1466 that 'felony is malice aforethought',[74] and another saying in 1470 that felony cases were the best example of the common law's ability to try 'the will, assent and intent of a man'.[75]

Secondly, much of the driving force and character of medieval criminal law seem to be embodied in two important, unquestioned rules. One was an autrefois acquit or double jeopardy rule. As Chief Justice Markham stated it in 1468: 'a man will not be twice put to respond for one same felony nor put his life in jeopardy but once'.[76] Lawyers applied this rule consistently over the fourteenth and fifteenth centuries.[77] It was the basis for many arguments about pre-trial process,[78] venue of trial,[79] pardons,[80] and standing to bring an appeal.[81]

Lawyers applied a second rule with equal strictness and with even greater frequency in felony cases. This was the rule that an accessary should not be made to answer until the principal was convicted and attaint.[82] Twice, the Year Books tell of wrongful executions, and each was a case of an

---

[71] Trin. 12 Edw. 2, pl. 29(e), 81 SS 123 (1319); Trin. 12 Edw. 3, RS 627; Lib. Ass. pl. 30, fol. 37; Fitzh. Corone 118 & 170; Brooke Corone [74] (1338). Courts refused to execute infants in Pasch. 25 Edw. 3, pl. 28, fol. 85; Fitzh. Corone 129 (1351); Mich. 3 Hen. 7, pl. 8, fol. 12; Fitzh. Corone 51; Brooke Corone 135 (1487); Hil. 3 Hen. 7, pl. 4, fol. 1, Fitzh. Corone 57; Brooke Corone 132 (1488).

[72] 26 Edw. 3, Lib. Ass. pl. 27, fol. 123; Fitzh. Corone 193; Brooke Corone 101 & 216 (1352).

[73] Trin. 15 Edw. 3, pl. 42, RS 263; Lib. Ass. pl. 7, fol. 43; Fitzh. Corone 116; Brooke Corone 80 (1341); Trin. 22 Edw. 3, Stath. Corone 86; Fitzh. Corone 261 (1348); 26 Edw. 3, Lib. Ass. pl. 23, fol. 123; Brooke Corone 100 (1352); 26 Edw. 3, Lib. Ass. pl. 32, fol. 123, 124; Fitzh. Corone 194; Brooke Corone 102 (1352); Mich. 44 Edw. 3, pl. 55, fol. 44; Lib. Ass. pl. 17, fol. 287; Fitzh. Corone 94; Brooke Corone 12 & 14 (1370).

[74] Mich. 6 Edw. 4, pl. 18, fol. 7; Brooke Corone 147 (1466).

[75] Trin. 10 Edw. 4, pl. 5, 47 SS 97 (1470) (Choke JCP). Also in Mich. 6 Edw. 4, B & M 327 (Fairfax Sjt) (in felony the intent and will of a man shall be construed).

[76] Mich. 8 Edw. 4, pl. 1, fol. 7; Brooke Corone 197 (1468).

[77] One exception allowed appeal after acquittal at the king's suit. Hil. 17 Edw. 3, pl. 6, RS 21; Lib. Ass. pl. 1, fol. 48; Fitzh. Corone 111 (1343). Contrary results are found in Trin. 45 Edw. 3, pl. 36, fol. 25 (1371); 8 Hen. 6, Stath. Corone 8n (1430) (noted in a 1347 case); Hil. 11 Hen. 4, pl. 6, fol. 41; Brooke Corone 29 (1410).

[78] Pasch. 19 Edw. 3, Stath. Corone 12, fol. 56a; Fitzh. Corone 444 (1345); Hil. 21 Hen. 6, pl. 12, fol. 28, 29; Brooke Corone 48 (1443).

[79] Pasch. 14 Edw. 3, pl. 61, fol. 155, 157 (1340); Pasch. 4 Hen. 7, pl. 1, fol. 5; Brooke Corone 139 (1489).

[80] Trin. 3 Edw. 2, pl. 4, 20 SS 153–56 (1310).

[81] Hil. 7 Edw. 2, pl. 17, 39 SS 72, 73 (1314); 8 Hen. 6, Stath. Corone 8n (1430) (noted in a 1347 case).

[82] E.g., Mich. 33 Edw. 1, RS 55, 63 (1305); Hil. 12 Edw. 2, pl. 45(d), 70 SS 92 (1319); Trin. 7 Hen. 4, pl. 5, fol. 16; Stath. Corone 33; Brooke Corone 18 (1406); Hil. 7 Hen. 4, pl. 4, fol. 35, 36; Brooke Corone 20 (1406).

accessary found guilty and hanged before the principal was tried and acquitted.[83] Lawyers more frequently combined the principal–accessary rule with the complexities of outlawry, royal pardons and benefit of clergy, and with the double jeopardy rule, to obtain outcomes favouring accessary defendants.[84]

Thirdly, in criminal practice, it is true that lawyers did not attempt special pleading. But that was because they were permitted double pleading. In appeals, defendants' counsel could plead that the plaintiff was not the deceased's widow (not lawfully married),[85] or was not the deceased's eldest male heir (appeals of death descended, we are told, in tail male),[86] or was not of age,[87] or was a felon,[88] an outlaw,[89] an excommunicant,[90] a villein,[91] or illegitimate.[92] Defendants' counsel could also plead that the defendant was misnamed in the appeal,[93] or was defending another pending appeal

[83] Trin. 3 Edw. 2, pl. 27, 20 SS 193, 196 (1310), also reported in Hil. 5 Edw. 2, pl. 10, 31 SS 42, 44 (1312) (Bereford CJCP recalls Hengham CJKB berating another justice for this); Trin. 18 Edw. 4, pl. 16, fol. 19; Brooke Corone 164 (1478).

[84] E.g., Hil. 13 Edw. 3, pl. 45, RS 153, 155 (1339); 27 Edw. 3, Lib. Ass. pl. 10, fol. 134; Fitzh. Corone 200; Brooke Corone 105 (1353); Hil. 9 Hen. 7, pl. 14, fol. 19 (1494).

[85] 27 Edw. 3, Lib. Ass. pl. 3, fol. 133; Fitzh. Corone 197 (1353); Pasch. 28 Edw. 3, pl. 4, fol. 15; Fitzh. Corone 140 (1354); Trin. 50 Edw. 3, pl. 5, fol. 15; Fitzh. Corone 106 (1376); Pasch. 3 Hen. 6; Fitzh. Corone 3, fol. 257v (1425).

[86] 2 Edw. 2, pl. 1, 17 SS 42, 43 (1309); Mich. 11 Hen. 4, pl. 24, fol. 11 (1409); Hil. 13 Hen. 4, Fitzh. Corone 235, fol. 268 (1412); Mich. 5 Edw. 4, pl. 11, fol. 6 (1465); Mich. 7 Edw. 4, pl. 3, fol. 15; Fitzh. Corone 28 (1467). Contra Pasch. 32 Edw. 1, RS 193, 195 (1304); Mich. 28 Hen. 6, Stath. Corone 54, fol. 57b; Fitzh. Corone 458 (1449).

[87] Mich. 33 Edw. 1, RS 95 (1305); Hil. 4 Edw. 2, pl. 58(f), 26 SS 130 (1311); Trin. 21 Edw. 3, pl. 16, fol. 23; Lib. Ass. pl. 4, fol. 76; Stath. Corone 8; Fitzh. Corone 114 (1347); 32 Edw. 3, Lib. Ass. pl. 8, fol. 196; Stath. Corone 124 (1358); 41 Edw. 3, Lib. Ass. pl. 14, fol. 254 (1367); Trin. 45 Edw. 3, pl. 36, fol. 25 (1371); Trin. 11 Hen. 4, pl. 56, fol. 93; Brooke Age 16 (1410) (repeats 1358 case); 8 Hen. 6, Stath. Corone 8n (1430) (noted in a 1347 case); 32 Hen. 6, Fitzh. Corone 279 (1454). An infant's appeal was postponed until the infant attained maturity, but did not preclude an indictment for the same offence.

[88] Hil. 1 Edw. 3, pl. 19, fol. 3; Brooke Corone 220 (1327).

[89] Mich. 18 Edw. 3, pl. 15, RS 51 (1344), also reported in 17 Edw. 3, Lib. Ass. pl. 26, fol. 53; Fitzh. Corone 175 (1343); Pasch. 20 Edw. 3, pl. 71, RS 429, 431–35 (1346); Hil. 21 Edw. 3, pl. 20, fol. 17; Stath. Corone 30; Fitzh. Corone 452; Brooke Corone 37 (1347). Or an abjurer 11 Edw. 3, Lib. Ass. pl. 27, fol. 33; Fitzh. Corone 167; Brooke Corone 210 (1337); Hil. 19 Edw. 3, Stath. Corone 11; Fitzh. Corone 443 (1345).

[90] Pasch. 3 Edw. 3, pl. 33, fol. 19; Lib. Ass. pl. 12, fol. 5 (1329); Pasch. 13 Edw. 4, pl. 3, fol. 8 (1473).

[91] Mich. 18 Edw. 3, pl. 4, RS 9 (1344); Mich. 1 Hen. 4, pl. 11, fol. 5 (1399); Trin. 11 Hen. 4, pl. 52, fol. 93 (1410) (repeats 1344 case); Trin. 29 Hen. 6, Stath. Corone 23, fol. 56a–56b; Fitzh. Corone 17; Brooke Corone 215 (1451).

[92] Mich. 28 Hen. 6, Stath. Corone 55, fos 57b–58a (1449).

[93] Pasch. 1 Hen. 5, pl. 8, fol. 5, 6; Brooke Corone 210 (1413); Pasch. 9 Hen. 5, pl. 3, fol. 1; Rogers 4, 5; Brooke Appeale 38 (1421); Mich. 5 Edw. 4, Long Quinto fol. 141, 142 (1465); Mich. 21 Edw. 4, pl. 56, fol. 71; Fitzh. Corone 43 (1481); Mich. 6 Hen. 7, pl. 2, fol. 7; Fitzh. Corone 64 (1490); Trin. 10 Hen. 7, pl. 14, fol. 27 (1495).

for the same crime.[94] The defendant who lost on any of these pleas could still plead not guilty to the offence.[95]

In indictments, defendants' counsel most often objected to flaws in the wording of the indictment, such as failure to specify correctly the victim's name, the defendant's name or description, the commission of the indicting authority, or the date, place, or precise nature of the offence. Defendants got the benefit of very technical, formal scrutiny of errors or omissions, if only to postpone the proceeding until a new grand jury could be convened.

Fourthly, lawyers reported in their Year Books several of the ways criminal defendants could avoid jury trials. It was the lawyers' business to know when defendants could choose trial by battle with their accusers,[96] what words the parties should use to offer battle, and how the preparations should be made.[97] Lawyers knew whether and when defendants could become 'approvers' by admitting their guilt and prosecuting all the other felons they knew, in hopes of postponing their own executions for a few days.[98] Lawyers also gathered much learning about benefit of clergy. In the early fourteenth century, a defendant could still be denied clergy if he had no clerical vestments or tonsure.[99] By the late fifteenth century, the justices excluded the bishop's representative from any role in determining whether a defendant had read 'well enough' to claim clergy.[100] Spelling

[94] This plea may never have been successful. Mich. 7 Hen. 4, pl. 7, fol. 30 (1405); Mich. 10 Hen. 4, pl. 14, fol. 4; Stath. Corone 97; Fitzh. Corone 269 & 465 (1408); Hil. 4 Hen. 6, pl. 15, fol. 15; Stath. Corone 18; Fitzh. Corone 4; Brooke Appeale 44 (1426).

[95] Pasch. 32 Edw. 1, RS 193, 195 (1304); Mich. 1 Hen. 4, pl. 11, fol. 5 (1399); Mich. 7 Edw. 4, pl. 3, fol. 15; Fitzh. Corone 28 (1467); Hil. 22 Edw. 4, pl. 1, fol. 39 (1483). Contra, Mich. 18 Edw. 3, pl. 4, RS 9 (1344); Trin. 14 Edw. 4, pl. 10, fol. 7 (1474).

[96] E.g., Hil. 12 Edw. 2, pl. 45(a), 70 SS 92 (1319); Pasch. 20 Edw. 3, pl. 4, RS 135; Fitzh. Corone 125 (1346); Mich. 45 Edw. 3, Fitzh. Corone 100, fol. 262v (1371); Hil. 13 Hen. 4, Stath. Corone 96, fol. 59a; Fitzh. Corone 230 (1412); Mich. 28 Hen. 6, Stath. Corone 56, fol. 58a (1449); Trin. 22 Edw. 4, pl. 46, fol. 19 (1482). Even so, the Year Book note from 1319 stated that the law was aware that a thief could vanquish a plaintiff by strength of body, and yet be guilty.

[97] Pasch. 15 Edw. 2, fol. 464; Fitzh. Corone 385 (1322); Hil. 17 Edw. 3, pl. 6, RS 21; Lib. Ass. pl. 1, fol. 48; Fitzh. Corone 111 (1343); Mich. 9 Hen. 4, pl. 16, fol. 3; Fitzh. Corone 78 (1407); Pasch. 10 Hen. 5, pl. 3, Rogers 54 (1422); Mich. 19 Hen. 6, pl. 74, fol. 35; Fitzh. Corone 6, Brooke Corone 46 (1440).

[98] E.g., Mich. 7 Edw. 3, pl. 87, fol. 1 (1333); 11 Edw. 3, Stath. Corone 116, fol. 59a (1337); Hil. 21 Edw. 3, pl. 21, fol. 17; Stath. Corone 24; Fitzh. Corone 447; Brooke Corone 38 (1347); 26 Edw. 3, Lib. Ass. pl. 19[f], fol. 122, 123; Fitzh. Corone 181, Brooke Corone 99 (1352); Mich. 47 Edw. 3, pl. 26, fol. 16; Stath. Corone 4; Brooke Appeale 14 (1373); 1 Hen. 5, Fitzh. Corone 441, fol. 273v (1413); 8 Hen. 5, Fitzh. Corone 439, fol. 273v (1420); Mich. 9 Hen. 5, pl. 25, Rogers 22 (1421); Pasch. 12 Edw. 4, pl. 26, fol. 10; Fitzh. Corone 37; Brooke Corone 156 (1472); Mich. 11 Hen. 7, pl. 22, fol. 5; Brooke Corone 227 (1495).

[99] Mich. 20 Edw. 3, Fitzh Corone 233, fol. 268 (1326).

[100] Hil. 7 Edw. 4, pl. 12, fol. 29 (1468); Pasch. 21 Edw. 4, pl. 1, fol. 21 (1481).

out the letters, or reading a word here and there, was enough.[101] From the 1340s onward, lawyers reported one further option for defendants, to refuse to put themselves 'on the country'. Defendants who stood mute were starved and crushed with iron or stone,[102] but lawyers explained that defendants would thereby avoid forfeiting their land and could thereby save their families' fortunes.[103] One topic wholly omitted from the Year Books is the process for obtaining the king's charter of pardon. Whatever role lawyers and justices may have played in that process, they did not regard seeking pardons as part of the professional learning to be preserved in their Year Books.

Fifthly, money, goods and land changed hands when a criminal proceeding ended. That topic, predictably, engaged the lawyers' interest. Lords received the lands of tenants attainted for felony. The king, or his grantee, received the goods of fugitives and attainted felons. After conviction in an appeal of robbery, the plaintiff could recover the stolen goods. On the other hand, after acquittal in an appeal, a defendant could get substantial damages from the plaintiff or those who abetted the plaintiff in making the false appeal. Also, after acquittal in an indictment, a defendant could seek damages in an action of conspiracy against those who procured the false indictment.

It is good to be reminded that defendants' necks were not the only interests at stake in criminal cases, and that acquitted defendants could emerge from the courts with damages. Parties thus had ample incentives to pay for professional advice and representation. A further stage when money probably changed hands was in the compromising of appeals, which must lie behind many of the nonsuits by plaintiffs. Only one or two Year Book reports mention compromises of appeals,[104] and none describes defendants paying plaintiffs to default. Apparently this brokering, like the pursuit of pardons, was not part of the lawyers' professional learning.

More generally, beyond these five topics, the Year Book reports of criminal law portray a contest between the king's role in indictments and private victims' roles in appeals. Should the king's indictment be postponed so the victim could prosecute an appeal against the same defendant for the same felony, or should the victim's appeal be discontinued so the king could prosecute an indictment?[105] Could the victim insist on hanging a

---

[101] Trin. 9 Edw. 4, pl. 41, fol. 28; Fitzh. Corone 32; Brooke Corone 55 (1469).

[102] Mich. 8 Hen. 4, pl. 2, fol. 1; Stath. Corone 49; Fitzh. Corone 71; Brooke Corone 21 (1406); Trin. 14 Edw. 4, pl. 17, fol. 8; Brook Corone 160 (1474).

[103] Pasch. 4 Edw. 4, pl. 37, fol. 19 (1464); Trin. 14 Edw. 4, pl. 10, fol. 7 (1474).

[104] One is Pasch. 4 Edw. 4, pl. 14, fol. 10; Fitzh. Corone 25; Brooke Corone 195 (1464).

[105] In Mich. 22 Edw. 4, Fitzh. Corone 44, fol. 259v (1482), the justices in Exchequer Chamber said that a homicide indictment should be postponed for a year to permit appeals and 'counselled all men of law to execute this as a law'. See Mich. 31 Hen. 6, pl. 6, fol. 11; Fitzh. Corone 18 (1452) (indictment went forward because robbery victim sued too late).

felon whom the king had pardoned?[106] Lawyers may not have agreed on all these questions, but they were clear about the different purposes of the two types of proceedings. Several cases point out that 'vengeance' belonged to the victim or the victim's heir and that vengeance was what motivated the private appeal.[107] Lawyers recalled that in earlier days the victim of a maiming took member for member from the defendant,[108] and that the widow and children of the deceased personally dragged the defendant to the gallows.[109] On the other hand, indictments were made possible because 'every Christian man must lawfully discover felony' and inform the justices.[110] An indictment was the 'people's action',[111] and it was also the king's action because the 'life and member' of every subject belonged to the king.[112] One report of 1488 explained carefully that the king had to execute murderers as an example to deter others.[113]

The double jeopardy rule, the principal–accessary rule, and the formalistic scrutiny of indictments are all instances of a pro-defendant sentiment running through the criminal proceedings in the Year Books. When lawyers reported that the courts gave defendants more peremptory challenges of jurors,[114] second chances to read as clerks,[115] reversals of outlawry,[116] and opportunities for double pleading,[117] they summed these up as instances of the common law's presumption 'in favour of life'. A series of cases culminating in the late 1360s, the 'Quadragesms' of Edward III, announced important procedural rights. One could not be arraigned, tried or arrested without an indictment, an appeal or other

---

[106] Only if the victim appeared personally to demand execution. Pasch. 12 Ric. 2, pl. 3, Ames 145 (1389).

[107] 32 Edw. 3, Lib. Ass. pl. 8, fol. 196; Stath. Corone 124 (1358); Hil. 41 Edw. 3, Stath. Corone 29, fol. 56b; Fitzh. Corone 451 (1376); Mich. 11 Hen. 4, pl. 24, fol. 11 (1409); Hil. 11 Hen, 4, pl. 23, fol. 48 (1410); Mich. 9 Hen. 7, pl. 1, fol. 5 (1493).

[108] Pasch. 18 Edw. 3, pl. 31, RS 131 (1344); Pasch. 12 Ric. 2, pl. 4, Ames 147 (1389). And death for death, in Hil. 21 Hen. 6, pl. 12, fol. 28, 29; Brooke Corone 48 (1443).

[109] Mich. 11 Hen. 4, pl. 24, fol. 11 (1409).

[110] Mich. 35 Hen. 6, pl. 24, fol. 14 (1456).

[111] Mich. 5 Edw. 4, Long Quinto fol. 141, 142 (1465) (indictment is a sort of popular action). See also Mich. 8 Edw. 4, pl. 1, fol. 7 (1468) (anyone can speak for the king).

[112] Trin. 29 Edw. 3, fol. 41; Fitzh. Corone 462 (1355); Trin. 10 Hen. 7, pl. 3, fol. 25 (1495). See also Pasch. 9 Hen. 6, pl. 5, fol. 2 (1431) (every indictment is the king's action).

[113] Hil. 3 Hen. 7, pl. 4, fol. 1, Fitzh. Corone 57; Brooke Corone 132 (1488).

[114] Hil. 32 Hen. 6, pl. 14, fol. 26 (1454); Pasch. 18 Edw. 4, pl. 31, fol. 6 (1478); Hil. 14 Hen. 7, pl. 8, fol. 19 (1499).

[115] Trin. 34 Hen. 6, pl. 16, fol. 49; Fitzh. Corone 20 (1456).

[116] Mich. 9 Hen. 4, pl. 12, fol. 3 (1407); Pasch. 4 Edw. 4, pl. 15, fol. 10, 11 (1464) (repeats 1407 case). But see Hil. 1 Hen. 7, pl. 27, fol. 13; Brooke Corone 127 (1486).

[117] Mich. 7 Edw. 4, pl. 3, fol. 15; Fitzh. Corone 28 (1467); Hil. 22 Edw. 4, pl. 1, fol. 39 (1483).

'due process'.[118] A person wrongfully imprisoned could obtain a writ to be brought, along with the record below, to appear before the King's Bench.[119] In the late fifteenth century, the courts elaborated the grounds of objective suspicion that would warrant a lawful arrest.[120]

Lawyers in the Year Books often referred back to earlier cases, and recopied early cases into later Year Books, sometimes at eighty or ninety years' remove.[121] Much is consistent in this body of law, and what is inconsistent calls for careful distinction. A list of all the points of criminal law and procedure to be found in these Year Book cases beckons the modern student of law to construct a coherent 'restatement' of medieval English criminal law.

There are valuable and humane ideas in the criminal law and criminal procedure of the fourteenth and fifteenth centuries. Once acquitted, no person should be tried again. An accomplice should not be found guilty before the principal has been found guilty. No person should be put to trial on an indictment that fails to specify the person and the offence with absolute certainty. No person should be imprisoned for a felony unless a valid indictment or appeal can be shown. No person should be arrested for a felony unless a requisite level of objective suspicion has been shown. No person should be found guilty of a felony unless a requisite mental intent has been shown. These achievements of the legal imagination should not be lost from view, or regarded as the idle speculations of a profession whose business was not crime.

4. Lawyers and the Whole of the Common Law

My fourth and final point is about the whole intellectual domain of law, as conceived by English common lawyers. The first line of the first chapter

[118] Trin. 1 Edw. 3, pl. 19, fol. 23; Fitzh. Corone 165; Brooke Corone 69 (1327), also reported in 3 Edw. 3, Lib. Ass. pl. 3, fol. 4 (1329); Hil. 2 Edw. 3, pl. 4, fol. 1; Fitzh. Corone 149 (1328); Pasch. 25 Edw. 3, pl. 32, fol. 85; Fitzh. Corone 131 (1351); 42 Edw. 3, Lib. Ass. pl. 5, fol. 258; Brooke Corone 194 (1368). Fifteenth-century courts were more reluctant to release prisoners against whom no indictment or appeal was found. Hil. 8 Hen. 4, pl. 1, fol. 17; Brooke Corone 23 (1407); Mich. 13 Hen. 4, pl. 33, fol. 10; Bryt's Reports, App. I, 48 *Camb. L.J.* 113 (1410).

[119] 41 Edw. 3, Lib. Ass. pl. 22, fol. 255; Brooke Corone 192 (1367).

[120] E.g., Mich. 7 Edw. 4, pl. 19, fol. 20 (1467); Trin. 11 Edw. 4, pl. 8, fol. 4 (1471); Mich. 17 Edw. 4, pl. 1, fol. 5 (1477); Trin. 20 Edw. 4, pl. 8, fol. 6 (1480); Pasch. 2 Hen. 7, pl. 1, fol. 15 (1487); Mich. 13 Hen. 7, Keilway 34, 72 Eng. Rep. 191 (1497).

[121] E.g., Pasch. 12 Ric. 2, pl. 4, Ames 147 (1389) reprints Pasch. 18 Edw. 3, pl. 31, RS 131 (1344); Trin. 11 Hen. 4, pl. 50, fol. 93; Brooke Corone 31 (1410) repeats Hil. [7] Edw. 3, pl. 29, fol. 12; Fitzh. Corone 143; Brooke Corone 31 (1333); Trin. 11 Hen. 4, pl. 54, fol. 93; Brooke Corone 33 (1410) repeats Trin. 15 Edw. 3, pl. 42, RS 263; Lib. Ass. pl. 7, fol. 43; Fitzh. Corone 116; Brooke Corone 80 (1341); Pasch. 4 Edw. 4, pl. 38, fol. 19 (1464) repeats Mich. 44 Edw. 3, pl. 57, fol. 44; Lib. Ass. pl. 21, fol. 288; Stath. Corone 2; Fitzh. Corone 95; Brooke Corone 13 (1370).

of the first treatise on English common law, the treatise we call *Glanvill*, announced that all pleas are either criminal or civil.[122] A century after the *Glanvill* treatise was written, English lawyers no longer used the canon law terms 'criminal' and 'civil' to divide their pleas, but they understood that all suits were either 'pleas of the crown' or 'common pleas'.[123] The hundreds of Year Book reports on points of criminal law assure us that criminal law, the category these lawyers occasionally named 'the law of the crown',[124] remained an important part of the whole that was the 'common law' of England.

English lawyers occasionally mentioned other systems of law — notably the law of the Holy Church, the law of the Romans, the law of the French — and they were well aware of an ideal legal system, the law of God or the law of nature. I suspect that these English lawyers would have said that an ideal body of law and every 'complete' body of law in existence had to have a criminal part as well as a civil part. I suspect that they believed that the business of lawyers, the 'common erudition' of those 'learned in the law', required their attention to all the important parts of the law.

My larger point is that England's common lawyers were in control of their intellectual domain and their means of improving it, just as they controlled their legal literature and their means of reporting it. The insights of modern legal historians reveal how one institutional factor — tentative special pleading in common pleas — spurred the development of many important legal doctrines. It is wrong, however, to confuse that single mechanism with the whole history of the common law. Our simple, functional explanations do not control how they — the active, intelligent lawyers of fourteenth- and fifteenth-century England — constructed their intellectual world. The business of common lawyers was what they made their business.

Year Book lawyers were innocent of jurisprudential worries about how and when to 'make' law, but they appreciated a good knotty legal problem. A legal problem was the application of a legal proposition to new facts, real or hypothetical. Problems of criminal law were not beneath them, or beyond them, or beside the point of their daily professional practice. Year

---

[122] G.D.G. Hall (ed. & trans.), *The Treatise on the Laws and Customs of the Realm of England Commonly Called Glanvill* (Oxford, 1965), bk1, ch. 1 at p. 3.

[123] See M.T. Clanchy, 'Magna Carta and the Common Pleas', in Henry Mayr-Harting and R.I. Moore (eds), *Studies in Medieval History Presented to R.H.C. Davis* (London, 1985), p. 219.

[124] Pasch. 15 Edw. 2, fol. 463; Fitzh. Corone 383; Brooke Corone 214 (1322), also in Pasch. 16 Edw. 2, 31 SS xxix–xxx & n. 1 (1323); Mich. 20 Edw. 2, Fitzh. Corone 232, fol. 268 (1326); Pasch. 8 Edw. 4, pl. 8, fol. 4 (1468). Pasch. 17 Edw. 3, pl. 8, RS 281; Lib. Ass. pl. 6, fol. 49 (1343), is a 'crown case'. The title 'Corone' is the largest in Statham's Abridgment and the Abridgment of the Liber Assisarum, and the third largest in Fitzherbert's Abridgment. See Percy H. Winfield, *The Chief Sources of English Legal History* (Cambridge, Mass., 1925), pp. 219, 222, 231.

Book lawyers knew a legal problem when they saw it. They knew that their business — their calling — was to dispute until they resolved it. The set of propositions that these lawyers consciously regarded as their intellectual domain — their responsibility and their prerogative — was the 'common law of England'.

3

Some Early Newgate Reports (1315–28)

J.H. Baker

I should like to dedicate this essay to the Goddess Serendipitas, who has invisibly regulated so much of my research in manuscript law reports. Twenty years ago I published a series of Newgate reports from 1616, which I had recently stumbled upon at Harvard, thinking they were the earliest of their kind.[1] Some time later, I found in the same remarkable Treasure Room a much shorter series two centuries older, from 1421. I thought these were unprinted until I acquired a copy of the very rare Year Book of 9-10 Henry V published privately by Rogers in 1948;[2] they are printed there, but I suspect they are still not widely known. More recently, while searching through manuscript Year Books in the British Library, looking for moots, I found several series from the reign of Edward II and the first year of Edward III. These, as I hope and believe, are not known at all. It was quite a startling find for me, because the cases are three hundred years earlier than those I began with. Unconscious censorship by printers and editors, including even Selden Society editors, has kept them largely from sight. Presumably they seemed superfluous to the Year Books, as later understood, and so they were treated as if they were not there. It seems opportune to announce that they *are* there, and to say a few words about them.

The first text (cited below as A) consists of eighteen cases which came before Spirgurnel J around 1315–17;[3] they are undated, and are dispersed within a larger group of criminal cases under the heading *Corone* in an topically arranged collection. Most of the other matter in A is from the eyre of Kent, but there are also three cases before Sir William de Goldington (who died *c.* 1319), one of them at Colchester;[4] and also a

---

[1] Harvard Law School, MS 112, pp. 295–99 (1616). Printed (with a few addenda of 1618–27) in J.H. Baker, 'Criminal Justice at Newgate, 1616–1627', *Irish Jurist*, 8 (1973), pp. 307–22; reprinted in *The Legal Profession and the Common Law* (London, 1986), pp. 325–40.

[2] Harvard Law School, MS 41, fos 178v–180r. They are printed without translation in R.V. Rogers ed., *Year Books of the Reign of King Henry the Fifth* ([Würzburg], 1948), pp. 21–22.

[3] BL, MS Harley 2183, fos 172v–175v.

[4] Ibid., fol. 172v. The third case is identified as a trailbaston case.

case, which came before Bereford CJ, of an eighty-year-old man who killed his wife against his will while chastising her ('auxi cum il la voleyt aver chastice').[5] The second of my texts (B), added in the lower margins of a Year Book, contains twenty-four cases before Spigurnel J in 1317–19;[6] this series begins with a dated caption, and many of the cases can be traced in the surviving Newgate gaol delivery rolls. These are known to me in only one version each. The third text (C) occurs in most of the manuscript Year Books of 15 Edw. II, though not in the Maynard edition, and contains eleven cases before Spigurnel J in 1321.[7] At the beginning of the next reign, we have a series of sixteen cases before Bourchier ('Bousser') J. in Lent 1327 (cited here as D), also to be found in more than one version;[8] indeed, half a dozen of them were printed in the vulgate.[9] There are some scattered Newgate cases from other years of Edward III; but Professor Seipp and I have independently searched the black-letter Year Books, and our combined efforts confirm that there is no year after 1329 in which more than two Newgate cases occur. Glancing through numerous manuscript Year Books does not raise hopes of finding much more unprinted material of this kind either, though in the British Library there is a series of fourteen cases before Sir Geoffrey le Scrop at York Castle in about 1328 (E);[10] in the Cambridge University Library may be found three cases before Thorpe and Knyvet at Newgate in 1362,[11] and in the Wiltshire Record Office there is a report of a single case at Newgate in the year 15 Ric. II.[12]

I wish I could claim that this type of material is wholly new to the legal historian, but of course it is not. In 1981 Dr Summerson gave us an interesting account of the criminal cases in the Latin reports of the Yorkshire eyre of 1293/94 and showed how they could be augmented

---

[5] Ibid., fol. 173r.

[6] BL, MS. Egerton 2811, fos 118v–123v: 'Deliberacion de Neugate par Sir Henry Spig' et alium die mercurii proximo ante dominicam in ramis palmarum anno decimo Regis Edwardi filii Edwardi.' The record of this delivery is in JUST 3/41/3 (caption on m. 6).

[7] Holkham Hall, MS 243, col. 694; BL, MS Add. 25183, fol. 69r; CUL, MSS Gg 5.20, fol. 137r; Hh. 2. 4, fol. 180r.

[8] BL, Cotton MS, Faustina C. VI, fol. 182r–v; MS Harley 739, fol. 45r–v; MS (Add. 12270, fos 4v, 39v, 41r; Lincoln's Inn, MSS Hale 116, fos 1v–2r; 137(2), fol. 302v. Some of the cases are recorded in JUST 3/43/1,3.

[9] YB Trin. 1 Edw. III, fol. 16 (six cases before 'Bousser', who sat at Newgate). These are also in the MSS of this term: e.g., CUL, MS. Gg. 5.1, fol. 6v; Hh 2.4, fol. 131r–v; Mm 2.17, fos 2v–3r. Four of them are printed in 98 Selden Soc. 790–91. Cf. also YB Mich. 1 Edw. III, fol. 25 (Bousser J); 1 Lib. Ass. 7–8; Fitz. Abr. [hereafter F.], *Corone*, pl. 157, 159–60.

[10] BL, MS Add. 12270, fos 139v–140v (fourteen York cases, and one or two others belonging to D, above).

[11] CUL, MS Hh 2.4, fol. 300r–v ('Devant Monsieur Robert Thorpe et Knyvet a la gaiole de Neugate deliverer', 36 Edw. III).

[12] Savernake Deposit, MS Bruce 11, fol. 60r ('A Newgate devant Sir Water Clopton, Charlton et plousours autres justices assignes . . .').

from the record.[13] There are plenty of criminal cases in other eyre reports, two quite full King's Bench trailbaston sessions (at York and Kingston on Thames) in the *Liber Assisarum*,[14] and a scattering of criminal cases, especially in the King's Bench, throughout the Year Books.[15] Even from Newgate there are about twenty fourteenth-century cases in the printed Year Books, and about a dozen from the fifteenth century.

All I can claim as a new discovery, therefore, is the existence of such reports in the form of a more or less continuous series limited to Newgate. For about ten to fifteen years, at the least, there was regular reporting of crown cases at Newgate. It must at present be a matter for speculation whether the series continued after 1328. It is possible that the stray cases in the vulgate were abstracted from continuing instalments of the same series, and that we have lost the main collection because its circulation was so much more limited than that of the regular Year Books. The stray groups from 1362 and 1421 might strengthen such a hypothesis, though it would be remarkable if reporting had been carried on for so long as a century with so few surviving remains. Be that as it may, even if we assume that regular Newgate reporting did not continue beyond the early years of Edward III, the existence of this stream of reports raises an interesting question about its purpose. The contents are also interesting, since we can in many cases identify the records, and the combination of report and record — despite the extreme brevity of both — helps to illuminate a dark corner in the history of the criminal law.

Unlike the eyres and the King's Bench, the sessions at Newgate had a purely criminal jurisdiction. We cannot therefore explain the reports as mere appendices to the regular reports, taken to while away the time by lawyers who were in court for other purposes. Lawyers at Newgate can only have been there for the crime. Yet we do not readily assume or expect the regular presence of counsel in the medieval crown courts. A well-known case in the 1293/94 eyre shows the rule already in place that counsel were not permitted to prisoners on indictment;[16] and we know that even in Tudor times capital cases were dealt with on circuit without the benefit of counsel on either side.[17] Our reports reveal that

[13] The reports only were printed, unidentified and without translation (from one MS), in A.J. Horwood (ed.), *Year Books 30 & 31 Edward I* (Rolls Series, 1863), pp. 528–45.

[14] The York session is in 22 Edw. III (beginning at pl. 39), and the Kingston session is in Mich. 27 Edw. III (beginning at pl. 3). Note also 33 Lib. Ass. 7 (?Sarum); 40 Lib. Ass. 39–40 (Oxford); 43 Lib. Ass. 30 (Hertford).

[15] There are also some little-known criminal cases (including circuit cases down to 32 Hen. VI) in the *Abridgement of the Boke of Assises* (1555 ed.), fos 65v–79v. Cited below as Abr. Ass.

[16] Horwood ed., *Year Books 30 & 31 Edward I* (Rolls Series), p. 530. Professor Seipp shows in his essay that there were many exceptions to this rule; but it remains doubtful whether counsel were routinely employed in criminal cases.

[17] Baker, *The Legal Profession and the Common Law*, pp. 286–87; J.B. Post, *Journal of Legal History*, 5, p. 23.

there were lawyers at Newgate besides the presiding judge. The references
to counsel are not numerous, and are mostly (it seems) to king's serjeants
acting either directly for the crown or for appellors. They represent the
crown in an administrative capacity, and are given directions as such —
for instance, in one instance they are told to sue out writs. But 'king's
serjeant' is not here a loose synonym for the clerk of the crown who
must also have been present.[18] The one king's serjeant mentioned by
name (Willoughby) is a serjeant of the coif. Appellees were presumably
entitled to representation, though the Newgate reports do not happen to
mention it; the York reports, on the other hand, mention counsel arguing
a point of law for a defendant indicted for murder.[19]

The only other lawyer mentioned is an 'apprentice' who, in text D, is
encountered asking a question. It is quite a good question. An approver
had brought an appeal, to save his life, but when the time came to sue his
appeal at the gaol delivery he successfully claimed benefit of clergy and
was delivered to the ordinary. The apprentice wanted to know whether he
could make his purgation, since he had already confessed his guilt before
the coroner when he became an approver. The judge answered that the
ordinary ought not to proceed to purgation *rege inconsulto*.[20] This mention
of an apprentice may help to answer our question about the reports. Of
course, he might have been some kind of junior counsel for the crown,
but in view of the employment of a king's serjeant at the London gaol
deliveries this seems to be an anachronistic concept. The word 'apprentice'
is more likely at this date to bear its original sense of a student, and it is
not too wildly imaginative to suppose the equivalent of a wooden crib at
Newgate, even if it was less crowded than that in the Common Bench.
Nor does it shock the imagination to suppose that students wanted to
know something of crown proceedings. The existence of the texts called
Placita coronae almost certainly indicate a criminal procedure course for the
apprentices, the set book (with practical examples) being doubtless based
on lectures. These apprentices were not, of course, aspiring to criminal
advocacy of the kind associated with Thomas Erskine or Marshall Hall.
The best fees, then as now, flowed from contests over material wealth. But
even wealthy serjeants at law needed to know their criminal law. Professor
Seipp has drawn our attention to the speech by the lord chief justice to the
new serjeants created in 1521. They were instructed, somewhat fancifully,
that their parti-coloured robes were blood-red on one side to indicate
the *causae sanguinis* in which they would be consulted, while the blue on
the other side represented the *causae pecuniariae*.[21] The 'cases of blood'

[18] Serjeant Willoughby is named in Mich. 2 Edw. III, F. *Corone* 157 (but not in the
MSS). D2 says: 'Le serjant le roi fust del conseil W. [the appellor]'. Other allusions to
king's counsel are in B21, C1, D1, D13.

[19] *William atte Beck's Case*, E9. The counsel was Scorborough.

[20] D9, printed in YB Trin. 1 Edw. III, fol. 16, pl. [3].

[21] J.H. Baker, *The Order of Serjeants at Law* (London, 1984), p. 287.

may have referred to their role as assize commissioners and members of Serjeants' Inn rather than to advocacy or advice; but none of these roles were confined to the order of serjeants, and they existed three centuries earlier. Many lawyers beneath the degree of serjeant could expect to be engaged on commissions, or as coroners, or as stewards of leets, or as clerks of courts with criminal jurisdiction, or as counsel in appeals;[22] a knowledge of criminal law and procedure was therefore a professional asset at most levels.

Why, then, was the series discontinued? The question is impossible to answer, given our lack of knowledge of the way ordinary Year Books were circulated, and why even Common Bench reports seem to have been teetering on the edge of extinction under Richard II. If we are right to associate the Newgate reports with the core subject of criminal procedure as taught to apprentices of the Bench, the answer may lie in the fourteenth-century reorganisation of legal education which resulted from collegiate decentralisation.[23] As elementary instruction passed to the Inns of Chancery, the Criminal Procedure course somehow disappeared, to be replaced by practical training under senior clerks. The only surviving medium for teaching criminal law was of a higher order, aimed at potential justices rather than clerks, in the form of readings in the Inns of Court; and it is notable that criminal law features prominently in readings from at least the mid fifteenth century onwards.[24]

Let us, then, turn from these speculations to the content of the reports, and with the aid of our seventy Newgate cases — eked out with parallel material from the same period — attempt to sketch the principal legal issues arising at the London gaol deliveries in the early fourteenth century.[25]

Modes of Prosecution: The Arraignment

Since these were gaol deliveries, we may suppose that the calendar consisted of the prisoners currently detained in Newgate. When each prisoner is put up for arraignment the first question raised is how he comes to be in gaol. The dominant method of prosecution still seems to be the appeal; and the usual incentive to appeal seems to be either to escape

---

[22] Counsel beneath the degree of serjeant could be engaged: e.g. Bluet in 22 Lib. Ass. 39.

[23] J.H. Baker, *The Third University of England*, Selden Society lecture (London, 1990).

[24] See 94 Selden Soc., introduction, pp. 302–3, 347–50.

[25] To avoid excessive citation, the four series are here referred to by the sigla A-e as indicated above, the cases being numbered within each series in the order in which they occur. (The sequence in D is based on the Cottonian MS) Fitzherbert's *Abridgment* is cited as F.

death by turning approver, or to recover stolen property.[26] The approver's bargain for his life is very strict. He must first confess the felony, and take an oath to accuse all his companions, without accusing anyone falsely (C1); he must then proceed within three days of commencing the appeal,[27] though the court generously interprets this as running from the formal accusation rather than from the confession (A5). His obligation to prosecute the appeal is so strict that in one case an appellor is hanged because the appellee has disappeared to Flanders (D11);[28] a few years later the same fate befalls an approver who mistakes the colour of a stolen horse in his count.[29] Appellors, other than approvers, who fail to prosecute may be fined (B7) and their pledges of prosecution amerced (B1, D1). If an appeal collapses, the accused is always arraigned at the king's suit if possible; but this must be done within a year and a day (B20), and it is not allowed in the case of theft unless the accused was taken with 'mainour' — the stolen goods found in the thief's possession (B1, B6, B23, D1 = D13).

Some prisoners are, however, accused by written indictment, which must be produced in court. Many prisoners in Newgate were there to answer indictments taken in other counties, and this raises the puzzling question of how the 'police' network functioned; often the indictment has not yet been received from the other county, but the court will not proceed to arraignment without it (B10, B15, B22, C1, C2, D2). Where there is no indictment, even if it is a homicide case, the accused is entitled to mainprise (B10, D1); freemen of London claim special privileges in this regard (B21). Those released on mainprise are still notionally in Newgate, and are therefore arraigned at the gaol deliveries. An indictment cannot allege an offence in a county other than that in which it is found (A2); but the court can if necessary send for a jury from a nearby county such as Essex (A2).

Perhaps of greatest technical interest are the exceptions to the rule, which was soon to be of constitutional importance, requiring an indictment or appeal before anyone could be tried for felony. In our first series, a suspected cutpurse was arraigned before Spigurnel J without indictment. The judge said that at one time cutpurses could not be hanged, but that the council had ordained that they should be arraigned and hanged wherever they were taken with the mainour. Since there was no mainour, however, the suspect was released.[30] Then, in 1321, we find the case of

---

[26] If the owner did not appeal, the goods went to the crown: 97 Selden Soc. 157 (1329).

[27] Cf. 97 Selden Soc. 155, where Cambridge JItin says there is no time-limit (1329).

[28] Printed as YB Trin. 1 Edw. III, fol. 16, pl. 4; 98 Selden Soc. 790.

[29] 26 Lib. Ass. 9.

[30] A9. The obscure reference to the council may be a garbled allusion to the Assize of Northampton: cf. Bracton's *constitutio antiqua*: fol. 137 (ii, 386).

a suspected horse-thief who was brought from Smithfield to Newgate, where Spigurnel J proposed to arraign him on the presentment of an inquest *ex officio*, without indictment. This time the summary procedure seems to have been warranted because the accused was brought directly from the scene of the crime; but the inquest said he was not guilty, and so he was not in fact arraigned. The use of an inquest of accusation, other than the grand jury, is unusual, and it may have been used here because the horse was not produced as mainour; the reporter queried whether the procedure was correct without mainour.[31] In both cases, therefore, we are seeing in operation the principle that a thief taken red-handed may be arraigned without indictment or appeal.[32] What Maitland called the 'barbaric justice' of the original rule has nevertheless now been brought under judicial control;[33] although the need for appeal or indictment is dispensed with, there must still be arraignment and jury trial, and in our second case there cannot even be an arraignment without a preliminary hearing. But we are seeing the judicialised summary procedure in its final stages. According to Hale, it did not survive the Edward III statutes of due process. The last example so far noted was in 1343.[34]

An accessory cannot be arraigned without the principal; there is a doubt as to what happens if the principal has benefit of clergy (A15), but certainly if the principal is acquitted the accessory must clearly be discharged without trial (B24) and this is soon held to be the position in the former case as well.[35]

Although appeals seem to account for about half the prosecutions, the Newgate reports and records show nothing of the factual detail or the technicalities of counting in appeals, as revealed in *Placita Coronae* or the eyre reports.[36] Indictments are even more obscure. The records do not

---

[31] C4 ('Nota qe un fust pris par suspecion pur un chival en Smytfeld et amené devaunt Sire Henry Spigurnel, et saunz enresoner il prist enqueste sil fuist coupable, et sil soit trove coupable donqes il serra resoné et il se put mettre et aver respons, qar le primer enqeste serra en lieu de enditement etc. Quere si home serra pris par suspecion sanz mayn oevere: credo quod non. Et lenqueste dit qil ne fust pas coupable').

[32] Another application of the principle is found in D7 (1327), when it was said that an accessory found selling the mainour in company with the principal could be arraigned without indictment or appeal: 'Si un homme seit pris ove meinovere ove un chival et arené . . . et si un altre seit trové en sa compaigne il serra arené par suspecion sil seit trové ové ly vendant le chival, tot neit il vers li apel nenditment.' Cf. *Sharneye's Case* (1329), 97 Selden Soc. 159. Another example may be 98 Selden Soc. 791 (before Bousser J, 1327).

[33] *History of English Law*, ii, p. 579.

[34] *Case of the Queen's Cup* (1343), YB Hil. 17 Edw. III, fol. 13, pl. 48; 17 Lib. Ass. 5; F. *Corone* 174.

[35] 97 Selden Soc. 157 (1329); Trin. 5 Edw. III, F. *Corone* 145 (5 Lib. Ass.); 18 Lib. Ass. 13 (F. *Corone* 176); Trin. 22 Edw. III, F. *Corone* 252; 26 Lib. Ass. 27 (F. *Corone* 193); Hil. 41 Edw. III, F. *Corone* 450.

[36] E.g. 24 Selden Soc. 100 (1331). 'Malice aforethought' is formally alleged in an appeal of death in B13.

recite their contents except in the briefest outline, and it seems from a report of the London eyre that they were not read out in court either.[37] These deficiencies in the records raise a serious obstacle to the study of early criminal law.

A further obstacle, though in no way surprising, is the lack of any details of trials. We have only fleeting glimpses of the proceedings before the jury, and must be wary of assuming that a 'trial', with witnesses, was usual. In one case a jury are locked up overnight without amenities because they cannot agree; the technique succeeds, and they reach a verdict in the morning (C8). In another case a judge mentions a piece of evidence to an inquest of office off his own head in the course of his direction.[38] But generally we hear little of the way juries were informed or went about making their decisions. In later theory that the judge acted as counsel for the accused; and certainly in one case we have Spigurnel J telling the defendant to shut up or he will hang himself.[39] But the same judge is not helpful to those who do not heed his advice and who try to be evasive; he may make vague threats — 'you will soon see what will be done'.[40] or 'you will learn the law of the crown'[41] — or send him to the *peine forte et dure* with a profane expletive.[42]

Perhaps the best view of a Newgate jury at work is provided by another case before Spigurnel J which seemingly reflects a sophisticated sense of fair play. Four down-and-outs were arraigned for various unspecified robberies in the region of St Giles in the Fields on the grounds that they were commonly seen wandering around late at night and early in the morning. There was no mainour, and the only additional evidence was that they lived in an empty house on the outskirts of the town. The suspicion here was too unspecific; the jury found them all not guilty.[43] It is not made clear whether the acquittal was encouraged by the judge; but we know that there was a growing judicial hostility to vague charges. Although it was still possible to be indicted as a 'common thief', we learn that the justices would direct the jury not to convict unless some specific

[37] 85 Selden Soc. 44 (1321).

[38] C1: '. . . Et *Spigurnel* dit de sa teste demene a lenquest . . .'

[39] B17: 'il vaut meuth qe vous lessez, qar volez vous pender meim?'

[40] C1: 'Et puis dit *Spigurnel* sil ne voleit conustre [ly] mesme estre laron il verreit bien tut ceo qil fereit.' The prisoner wished to turn approver without formally confessing the felony. (Cf. note 42, below.)

[41] Mich. 20 Edw. II, F. *Corone* 232, *per* Scrope CJ ('si nous [d]ussoms ciens ceo que nous faut, vous duisses apprendre ley del corone').

[42] B18 ('Dunques a sa penance, de parte Dieux!'). The prisoner had already been sentenced to the *peine forte et dure* but wanted to become an approver before the coroner without returning to confess before Spigurnel; this was refused.

[43] B14. Identified as *Simon Braban's Case*, JUST 3/41/1, m. 12d.

fact was proved.[44] By the middle of Edward III's reign, the courts would strike down the indictment itself for generality.[45]

More informative are two cases, in our York reports,[46] which show the kind of interchange between judge and jury which Judge Arnold identified in civil cases later in the reign.[47] In the first case, the prisoner was indicted for battery and for being a common wrongdoer. The jury acquitted him on the latter charge, though we cannot tell whether this was at the court's suggestion in pursuance of the policy just mentioned. On the battery charge, however, we are given more detail. The jurors found that the prisoner was playing a ball game (*pelot* — perhaps handball) and gave his partner a biff (*un boef de sa mayn*), for which they later made up. Scrope awarded that the prisoner be discharged (*qil alast quit*), even though he struck the other person against the peace. It is not clear from the report whether this was a special verdict, a general verdict of acquittal, or a conviction with judicial discretion exercised at the sentencing stage.

The second case, immediately following in the manuscript, provides another example of what looks like a tentative special verdict. The prisoner pleaded not guilty to murder, and put himself on the country. The jury said that the deceased had struck the prisoner in a tavern with his stick, and the prisoner had drawn his knife and put it up to ward off the blow; the deceased had then struck his arm against the knife and suffered a fatal wound. This, of course, was an attempt to shift the causation on to the deceased; but Scrope decided to treat it as a case of self-defence and questioned the jurors as to the chance of retreat:

Scrope	When he drew the knife and put it up against the blow, could he not have escaped in some other way?
The Inquest	No, sir.
Scrope	Was there only one door in the house?
The Inquest	Sir, there were two, but one was shut so that he could not get out.
Scrope	Let him be remanded to prison to await the king's grace.

This is the inquest of life and death speaking, not the grand jury, and yet the impression given is that they have already made some enquiry in advance. There is no mention of evidence given in court. Of course, it may

[44] 24 Selden Soc. 141 (1313): 'Nota qe home pris pur suspeccion ou endite com comune laron e de ceo arené, les justices dirroit a la [dozein] qil ne les soilent sil ne soit pas certain fait'. Bolland was surely nodding when he translated the last words as 'certain of his guilt'.
[45] J.H. Baker, *An Introduction to English Legal History* (3rd edn, London, 1990), p. 577.
[46] E11–12.
[47] M.S. Arnold, 'Law and Fact in the Medieval Jury Trial: Out of Sight, Out of Mind', *American Journal of Legal History*, 18 (1974), pp. 267–80; 'The Control of the Jury', 100 Selden Soc. x–xxxi (1985).

be that Scrope has heard the evidence himself and is simply putting formal
questions of the kind we associate with modern trials. But that would be to
read a Victorian sophistication into simple words which suggest that the
jury may still have been, at any rate in some cases, self-informing. The
outcome is equally unclear, but since a pardon was to be obtained it may
have been a formal special verdict.

Whatever form the jury investigation took, it had certainly become the
usual mode of trial. Battle is occasionally proffered, but it seems to be
hedged around with more restrictions than in Bracton's account, and the
judges seem hostile to it as a potential means of escape. In one case the
judge refuses to allow it in robbery on the explicit ground that it would
encourage the strong to rob the weak (A8). And it is not allowed to a
defendant who broke the king's prison (D2,[48] D13,[49]). Moreover, battle is
only allowed in an appeal of robbery if there is mainour (D2, D13, D16).[50]
There is no evidence in the Newgate reports of any battle actually being
fought.

Capacity of Parties

A number of infants are arraigned, one as young as eight, but four cases
state that they are not to be sentenced if under the age of twelve (A3, A10,
B8, D17). This age may be significant because, as is pointed out in one case
(A3),[51] it is the age of joining frankpledge; one cannot be outlawed under
twelve, because one is not in law. Our texts also give as the reason that
infants under twelve are not of an age to suffer judgment (A3, B8, D17);
and on this theory a child of seven could still be tried but not sentenced
(D17).[52] This could be taken to mean that he would be sentenced when
of full age, as apparently happened in a case of 1351.[53] The record in
one of our Newgate cases, however, puts it on the ground that no felony
or 'sedition' (disobedience to law) can attach to such a child, and so the
child is discharged without trial (B8). This is borne out by a Latin report
from Edward I's time, when a judge said of a small boy who accidentally
killed a woman with an arrow, 'Since he is not twelve years of age, he is
not a felon but good and lawful'; and because he had run away it was

[48] Identifiable as *Whytecroft* v. *Whyting*, JUST 3/43/1, m. 8d.

[49] YB Trin. 1 Edw. III, fol. 16, pl. 6 (F. *Corone* 154, 281).

[50] Cf. also 4 Lib. Ass. 1 (F. *Corone* 144); 36 Edw. III, CUL, MS Hh 2.4, fol. 300.

[51] Likewise in 24 Selden Soc. 108 (1313).

[52] Cf. 24 Selden Soc. 109 (1313): an infant of seven shall not bear judgment ('ne portera nul juyse') though attainted (presumably meaning convicted by verdict), because he does not know good and evil. Cf. ibid. 148 (boy of eleven, mentioned below).

[53] YB Pas. 25 Edw. III, fol. 85, pl. 28 (F *Corone* 129).

proclaimed that he should come back again without being charged.[54] On the other hand, in the time of Edward II, when a boy of eleven killed another child and hid the body under some cabbages, this was taken as proof that he knew right from wrong and therefore deserved to die.[55] The notion that *malicia supplet aetatem* is found in later cases, but perhaps only when the infants were over twelve.[56]

There was no objection to an infant being an accuser, and this may have represented a change since Bracton's time. Bracton took the view that, since an infant could not fight a battle, an appeal would have had to await his full age; but in our period it is up to the appellee whether he stays in prison in order to fight later or elects to have jury trial at once (D17).

Although our Newgate reports do not mention insanity, the York series affords an instance (E3) of a woman who strangled her ten-year-old child while temporarily out of her senses ('hors de son sen et enraggée par xv jours'). She was remanded to await a pardon, and the judge offered to help obtain one if she had no friends to do so.[57]

A married woman has some kind of defence if accused with her husband, though the theory is not here stated (A14).[58] The reporter in one case wonders whether the rule is confined to receiving her husband after the fact (D6). A married woman can bring an appeal for her goods stolen while she was single; but she must join with her husband for this purpose (A14; and cf. C5).

A woman convicted of felony may plead pregnancy as a ground for respiting execution.[59] The practice in such a case was not to enter the judgment of death at once on the roll, but to enter a clause of respite 'until she be delivered' (C7).[60] At this date apparently the woman could be further respited if she became pregnant again before the authorities caught up with her; and if she managed to arrange a series of repeated pregnancies which took her into the next reign, it would be impossible to sentence her without an elaborate procedure for getting the record

[54] BL, MS Royal 10.AV, fol. 155v: 'Nota. Quidam puer nomine Johannes de B. etatis xii annorum stetit infra quandam domum et sagittavit ad quandam metam extra domum et per infortuniam quandam mulierem Rosam nomine interfecit. *Justiciarius*: Quia non est xii annorum non est felo sed bonus et fidelis. Et quia se subtraxit proclamatum fuit pupplice quod reveniret si vellet sine occasione.'

[55] 24 Selden Soc. 148 (earlier case recollected in 1313). There is also some emphasis on spontaneity, and an implicit hint that a child might be excused by parental coercion: see p. 149.

[56] 12 Lib. Ass. 30 (F. *Corone* 118). This was a recollection of a case before Spigurnel J: the defendant 'se mucha', but his age is not stated.

[57] Cf. 26 Lib. Ass. 27 (F. *Corone* 193): pardon for killing while *enragé*.

[58] Cf. 97 Selden Soc. 179 (1329).

[59] It could only be pleaded on conviction, not as a way of avoiding trial: 22 Lib. Ass. 71 (F. *Corone* 180).

[60] Cf. also the *Case of Alice Beyond-the-Brook* (1329), 97 Selden Soc. 179. If the pregnancy was not obvious, it was tried by a jury of women: 22 Lib. Ass. 71 (F. *Corone* 180, 240).

from the judge before whom she was tried (D6).[61] Perhaps because of
this problem in 1328, the courts in the first half of Edward III's time
adopted the sterner view that the benefit of pregnancy could only be
claimed once.[62] No one mentioned the rights of the unborn child.

Benefit of Clergy

Benefit of clergy is one of the most legally interesting topics recurring
in the criminal reports of the early fourteenth century, and the subject
deserves some attention because Miss Gabel was unaware of the case law of
this period when she wrote her classic essay on *Benefit of Clergy in England*
in 1928. The privilege was very frequently claimed, even in one case by a
child under twelve, though the child was not handed over to the ordinary
(A10);[63] but the court was not usually disposed to facilitate claims, and any
tension with the ordinary arose from the judges' perception that claims
were too readily allowed rather than the reverse.

Clergy was still usually claimed on arraignment, and an 'inquest of
office' taken.[64] According to the entry on the roll, the inquest was to find
out in what sort the prisoner should be delivered (*ut sciatur qualis liberari
debet*); if the inquest acquitted the accused, he was discharged without
being handed over (B13);[65] if it declared him guilty, he became a clerk
convict. Conviction in this sense did not bind the church court but had
the practical effect that the crown obtained the convict's chattels pending
purgation,[66] and the procedure also enabled the court to determine the
fate of any mainour (A11; C5). The later practice of claiming clergy after
a substantive trial — that is, where the prisoner pleaded not guilty and
put himself on the country — was not yet regarded as proper. In the
Kent eyre of 1313, several prisoners were forced to elect between jury
trial and clergy, and the judges refused to allow a submission to trial with

[61] Abridged in 1 Lib. Ass. 8.

[62] 12 Lib. Ass. 11 (F. *Corone* 168); 23 Lib. Ass. 2 (Trin. 22 Edw. III, F. *Corone* 253); YB
Pas. 25 Edw. III, fol. 85, pl. 30 (F. *Corone* 130). The vulgate text of the last case misprints
'enseintes' as 'enfants'.

[63] Fitzherbert says that a *woman* was demanded as a clerk by the ordinary in 1348, but
was remanded because other indictments were pending: Hil. 22 Edw. III, F. *Corone* 461.
Can this be a misreading?

[64] This term is used in B13; C5; 5 Lib. Ass. 5; 97 Selden Soc. 188, 192. The procedure
is mentioned in *Britton*, I, 27, and is that usually found in the records since at least
the 1240s.

[65] Cf. *Marche's Case* (1321), 85 Selden Soc. 103, where Herle J proposes to hand over a
clerk acquit, but the ordinary discharges him without purgation.

[66] See 24 Selden Soc. lxxiii, 107, 141 (king keeps chattels if convict dies before purgation),
149, 154 (1313); 97 Selden Soc. 165, 202 (1329); L.C. Gabel, *Benefit of Clergy* (Northampton,
Mass., 1928), pp. 41, 60.

a saving of clerical privilege;[67] if the party elected to plead not guilty and submit to jury trial, he could not later plead clergy.[68] In the London eyre of 1321, the court asked the ordinary where he had been sleeping when he failed to claim the prisoner until after the inquest, and a trick was suspected.[69] The objection seems to be related to waiver, or estoppel, in that a plea to the jurisdiction ought to be taken in good time. If the prisoner submitted to a jury *de bono et malo* he had necessarily waived the claim of ecclesiastical jurisdiction; and even if the claim was regarded as belonging to the ordinary, rather than the prisoner, it could likewise be treated as waived if not taken in time. A similar objection arose in the case of a person who had abjured; if he was subsequently arraigned and prayed clergy, it seems he could neither be executed nor handed over to the ordinary, but was liable to suffer perpetual imprisonment unless he could obtain a pardon for the return to England, in which case he would be handed over (B17, D5,[70] but cf. A7, B2). The related problem of the approver — the problem, it will be recalled, which lay behind the question of our 'apprentice' — was resolved in favour of benefit of clergy by the king's sixteenth answer to the Articles of the Clergy in 1315, though the point still arises in the reports and seems not to be free from doubt.[71] In due course the other cases were all held to fall within the equity of this enactment, and so this may have been the turning-point.[72]

By 1340 there was no waiver or estoppel merely because a prisoner had put himself on the country without claiming clergy on arraignment.[73] Once it was accepted that there was an election, however, it could be seen as a disadvantage to claim clergy on arraignment, if only because the defendant had no challenges to the jurors *ex officio*.[74] It seems to have been increasingly common to claim clergy after conviction in the 1360s and 1370s,[75] when it was held that in such a case judgment of

[67] 24 Selden Soc. lxxv-lxxvi, 114–25, 151, 154. Cf. ibid. 112, where Spigurnel J sends a prisoner to the *peine forte et dure* because he will not elect between pleading a pardon (which would acknowledge the jurisdiction) and praying clergy.

[68] *Foljambe's Case* (1313), 24 Selden Soc. 154. The apparent statement to the contrary on p. 119, *per* Bereford C.J., may be a mistranslation by Bolland; the meaning seems to be that clerks often submit themselves to jury trial *instead of* claiming clergy. There are other examples of this occurring on pp. 125 and 151.

[69] 85 Selden Soc. 82 (1321).

[70] Abridged in 1 Lib. Ass. 4 (Mich. 2 Edw. III, F. *Corone* 155); YB Trin. 1 Edw. III, fol. 16, pl. 4; 98 Selden Soc. 791.

[71] An approver is delivered to the ordinary in A6; C11; *Wodhull's Case* (1329), 97 Selden Soc. 162; *Anon.* (1351) F. *Corone* 128. For doubts, see B3; D5; D9 (98 Selden Soc. 790.)

[72] Sta. P.C. 124G.

[73] *Lacy's Case*, cited in YB Trin. 12 Edw. III (Rolls Series), p. 599, *per* Aldeburgh J.; misdated 22 Edw. III in F. *Corone* 257.

[74] 9 Hen. [V] ('VI'), Abr. Ass., fol. 78.

[75] Cf. 36 Edw. III, CUL MS Hh 2.4, fol. 300, where the defendant (who had unsuccessfully proffered battle) said he would rather suffer the *peine forte et dure* than submit to a jury, but then read as a clerk and was acquitted by the inquest *ex officio*.

death would be given and the prisoner handed over *absque purgatione*.[76] Tradition at the end of the fifteenth century attributed to Prysot CJ (in the time of Henry VI) the complete reversal of policy which not merely tolerated but *required* a substantive trial before clergy was pleaded.[77]

A claim could be barred by a counterplea of bigamy. Bigamy — meaning marriage to a widow, or taking a second wife — became a bar to a claim of clerical privilege by a constitution of the council of Lyon (1274), which was impliedly incorporated into English law and extended in scope by the statute De bigamis 1276.[78] There is an example of its operation, to the benefit of the lay jurisdiction, in the Newgate reports for 1321. A jury is sworn to try the first marriage, and there is some discussion in court of the way the question is to be put, doubtless reflecting the need to ask a temporal rather than a spiritual question (C1). By this means, clergy could be ousted without referring the matter to the ordinary. But this caused conflict with the church, and in 1327 the king conceded that the question of bigamy in such cases was to be tried by the spiritual court; the concession was confirmed by Parliament in 1344.[79]

The claiming of clerks belonged to the 'ordinary'. The ordinary of Newgate was a duly appointed representative of the bishop of London, invariably a London parish priest.[80] It is evident that the judges did not believe in making things easy for the ordinary. He had to be present in court, with his authority in writing, to claim the clerk, and if he was not so prepared the prisoner was remanded.[81] On one occasion the ordinary was sharply rebuked for arriving late and without an up-to-date commission.[82] The judges required a precise commission, and this led them to insist that it should name the justices before whom it was to be executed. This was

---

[76] YB Mich. 40 Edw. III, fol. 42, pl. 23 (F. *Corone* 91); Mich. 12 Ric. II (Ames Fdn), p. 40, pl. 5 (F *Corone* 109).

[77] YB Mich. 3 Hen. VII, fol. 12, pl. 10, *per* Bryan CJ; Sta. P.C. 131A.

[78] 4 Edw. I, *De bigamis*, c. 5 (extended to clerks who became *bigami* before 1274). For examples, see 24 Selden Soc. 140 (1313); Mich. 40 Edw. III, Abr. Ass., fol. 79.

[79] *Rotuli parliamentorum Anglie hactenus inediti*, ed. H.G. Richardson and G. Sayles (1935), p. 109 ('Gravamina prelatorum' of 1327, no. 11); 18 Edw. III, stat. 3, *Pro clero*, c. 2.

[80] E.g. the parson of St Mary Gracechurch in *Reynberd's Case*, JUST 3/43/1, m. 11; perhaps D5. The rector of St Mary Woolnoth in *Abingdon's Case*, JUST 3/41/1, m. 13; perhaps B13. The rectors of St Peter Cornhill and St Benet Gracechurch were appointed in 1321: 85 Selden Soc. 103.

[81] B4. This is perhaps *William de Garscoigne's Case*, JUST 3/41/1, m. 6 ('Et quia nullus ordinarius ipsum petit nec potest constare justiciariis hic de clericatu etc. remittitur prisone etc. salvo custodiendus quousque etc. Postea obiit in gaola hic etc.'). Cf. *Ralph de Bereford's Case* on the same membrane ('Et quia non constat justiciariis hic de clericatu ipsius Radulphi nec aliquis ordinarius ipsum petit, ideo remittitur prisone salvo custodiendus tanquam de sua cognitione convictus etc. quousque per ordinarium petatur etc.').

[82] D5 (Cotton MS): '. . . Et pus vint lordinare et fust blamé pur ceo qe il aveit taunt demoré. Et il dist qil naveit nul comission fors cele qil aveit en temps lautre roi. Et *Bours*' dist qe ceo ne valut ren, et li dist qil alast quere novel en hast et qil deliverast la prisoné.' Cf. the similar situation at Newgate in 1307 cited in Gabel, *Benefit of Clergy*, p. 52.

particularly difficult to comply with, since the judges kept changing, and another concession made by the king in 1327 was that commissions for demanding clerks should be effective without naming the judges.[83]

Upon a proper claim being made, the clerical status had to be tried. The reading test seems to have been generally in use (C5, C11, D19),[84] but not if the accused appeared in lay costume (A12, B2, B3, D14), in which case he was given time to prove his orders with written evidence from the bishop (A12).[85] There are four such cases in the reports, clearly demonstrating that the privilege is not yet supposed to be available to literate laymen. Spigurnel J even armed himself by having in court the relevant decretal, which he caused to be read.[86] We can only suppose that this remarkable precaution was necessary to deal with any attempt by the ordinary to make an illicit claim.

The text in question was the recent decretal *Si judex laicus* of Boniface VIII (1295–1303), which provided that clerks arrested without clerical dress or tonsure were not to have the *privilegium clericale*.[87] This was not a new principle, since there was an English constitution of 1261 to similar effect,[88] but its re-enactment by papal authority seems to have been taken more seriously by the king's judges and to have provided an opportunity for restricting the use of the privilege. The 'nova constitutio' was expressly mentioned in the plea rolls in a case of 1301, when clergy was claimed by an appellee who had been arrested in lay dress and without the tonsure. Because the court was uncertain whether the king would have the papal constitution applied in his realm, the case was adjourned for consultation with the king. In the event the appellee pleaded and put himself on the

---

[83] *Rotuli parliamentorum Anglie hactenus inediti*, p. 107 ('Gravamina prelatorum' of 1327, no. 5).

[84] Cf. 24 Selden Soc. 151 ('le ordynare ly bailla le livvre et il lust ii vers').

[85] Cf. D14 ('Item, un homme fuit appellé de mort de homme et il dit qil fut clerk et non habuit habitum nec tonsuram clericalem nec bene sit legere. *Bours'*: Mettez vous ordinare claym sur lui? [*Ordinary*:] Sir, en tiel cas ou il nad coroune ne habite de clerk il serra enquis sil seit clerk pur favour de clergie. Et *Bour'* demanda de qil fuit coroune. Il dit que del eveque de N. a coroné benet. *Bourc'*: Si homme maunde al evesque et il responde en tieu cas quod non est clericus quia non sunt in registro et ideo quere qualiter erit.'). The last sentence is not fully intelligible.

[86] A12 ('Item, ibidem un homme se prist a sa clergie. *Spig'*: nous vous trovoms en abite de lay, et la decretal veut qe si clerk seyt trové en abit de lay qil prover[oit] ses orders. Et fist lire la decretal devant ly. Et vous dites estre ordinere del evesqe de Londres, en qy eveschie vous estes, par quey entre cy e nous procheynes venues proves les ordres devant le evesqe etc. Et probatio erit qil monstra avant [lettres] <*reads* auteres> qe ly temoignent qil fust ordiné').

[87] *Sext* 5.11.12. Cf. *Sext* 3.2.1, which is concerned primarily with preserving benefit of clergy for married clerks, but adds at the end that clerks who 'tonsuram vel vestes deferant clericales' should not enjoy the privilege.

[88] Lyndwode, *Provinciale* (Oxford, 1679 ed.), p. 68: constitution of Boniface, archbishop of Canterbury.

country, and so it seems that the new constitution was observed.[89] Not long afterwards, a defendant was put to the *peine forte et dure* because he prayed clergy after being found in lay dress and without a shaven crown.[90] Perhaps, then, it was a conciliar decision which led our Newgate judges to keep copies of the decretal to hand.[91] The identification of lay dress seems to have been primarily a matter of colour: certain bright colours, or colours used in combination (as in parti-coloured garments), were fatal. Some interesting *jurisprudence* was developed in late fourteenth-century Toulouse on the definition of lay dress: a parti-coloured hood worn over plain dress was enough to distinguish a lay habit,[92] as was the use of blue trimmings on a houpelande.[93] Our Newgate records tell us only that cloth of ray — that is, cloth with stripes woven into the fabric[94] — was the principal indication of lay dress in early fourteenth-century England (A12, B2, B3, D14, below).

Two fully reported cases from manuscripts of the 1320s confirm vividly the restrictive judicial attitude towards claims to clergy which the Newgate reports indicate. The first was an incident before one of the Scropes, probably in the King's Bench before Sir Geoffrey as chief justice.[95] It is related in a manuscript in the Wiltshire Record Office,[96] and a much

---

[89] *Dewesburi* v. *Erdeslowe* (Oxford, 1300–2) CP 40/131, m. 21d ('dicit quod clericus est. Et quia curia Romana novam in hujusmodi casu edidit constitutionem que evidenter distinguit quo casu hujusmodi malefactores qui coram judice seculari se dicunt esse clericos etc. curie ecclesiastice tradi debent, et quo casu coram judice seculari respondere, nec constet curie hic utrum dominus rex constitutionem illam in regno suo observare voluerit etc., datus est dies . . . et interim loquendum cum domino rege etc. . . .'). This was drawn to my attention by Dr Paul Brand, who kindly provided a transcript.

[90] *R.* v. *Huntyngdon* (1304–05), BL, MS Add. 31826, fol. 379r; CP 40/150, m. 207. (For this also I am indebted to Dr Brand.) On fol. 318r of the MS another appellee who claims clergy is told by Brabazon J, 'We have seen you before now in lay dress and you have comported yourself as a layman and have no clerical tonsure' ('avant ces oures vus avum veu en robe de lay e estis porté cum laie vus navez pas tonsure de clerk'); the appellee, Hamon Grossy, may be the serjeant counter of that name (see Baker, *Serjeants at Law*, p. 148; inf. Dr Brand).

[91] Dr Brand points out that the new constitution is copied in the same Year Book MS as the two cases cited in the previous note, at fos 316v–317r.

[92] So held by all the doctors of the Toulouse law faculty in 1394: *Decisiones Magistri Stephani Auffrerii* (1508 edn, fol. 54r, qu. 227). The reports were from the archiepiscopal court of Toulouse.

[93] Ibid., fol. 60r, qu. 252 (*faupelanda de cadifio* with blue collar, cords and *folrata*).

[94] See Baker, *Serjeants at Law*, pp. 63–74. It was common for parti-coloured robes to have ray on one side; this dress was particularly favoured by lawyers and city liverymen.

[95] The ordinary is said to be the abbot of Westminster. The abbot's archdeacon was ordinary in the courts in Westminster Hall: 24 Selden Soc. 122, 123 (1313); YB Hil. 17 Edw. III (Rolls Series), p. 213n; 27 Lib. Ass. 42 (F. *Corone* 205); YB Hil. 10 Hen. IV, fol. 9, pl. 9 (F. *Corone* 467); Trin. 34 Hen. VI, fol. 49, pl. 16 (F. *Corone* 20).

[96] Savernake Forest Deposit, Bruce MS. 11, fol. 58v. Henry le Scrope was CJKB, 1317–23. Geoffrey le Scrope was CJKB, 1324–38, apart from two brief intervals.

abridged version in Fitzherbert dates it to Michaelmas 1326.[97] A prisoner indicted for larceny prayed clergy on arraignment, but because he was in ray clothing Scrope asked him whether he had anything else to say. He replied that he could do nothing without his ordinary. Scrope then asked him to show his head. There was no tonsure, and since no ordinary was present to claim him, Scrope asked whether he would be tried by the country. He again insisted on his clergy, and so Scrope spoke to him in Latin: 'Quomodo vetaris?' He did not know what to say, so Scrope tried again in French, with no better result.[98] We may well suppose that, like the knight who claimed clergy in the 1293 eyre and then let slip that he could not read, our prisoner *stetit quasi confusus*.[99] At this point, however, a monk belatedly turned up from Westminster Abbey to claim the prisoner as a clerk. Scrope gave him a stern warning: 'If you claim him as a clerk, where he is not claimable, I want you to know that you will be liable to the following penalty; namely, that all the temporalities of the abbey within the bishopric shall be forfeit to the king,[100] and that the abbot will never again be received to claim anyone here as a clerk. Do you still want to claim him, or not?' The monk, whose enthusiasm must have been somewhat dampened by this welcome, gave the sensible answer: 'If he is a clerk we claim him, but you sir, should make him read and test him.' Scrope, however, was not willing to proceed to the reading test, and so no demand was made. Since the prisoner persisted in his refusal to plead, Scrope told him that the law of the crown required him to be put to his penance (the *peine forte et dure*), but that the law of the crown was so favourable and generous that before committing himself he would be told what the penance was. The judge duly obliged him with all the gruesome details, but the prisoner still refused to plead and was awarded to undergo the *peine forte et dure*. The case shows the lay court firmly in control of the clergy test.

The second case occurred at the gaol delivery at York castle in 1328, before Sir Geoffrey le Scrope, the chief justice of the King's Bench.[101] William Dautre was convicted of felony, and on a later day the ordinary came and claimed him. Scrope replied that he had been convicted on his own submission to jury trial and that he thought he had been hanged. The ordinary reported that he was still in the castle, and the case was adjourned for advisement. The case was stronger than that in the London eyre of

[97] Mich. 20 Edw. II, F. *Corone* 233 (and cf. pl. 283). Cited as Trin. 19 Edw. II (the previous term) in 1469: next note.

[98] Cf. YB Trin. 9 Edw. IV, fol. 28, pl. 41: '... Vide Trinitatis 19 Edwardi secundi de clergie, comment lordinarie fuist mis a son peril de challenger felon come clerk, sans oyer luy lier. Mes vide la que lordinarie [*sic*] devaunt parla al felon en Latin et en Frauncois et il ne scavoit responder a luy.'

[99] Horwood ed., *Year Books 30 & 31 Edw. I* (Rolls Series), p. 532.

[100] Cf. 24 Selden Soc. 86 (1313).

[101] El. Cited as Trin 2 Edw. III in YB Trin. 9 Edw. IV, fol. 28, pl. 41. Scrope is identified as Sir Geoffrey in E14.

1321, since the clerk was not merely convict but attaint. However, the question was probably much the same, because the objection to delivering him to the ordinary is that he has waived the privilege by submitting to jury trial on the general issue.

The next day the archbishop of York came and prayed that he might examine the prisoner to see whether or not he was a clerk. Scrope warned that, since Dautre had already been sentenced, the archbishop would risk the forfeiture of his temporalities if the court found that he was not a clerk. The archbishop, like the monk in our first case, answered that he was merely seeking an examination to see whether the prisoner could be claimed: in other words, it was suggested that the test should precede the claim. Scrope 'willingly' conceded that, and the test was conducted by the archbishop, presumably out of court. We are not told what form it took, but it probably included a head-examination. The prisoner passed, and the archbishop prayed that he be handed over. Scrope, like Spigurnel, had by now prepared himself with canon law. 'Sir,' he answered, 'the decretals are contrary, that he who is found not dressed as a clerk and without tonsure, and who does not bear himself like a clerk, shall not enjoy the benefit of Holy Church.' The archbishop said he had found him wearing only breeches and a shirt, but that there appeared to be a tonsure on his head. When Scrope offered to check this, the archbishop said that the examination belonged to him. Scrope replied that to deliver the prisoner to him would be a judgment to the detriment of the crown, and the crown ought not to be injured without a cause proved to the court. So the prisoner was examined by the court and, fortunately for the relations between church and state, he managed to read and was also found to have a tonsure — reading between the lines, a crisp new tonsure. The impression which comes down to us is that Scrope was not best pleased with this outcome. He turned to the marshal and said he would have to be amerced grievously because the prisoner's crown had been shaved while in his custody.[102] And to the archbishop he said, 'We deliver to you this William, who on his own submission and in the dress of a layman has been attainted of felony, as someone who has refused clergy and the freedom of Holy Church.' The archbishop retorted: 'We receive him as a member of Holy Church, and not as a felon, for you are not his judges.' The law had thus reached something like its classic position. The reading test was available at the court's discretion, even if the prisoner was improperly dressed, but it was subject to the supervision of the lay court; if the test was passed, however, the jurisdiction passed exclusively to the spiritual court. It may be added as a postscript that when another member of the same family (Marmaduke Dautre) claimed clergy at York ten years later, before Scot J, the ordinary said he did not wish to claim him again

---

[102] Cf. the earlier case in Gabel, *Benefit of Clergy*, p. 64. The archbishop's court of Toulouse held in 1393 that a tonsure acquired in prison did not count: *Decisiones Auffrerii*, fol. 60, qu. 252.

because he had been handed over twice in the past and on both occasions had broken out of the archbishop's prison. The court, after taking advice, accepted this denial, saying that they could not know more than was put before them and that they ought not to oust the lay jurisdiction without a claim by the ordinary.[103]

The judges were taking the same hostile stance in 1352, when Shareshull CJ at Newgate held that an ordinary would forfeit his temporalities if he claimed a layman as a clerk, and moreover that 'litteratura non facit clericum nisi habeat sacram tonsuram'.[104] For the next hundred years, there is a silence in the reports. When it ends, we are in the more familiar world in which the courts have assumed complete control of a reading test which has become available to all, whatever their appearance, and even if their ability to decipher the psalter was embarrassingly feeble.[105] We now know that this remarkable change of approach was to have a pervasive and benign, if counter-productive, effect on the development of criminal law for the next few centuries. What caused it is still a mystery. But we can at least now date the change to the period between 1350 and 1450.

The most interesting feature of these reports, perhaps, is their very existence rather than any of their specific contents. We should not try to compare them with those of 1616. There is very little indication of law being made off the record: that is, of legal rulings upon the facts as they appeared at the trial rather than upon the bare Latin record. The emphasis is heavily on procedure. But that is equally true of the ordinary Year Books, and it would have been far more surprising if our Newgate reports had been strikingly different. The criminal law was a body of procedure before it became a body of sophisticated distinctions.

It seems to me, nevertheless, that a good case could be made out for printing a careful edition of these reports with the corresponding records. I have prepared a draft text and translation, and found many of the corresponding records. They now need an editor more familiar with the period, and with gaol delivery records in general, to put them into a publishable shape.

[103] *Duket Dautre's Case* (Mich. 12 Edw. III), BL, MS Add. 12270, fol. 200v; probably the anonymous case more briefly noted in YB Mich. 12 Edw. III (Rolls Series), p. 69, pl. 31 (12 Lib. Ass. 39; F. *Corone* 120); cited in YB Trin. 12 Edw. III (Rolls Series), p. 599 (F. *Corone* 117), as 'Cukette Dancri'; and in 27 Lib. Ass. 42 (F. *Corone* 205), as 'Marmeduke D.'; perhaps misdated as Trin. 22 Edw. III, F. *Corone* 254. Cf. *Lacy's Case*, cited in YB Trin. 12 Edw. III (Rolls Series), p. 599 (dated 22 Edw. III, F. *Corone* 257), where the court would not sentence an unclaimed clerk to death.

[104] 26 Lib. Ass. 19 (F. *Corone* 191). Cf. similar statement dated Pas. 34 Edw. III, Abr. Ass., fol. 71v.

[105] YB Trin. 34 Hen. VI, fol. 49, pl.16; Hil. 7 Edw. IV, fol. 29, pl. 12; Trin. 9 Edw. IV, fol. 28, pl. 41; Mich. 22 Edw. IV, F. *Corone* 44. Cf. the odd case where the prisoner read but the ordinary found that *non legit ut clericus pro diversis causibus*, and this was accepted: YB. Pas. 21 Edw. IV, fol. 21, pl. 1.

4

The Acts of the Scottish Lords of Council in the Late Fifteenth and Early Sixteenth Centuries: Records and Reports

William M. Gordon

The purpose of this essay is to make a beginning with an exploration of the content and layout of a register mainly containing decisions of the Scottish lords of council which for simplicity I shall refer to as 'the Register'.[1] This Register apparently existed in the sixteenth century but is no longer extant; at any rate, if it has been misplaced rather than lost or destroyed, it has not yet emerged from its hiding place. The main and, as will appear, perhaps the only direct source of our knowledge of it is the work known as Balfour's *Practicks* which was compiled in the sixteenth century by Sir James Balfour of Pittendreich and first printed in 1754.[2]

In these *Practicks* decisions are usually referred to not only by their date and by the names of the parties but also by a chapter number in one of two volumes which for the most part contained decisions (along with some Acts of Parliament or council). An example of such a reference is '15 *Octob.* 1478, Williame *Lord* Creichtoun *contra* Herbert Johnstoun, 1 *t. c.* 21' which is recorded in the *Practicks* in the second half of c. VI of the title 'Of milnis and multures' (p. 494). The question to be addressed is how these volumes were compiled and the essay falls into three parts. The first is a brief introduction to the lords of council and session; the second

---

[1] The exploration is part of a larger project initiated by my colleague, Robert Sutherland, formerly of the Department of Private Law and a Senior Research Fellow in the Department of Jurisprudence in Glasgow University. His aim is to reconstruct the Register as far as possible as a step in relating the development of Scots law to the surviving records of Council and Session.

[2] For details see the reprint edited by P.G.B. McNeill for the Stair Society, xxi and xxii (Edinburgh, 1962 and 1963). The introduction includes a biography of Balfour who, in the course of his varied and stormy career, held the offices of Clerk Register and Lord President of the Session.

Balfour's *Practicks* are an example of what have been called 'digest practicks', containing not only decisions of the lords of council and later of the Session but statutory and other material, as opposed to 'decision practicks' containing only decisions: see H. McKechnie, 'Practicks, 1469–1700', *An Introductory Survey of the Sources and Literature of Scots Law*, by various authors, Stair Society, 1 (Edinburgh, 1936), pp. 25–41.

deals with the surviving records of their work and the publication of those records for the period from 1469 to 1503; the third is an examination of the Register in the period from 1469 to 1503 and a brief comparison with the published records.

The lords of council of the late fifteenth and early sixteenth centuries, dealing with judicial business in sessions devoted to that purpose (and hence referred to as lords of council and session), are the ancestors of the modern Court of Session, the supreme civil court within Scotland. The official date of birth of the Court of Session is 1532 when, by the College of Justice Act 1532 (c. 2)[3] James V announced his intention 'to institute ane college of cunning and wise men baith of spirituale and temporale estate for the doing and administracioune of justice in all ciuile actionis'. At the same time, as an interim measure, he nominated fourteen persons – half spiritual and half temporal – plus a spiritual president, the abbot of Cambuskenneth, to 'sitt and decyde apoun all actiouns ciuile'. The institution was then ratified by James in parliament in 1541 'eftir his parfite aige of xxv yeris' on the narrative that it had been 'rycht profittable to his grace and all the haill realme'.[4] But this official version of the birth of the Court of Session, like many official versions of events, does not reveal the whole truth. In fact the main reason for the formal institution of a College of Justice was not so much to provide a central civil court as to secure from the papacy, against a promise of loyalty to the Catholic faith, a subvention towards the cost of providing it, payable by the prelates of the Scottish church — a subvention much of which ended in James's own pocket so that the institution was indeed in a financial sense 'rycht profittable to his grace'.[5] The institution of the College of Justice, therefore, did not represent a wholly new development in the provision of a centralised system of civil justice, as is now generally recognised by historians.

The Court of Session (or the Session as it was more usually referred to until the eighteenth century when the fuller title came into common use), even in the form given to it by James V's legislation was not really a new institution. Its creation was more a formalisation of a practice of appointing specialist members of the king's council to sit in sessions to administer civil justice. In particular, looking at the period immediately before 1532, in 1526 lords of council were appointed specifically to sit on

---

[3] *A[cts of the] P[arliaments of] S[cotland]*, ed. T. Thomson and Cosmo Innes (Record Commission, 1814–75), ii, p. 335.

[4] The College of Justice Act 1540 (*APS*, ii, p. 371, c. 10), passed on 14 March 1540/41; at this time the new year began on 25 March, as it did in Scotland until 1 January 1600. There was a further ratification after the succession of Mary, Queen of Scots, in 1543, ibid., ii, p. 443, c. 7.

[5] For the full story see *The College of Justice: Essays by R.K. Hannay*, edited with an introduction by H.L. MacQueen, Stair Society, supplementary vol. 1 (Edinburgh, 1990).

the session and in 1528 those members of the council not so appointed were excluded from the judicial sittings. Of those appointed to the session in 1531 fourteen were among the fifteen named in the College of Justice Act 1532. In fact the tendency towards the creation of a specialised group of councillors to deal with judicial business and to do so in special sessions for that purpose goes back into the fifteenth century. At this time more judicial business was coming before the king's council, some of it carried forward from the parliamentary auditors of causes and complaints who dealt with actions brought to the king in parliament.[6]

The process of specialisation in the period 1460–1513 has been studied in detail by Trevor Chalmers and it is not necessary to go over in detail the ground which he has already covered.[7] It is sufficient to note his comments on the growth within this period of a 'judicial council' containing members who could gain legal expertise from regular attendance at sittings even if they had no formal training in law, such as clerical members might have, and the appearance in the last decade of the reign of James IV (1503–13) of what he calls (p. 311) 'the nucleus of a truly professional judicature', both lay and clerical. James IV, he observes, preferred investment in armaments to investment in civil justice and, after his death at Flodden in 1513, there was a period of regression during the earlier years of the minority of James V. The measures taken in 1526 and 1528 then represent a return to the arrangements developed in the latter part of James IV's reign. These in turn are further formalised with the erection of the College of Justice. There was, therefore, the beginnings of a central court even before 1532 and some possibility of a case law developing out of its proceedings. The questions which arise are whether the Register reflects the recording of the proceedings of the judicial council as part of the process of developing a case law; and whether it thus represents our first evidence of law reports in Scotland.

The earliest case in the Register is dated 17 May 1469. The original *acta* of the council, however, are now available only from 1478 and even then there are gaps. When any formal records of the work of the council began to be kept is uncertain but we do know that at one time there were records which went back before 1478, because there exist notes on such records made by Sir Robert Spottiswoode, who was created Lord of

---

[6] See on all this A.A.M. Duncan, 'The Central Courts before 1532', *An Introduction to Scottish Legal History*, by various authors, Stair Society, 20 (Edinburgh, 1958), pp. 321–40, esp. at pp. 334–39.

[7] Trevor Chalmers, 'The King's Council, Patronage and the Governance of Scotland 1460–1513' (unpublished Ph.D. thesis, University of Aberdeen, 1982). See also Alan R. Borthwick, 'The King, Council and Councillors in Scotland *c.* 1430–1460 (unpublished Ph.D. thesis, University of Edinburgh, 1989) and H.L. MacQueen, *Common Law and Feudal Society in Medieval Scotland* (Edinburgh, 1993).

Session in 1622 and Lord President of the Session from 1633.[8] These show that in his day there was material predating 1478 which was available for consultation. He refers to a quarto volume, which has not survived, which covered the period 17 May 1469 to 22 November 1470 and which perhaps continued a quarto series. Even after 1478 the record is less complete than it was when Spottiswoode wrote because he also refers to a further four folio volumes for the reign of James III (1460–88): one covering the period from 5 October 1478 to 2 October 1480; another the period from 13 February 1480/81 to 3 November 1483; a third the period from 9 March 1483/84 to 13 April 1485; and a fourth the period from 25 October 1486 to 15 November 1487. Of these the fourth is missing completely while of the second and third only the record for 10 March 1482/83 to 27 July 1483 and 17 March 1483/84 to 13 April 1485 (with gaps) survives. On the other hand five sittings in the period 13 April to 21 April 1485 not known to Spottiswoode have been recovered. For James IV's reign (1488–1513) the records are fairly complete, although in the period up to 1503 a diet in 1499 is missing and there are other gaps.[9]

The surviving records have been published in series only as far as 1503.[10] In 1839 there appeared the *acta* of the council for the period from 5 October 1478 to 15 November 1495, so far as extant, including the additional sittings between 13 and 21 April 1485. These were edited by Thomas Thomson.[11] In this edition the entries appear in full but in record type. In 1918 the *acta* for the period from 14 June 1496 to 24 March 1500/1 appeared, edited by G. Neilson and H. Paton.[12] In this edition record type

---

[8] These, entitled 'Some Things extracted out of the Books of Decreets and Acts that are kept in the Castle of Edinburgh, for informing of the manner of Justice administrat in Civil Causes, before the erecting of the College of Justice', are printed in *Acts of the Lords of Council in Civil Causes*, ed. G. Neilson and H. Paton (Edinburgh, 1918) (= *A[cta] D[ominorum] C[oncilii]*, ii), introduction, pp. xcviii–c, as well as in the eighteenth-century edition of Spottiswoode's *Practicks* (by his grandson John Spotiswoode, Edinburgh, 1706), pp. 360–61.

[9] Chalmers, 'The King's Council', p. 199 notes the absence of a diet in 1505, a break in March/April 1505 which may be either a recess or a gap, and a gap in October 1511 to November 1512.

[10] Selected cases from 1532–33, edited by I.H. Shearer, were published as *Selected Cases from Acta Dominorum Concilii et Sessionis* by the Stair Society as Volume 14 (Edinburgh, 1951).

[11] *The Acts of the Lords of Council in Civil Causes* (Edinburgh, 1839), cited as *ADC*, i. Some of the entries for November 1495 are displaced and should appear in 1490: see A.A.M. Duncan and M.P. McDiarmid, 'Some Wrongly Dated Entries in the Acts of the Lords of Council', *Scottish Historical Review* 33 (1954), pp. 86–88.

Thomson also edited the *acta* of the parliamentary auditors of causes and complaints for the period 1466–94 as *The Acts of the Lords Auditors of Causes and Complaints*, which likewise appeared in 1839.

[12] The edition covers the manuscript volumes CS 5/7 to fol. 60v of CS 5/10.

is abandoned but the entries are still given in full until 27 June 1498 (p. 239). Thereafter the text is contracted except where it was thought essential to give the exact wording. In the introduction (pp. ci–cxxxiii) are printed *acta* for the period from 10 March 1482/83 to 22 April 1483 (with some additional material), which in terms of chronology should have appeared in *ADC* i but which had only been discovered since its publication. In 1943 the Stair Society published a continuation of *ADC* ii to 5 January 1502/3 (with an additional entry for 27 January).[13] This follows the same principles, giving only abbreviated entries, but it has been found inaccurate in detail and has been superseded by an edition published by the Scottish Record Office which takes publication forward to 11 March 1502/3.[14] The text has been prepared by A.B. Calderwood and it contains an introduction by the former keeper of the records, Athol Murray, which clarifies the original arrangement of the records which was obscured by the interventions of Thomas Thomson in his capacities both as keeper and as editor of the records.

It is evident from inspection that the *acta* are not law reports in the sense even of notes of points of law arising in the cases which came before the lords of council. They are simply records of the proceedings. There are decreets deciding a case or continuing it to a later diet (at which there may or may not be a further record of its fate). Protestations by parties who are or may be affected by proceedings are recorded, as are citations to parties to appear at a later diet, warnings *apud acta* as they are expressed. There are acts recording a general continuation of causes and sometimes documents are engrossed, such as submissions to arbitration. These include some of the rare references which indicate directly the knowledge of the learned laws by participants in the proceedings which is clear to any reader of the *acta* who is familiar with these laws.[15] Often when a case is decided it is decided on the basis of findings in fact and issues of law do not arise as contentious issues. Where an issue of law is raised and decided it is not often made clear on the basis of what authority or authorities the decision was given that the law was as stated.[16] Is, then, the Register evidence that an attempt was made to record decisions as case

---

[13] *Acta Dominorum Concilii 26 March 1501–27 January 1502–3*, transcribed by J.A. Crawford and edited with an introduction by J.A. Clyde (formerly Lord President), Stair Society, 8 (Edinburgh, 1943). This completes CS 5/10 and continues to fol. 162v of CS 5/11.

[14] *Acts of the Lords of Council in Civil Causes*, iii, *A.D. 1501–1503*, ed. A.B. Calderwood, with an introduction by A. Murray (Edinburgh, 1993) = *ADC*, iii.

[15] See, for example, a submission to arbitration referring to a style in Durantis's *Speculum iudiciale* — *ADC*, ii, pp. 281–82.

[16] There are exceptions especially where an act or acts of parliament are referred to — see, for example, *ADC*, ii, p. 82 or p. 368. Cf. the observations of A.L. Murray, 'Sinclair's Practicks', *Law-Making and Lawmakers in British History: Papers Presented to the Edinburgh Legal History Conference 1977*, ed. A. Harding, Royal History Society Studies in History, 22 (London, 1980), pp. 90–104 at p. 102.

law offering guidance on points of law to the judges or to the parties and their representatives or even to a wider audience?

We know that after the institution of the College of Justice guidance on what the court considered the law to be was indeed provided in the form of the so-called 'decision practicks'. These were collections of notable decisions recorded by judges and, it seems, intended at least initially for their own guidance or for the guidance of the court or for both purposes, although some obtained wider circulation. The work of editing some of these decision practicks has begun but none has yet been printed. However, in a paper given by Athol Murray to the 1977 British Legal History Conference, there is an account of the earliest of them which has survived as the work of a named reporter, that is, Sinclair's *Practicks*. Of Sinclair, Murray remarks that 'historians of Scots law may accord him [John Sinclair][17] a special place as the first known reporter of legal decisions'.[18] The decisions recorded, and in this case apparently recorded primarily for Sinclair's own use, are recorded chronologically and indicate the points of law arising and some at least of the authorities relied on or referred to, giving greater insight into the work of the court than is usually available from the court records themselves. That some such record would be made is hardly surprising once the composition of the court was reasonably clearly settled, as it was by 1540 when Sinclair took his seat on the bench and his *Practicks* begin. By this time papal provision for finance had been made, leading to the ratification of the court's constitution, with minor modification, which took place in 1541 as noted above.

Although Sinclair's *Practicks* are the earliest known decision practicks, the so-called 'digest practicks' record decisions from the period before 1540. In particular, Balfour's *Practicks* record them as contained in what Peter McNeill, the editor of the Stair Society's reprint of the 1754 edition of these *Practicks*, has described as 'the elusive *Registrum Scotie*',[19] the Register with which this article is concerned. What, then, was the nature of this Register? We may start by quoting the beginning of McNeill's observations on it, including the relevant footnotes (renumbered from his n. 82 on p.lxi onwards to fit into the present sequence of notes):

> The ultimate source of most of the decisions quoted in Balfour is the acts and decrees of the lords of council and session which are extant in varying degrees. Their immediate source — the *registrum*[20] — is, however, not extant; but from

[17] He was appointed a lord of Session in 1540 and performed his duties until 1561. He is thereafter recorded as absent and in 1562 as being in France, to which he had retired or fled in consequence of the Reformation. He returned in 1565 and was briefly Lord President in succession to his brother Henry, to whom the *Practicks* are sometimes attributed, until his death in 1566: see Murray, 'Sinclair's *Practicks*, pp. 93–95.

[18] Ibid., p. 95.

[19] Balfour's *Practicks*, introduction, p. lviii.

[20] E.g. pp. 426, 562 ('*Et passim in regro*'), 441 ('*Ex registro*'); 102 ('*qualiter reperitur in registro post ult.* Sept. 1517'); p. 113 ('and nothing done in the register thairintill').

a perusal of the subject matter of the decisions and the chapter references we can hazard a description of what has been called Balfour's register of acts and decreets[21] or *registrum Scotie*.[22] Skene also cites cases from a *registrum*[23]: this extends to the 1590s; but in the earlier part many of the cases are also cited by Balfour.

The Register was a two volume work. Both volumes were arranged as digests under subject matter either alphabetically or according to a subject plan. The first tome — which was by far the larger — had 1392 titles (several of which are prayed in aid of more than one proposition) and extended from 1469 to 1579. The second volume had 856 titles and extended from 1540[24] to 1577.[25]

He goes on to suggest that the compiler of the digest probably did not go back to the manuscript acts and decreets but relied on early collections of decision practicks, including Sinclair;[26] he assumes that still earlier collections than Sinclair were to be found. So far as the sea laws are concerned he notes that Balfour includes citations of cases from the Register like Wellwod but that, while Wellwod gives the same volume and chapter as Balfour, he calls the Register '*Registrum Scotie*'; Wellwod, whose work was printed in 1613 could have copied Balfour but may have gone back to the Register himself.[27]

The first question which arises is whether there is any evidence for the Register apart from Balfour, who is certainly our main source. Starting with the case of Wellwod, it is clear that he does refer to decisions which are in Balfour and that he gives references to a *Registrum* which generally correspond with those of Balfour. He does not always give the chapter number, however, and there are occasional variations in chapter numbering which may represent typographical errors, such as his reference (at p. 55) to the case of *The King of Scotland and Maubray*. This bears the marginal note 'Tom 1 c 24 regist Scot'. In Balfour, who refers to the case as '*The King* contra Andro Murray *and utheris*' (p. 637),

21 McKechnie ['Balfour's Practicks', *Juridical Review*, 43 (1931), pp. 179–92], p. 183.

22 Wellwod, *Abridgement of All Sea Lawes*, London, 1613, p. 10 and passim. (Wellwod was professor of civil law in the university of St Andrews but was deprived in 1597. His earlier work *Sea Laws of Scotland* appeared in 1590.)

23 E.g. *Gorthie* v. *Methven*: Balfour, p. 121 *etc*; Skene, *De Verborum [Significatione]*, *s.v.* 'Curialitas'. Craig also cites cases which are in Balfour (e.g., *Aikman* v. *Aikman*: Balfour, p. 223; Craig, *Ius Feudale*, ii.14.11) but does not refer to the Register. (Sir John Skene became Clerk Register and a lord of Session in 1594. His *De verborum significatione* appeared in 1597.)

24 There are three stray decisions of earlier date: 1494, 1517 and 1534.

25 Some of the titles appear to have been sufficiently lengthy to divide into *prima pars* and *posterior pars*: pp. 432–33. (This could, however, refer to an earlier and later part of the same report.)

26 Murray, 'Sinclair's *Practicks*', p. 104, observes that Balfour did not use Sinclair directly.

27 McNeill, p. lxii.

the reference is to c. 34 of volume one of the Register. But there are indications that if Wellwod did take his references from Balfour he may also have gone from Balfour either to the Register or to the original acts and decreets. In particular he refers (at p. 50) to a case as 'Couper and Seagy anno 1498 mense Iulii' with the marginal note 'Tom 1 regist Scot' which appears in Balfour (at p. 626) as '4 *Julii* 1498, Alexander Meldrum *of* Segie, *contra Burgh of* Cowper, 1 *t. c.* 98'. This case is to be found in *ADC*, ii, p. 245 (continued from p. 187) as an action between the bailies and community of the burgh of Cowper and Alexander Meldrum of Segy, in which the burgh complained that Meldrum had interfered with the loading of goods on to ships anchored by the shore, claiming anchorage dues. The decision (which corresponds with and may have been based on Roman law) was that Meldrum was not to interfere with public access to and loading on to ships anchored within the floodmark but that he could claim anchorage dues if anchors were attached on his land or his land was occupied above the floodmark. Balfour gives the legal point accurately but his reference suggests that Meldrum was the pursuer, whereas the record shows that the burgh was the pursuer and Meldrum was the defender and made a counterclaim. In this respect Wellwod's reference is more accurate than the printed version of Balfour. He may, of course, have used a manuscript of Balfour with the names of pursuer and defender in the correct order, or the order may have been correct in the Register and he checked that, but it is also possible that he checked not the Register but the original record.

Skene in his *De verborum significatione* also refers to cases which he sometimes says are in the register or *in Registro*, but more usually he simply gives the date and parties and he does not refer to a two-volume register as such. He may have used Balfour as a source so far as his material extended because there are cases which are common to both. For example, under 'WARE' he deals with the use of the sea shore in a way very close to Balfour's treatment in his title 'Sea lawis: Anent the flude mark', cc. LVI and LVIII (p. 626), quoting the same two authorities but conflating the statements of the law found in Balfour's two chapters. Only one of the two cases cited has a Register reference in Balfour and Skene does not give Balfour's Register reference for it. It is not clear whether he went to the record for the other, *The King* v. *Laird of Seafield*, 29 July 1500 which is to be found in *ADC*, ii, p. 416 as an action by the king against John Multrare of Seyfeild. The fact that Skene refers to the defender as the laird of Seafeild, using a similar spelling for his lands, is hardly significant. On the other hand there is clear evidence that Skene did go directly to the records in some cases (as one might expect of a man who held the office of Clerk Register). For example, in the entry 'SOK', when giving an example of the reduction of the decree of a lower court by a higher one, in particular the reduction of a decree of the justice-court by parliament, he quotes almost verbatim the record of a case of

7 October 1476, which he cites as a case, 'before the Lordes, called *Auditores querelarum*, in this maner conteined in the register'.[28]

There appear to be no other users of the two-volume Register independent of Balfour among known collections containing early material. A possible candidate is a digested collection of decisions known as the *Lord Chancellor's Practiques*, to be found in the National Library of Scotland's Advocates' MS 22.3.4,[29] which cites some early decisions which are also to be found in Balfour. For example, under 'King' is cited a case '1498 Alexander Gordon contra William McClellan' which appears in Balfour in the title 'Of the Kingis patrimonie', c. VIII (p. 134) as '20 *Julii*, 1490, Alexander Gordoun *contra* Williame Makclellane, 1 *t. c.* 104'. However, there is no reference to the two-volume Register in this or other citations of cases in the *Practicques* and so no evidence that the Register was used. It may be noted that the correct date of the case of *Gordon* v. *McClellan* is 1498 and not 1490 because the case appears in *ADC*, ii, p. 284 on 20 July 1498 (as *Gordon* v. *McClelane*). This demonstrates the unreliability of some of the dates given in Balfour, a point which is discussed more fully below. It then appears that there are no references to the Register which are indubitably independent of Balfour and so the Register can indeed claim to be in this sense Balfour's Register.

How, then, was the Register arranged? McNeill suggests an alphabetical or subject plan and Athol Murray either follows him or agrees independently with the idea of a subject collection.[30] Goodal, the original editor of Balfour, on the other hand suggests, by implication at least, that the main arrangement of the Register was chronological, although he points out that there are many errors which may mislead the user. I quote:

> It doth not appear clearly that there had been any Decisions here noted later than the Beginning of the Year MDLXXIX and perhaps the Register had not then been continued any further: For although in Page 400 there is one noted 23d *July* 1580, yet *by its Place in the Register*, [emphasis supplied] it would seem to be an Error for 1480. In the vast Number of Citations and Dates, many such Errors have crept in, while through the numerous Transcripts that had been made of this useful Book, the Errors in the former, as usually happens, were all copied in the later, and new ones superadded.[31]

---

[28] See *The Acts of the Lords Auditors of Causes and Complaints*, ed. T. Thomson (Edinburgh, 1839), p. 57.

[29] See McKechnie, 'Practicks', pp. 25 and 35.

[30] 'Sinclair's Practicks', p. 96, where he refers to Balfour's use of a 'two-volume subject collection', and again at p. 104 where he says that Balfour did not use Sinclair but a secondary source 'the two-volume subject collection'.

[31] Preface, pp. x–xi. The preface, understandably, because much of it gives biographical information on Balfour which is superseded by McNeill's introduction, but nevertheless regrettably, is not reprinted in the Stair Society edition.

So far as the order is concerned there are, in fact, three interconnected questions:

(a) Was the Register a contemporary record like the later decision practicks, such as Sinclair?
(b) If it was not such a record, how was it made up, from the original registers, or from earlier collections?
(c) Was the order of the Register chronological or not?

As will appear the possible answers to these questions are intertwined but addressing them in order the following answers may be suggested.

(a) The probabilities seem to be against a contemporary record at least for the period up to 1503 or so with which we are immediately concerned. The surviving decision practicks date from a period when the Session was settled in its composition and sitting regularly with much the same personnel. There were then persons available to record significant decisions, a greater incentive to record decisions of legal interest and even a desire to mould the law. There are indications that after the foundation of the College of Justice the Session did assert itself in areas where previously it could not or would not, as in dealing with questions of fee and heritage.[32] In the early days of the development of the council's jurisdiction, there was not the same continuity of personnel and the prevailing view nowadays is that the increasing use made of the council as a central court was more reactive than proactive. It does not reflect a policy of creating a central supreme court with a view to at least partially displacing local jurisdictions, thereby providing control over the development of the law. Again, the fact that the council did not deal directly with issues relating to fee and heritage meant a substantial restriction of its influence on an important part of land law, one of the central areas of the law at this time. The same could be said of its refusal to deal with matters appropriate to the church courts. Against this it might be said that a fluctuating personnel would have had more need of guidance but there were the official records which inevitably were less extensive in the early years of record keeping. The evidence of the later practicks is that it was judges who were first motivated to keep a record of important decisions on issues of law. The possibility of a contemporaneous record would increase with the increasing regularity of meetings of the judicial council, which is noted above, but it may be significant that while the *Lord Chancellor's Practiques* records at least one decision from 1501 as well as the decision of 1498 already cited, such early decisions are not numerous in that collection.

---

[32] See Murray, 'Sinclair's Practicks', pp. 98ff; H.L. MacQueen, 'Jurisdiction in Heritage and the Lords of Council and Session after 1532', *Miscellany Two*, by various authors, ed. D. Sellar, Stair Society, 35 (Edinburgh, 1984), pp. 61–85; and idem, *Common Law and Feudal Society in Medieval Scotland* (Edinburgh, 1993), ch. 8.

(b) If the probabilities seem to be against a contemporary record at least for the earliest cases, is there any indication of use of or derivation from the original acts and decreets? The evidence does seem to point in this direction. In Balfour there are four cases dated in 1469 and numbered as 1, 3, 4 and 5 in volume one of the Register. There are then four cases dated in 1470 and numbered 6 to 9 in the Register. The next two cases in chronological order are dated 1474 and 1476. The first (recorded on p. 493 of Balfour) is *Cochrane* v. *Wallace*, a case involving withdrawal of water from a mill, and it is dated 31 July 1474 and numbered as 66 in the Register. If the Register were ordered chronologically the number 66 would suggest a date in 1491. There is no record of a case on 31 July 1491 in *ADC*, i, but Wallace and Cochrane appear as litigants over the withdrawal of water of the River Cart from the mill of Johnstone in 1493 (*ADC*, i, p. 318) and 1494 (*ADC*, i, p. 345). The former entry refers to a decree given before in respect of which there had been an inquest by a jury presided over by the sheriff. An error in the dating in Balfour, comparable to the error in the dating of *Gordon* v. *McClellan* already pointed out, must therefore be suspected; there is no doubt that Goodal is correct in supposing quite numerous errors and in his explanation of them, or many of them, as faults of transcription.

The case recorded in 1476 again appears to have been wrongly dated and thus to provide further evidence of the unreliability of the dates which appear in Balfour. It is *Wauchope* v. *Lord Seytoun* and it is dated 6 November 1476 and numbered 19 in volume one of the Register according to Balfour (p. 113). This number would suggest a date in 1478 or 1479 if the Register were chronological. The case referred to can indeed be found in *ADC*, i, p. 41, under the date 6 November 1479. In this case the simple explanation may be that the printer placed a 9 upside down. The possibility of such an error is very clear when the 6s and 9s in the typeface of the 1754 edition are compared.

After these two cases the cases in the Register run from 1478 to 1480, with their numbers in the Register in general following chronological runs, subject to what is said below on numbering when more than one case is cited for a particular proposition.[33] After 1480 comes a case dated 8 July 1484, *The King* v. *The Bishop of Galloway*. This appears in Balfour on p. 565 along with another case in 1500, both dealing with wrongous cursing of the king's officers. The Register number, apparently of both of these cases, is 67. The bishop of Galloway's case is to be found in *ADC*, i, pp. 362–63 but under the date 8 July 1494, which would be more consistent with the Register number if the numbers ran chronologically. After this, the sole case dated in 1484, there come four cases dated in Balfour to 1486,[34]

---

[33] 1478: 11, 12, 13, 21, 22, 17; 1479: 10 (?) — see text below; 18, 19, 20 (also 1358), 24, 33; 1480: 25, 26, 27, 28, 32.
[34] 1486: 29, 31, 33, 39.

a number from 1487 (including three in January 1487/88, a period for which there are no surviving official records)[35] and others from 1488 to 1492.[36] There are no cases from 1493 but thereafter there are cases in every year from 1494 to 1503.

Comparing all this with what is known of the records of the council's judicial activity, it looks very much as if the collection in the Register may have been put together from the surviving records, at least for the period up to 1503. The only cases which do not have a corresponding record are the three in January 1487/88, assuming that these are correctly dated. The correspondence with the records known to Spottiswoode is not complete, however. He gives a volume for the period from 1481 to 1483 for which there seem to be no cases recorded in Balfour, nor does there seem to be anything from 1484 and 1485, Spottiswoode's fourth volume, once the correction noted above with regard to the bishop of Galloway's case is made. On the other hand there are cases from 1486 and 1487, a period for which there is now no surviving record but for which records existed in Spottiswoode's time.

(c) It is implicit in what has been said about errors in dating that it appears to be the case that the early part of the Register was arranged chronologically and probably compiled from the records (or from an extract from them which followed the same order). It is now time to examine the chronology of the cases more closely. For a start, it seems more than coincidence that the first chapter of volume one of the Register bears the same date as the first known record of the council's judicial activity, 17 May 1469. Subsequent chapters generally follow chronologically, bearing in mind that the year began on 25 March until 1600. Thus, c. 3 is dated 11 January, c. 4 is dated 18 October and c. 5 is dated 17 March, which makes c. 4 out of place, assuming it is really to be dated to 18 October 1469. The actual entry in Balfour listing the authorities for the proposition to be vouched (p. 494) runs as follows: '18 *Octob.* 1469, James Scrymgeour *Constable of* Dundie, *contra* Thomas Wintoun. 8 *August.* 1526, *Abbott of* Cambuskynneth *contra* Henrie Crawfurd. *Ult Maij*, 1567, Robert Liddel *contra Ladie* Zester, 1 *t. c.* 4'. In the index to McNeill's edition it is assumed that the Register entry number 4 relates to the last case and not to the case on 18 October 1469. The basis of this assumption seems to be that the Register entry was a proposition gathered from a number of authorities and set out in a subject digest with the authorities annexed. This would help to explain why the Register was thought to be arranged by subject. It seems equally possible, however, that the proposition is derived from the first of the cases cited and that the later authorities are additional vouchers added to a chronological list, even if

[35] 1487: 34, 35, 36, 737 (*recte* 37), 38, 39, 41, 44, 45, 52, 53, 54.
[36] 1488: 55 to 60; 1489: 42, 43, 47, 48; 1490 (*recte* 1498): 104; 1491: 51, 68, 69, 71, 62, 72, 78, 80, 73, 61, 68, 40; 1492: 81, 82 (two cases), 90, 93, 109.

such an order is not invariable.[37] 'Chapters' in the Register would then be understood not as titles but as case entries, or as propositions derived from cases where more than one proposition can be vouched by the same case as in numbers 95 and 96 in the Register, which are both derived from the case of *Cockburn* v. *Ramsay* (Balfour, pp. 442 and 443).

Moving on to 1470, chapters 6 to 9 of the Register appear in the order of dates as 28 May, 29 March, 17 October and 6 October. At first sight this is a random order but it seems possible that there has been a scribal confusion of May and March. The months in Balfour are given in Latin in the genitive case and there is not a great deal of difference between 'Mart' for March and 'Maij' for May. There would then be only one displacement. The next entries chronologically are in 1478 and 1479. Here chapters 10 and 11 appear to be in the wrong order because 10 is dated 5 October 1478 and 11 is dated 6 October 1479. However the original acts and decreets now become available for comparison and there is no recorded sederunt for 6 October 1479. But there is one for 6 October 1470, as appears both from Spottiswoode and from chapter 9 which bears that date. Another error seems probable. After chapter 11 the relatively neat progression does not continue because 1478 and 1479 seem to run together. In 1478 appear as already noted (in date order which can be confirmed from *ADC*, i) chapters 11 to 13, 21 and 22 and 17; in 1479 chapters 18 to 20, 24 and 33. The last is perhaps a further mistake because there is another c. 33 in 1486 and the case in Balfour appears in *ADC*, i before the case in c. 18.

There is a similar pattern for 1480 and 1486. Chapters 25 to 28 appear in order in 1480 and then comes c. 32; in 1486 are chapters 29, 31, 33 and 39 (but the 39 could be 30 if 9 was sometimes confused with 0 and it would then fit in, as it has the same date as chapter 29). Thereafter this pattern of interrupted neat chronological runs continues, but with some serious irregularities or apparent irregularities, such as the appearance of chapter 745 under the date 31 July 1499 (the 737 on 13 October 1487 is almost certainly a mistake for 37, coming as it does between chapters 36 and 38). While some of the apparent irregularities can probably be explained as errors by copyists or the printer, the pattern of interrupted runs also seems to point to excerpting by more than one hand to produce the Register. It is inherently probable that more than one clerk would have been used to trawl through the records if that is what happened. There were in fact at least two occasions for such a trawl involving Balfour when commissions, of which he was a member, were set up to revise the law in 1566 (renewed and it seems extended in scope in

---

[37] See, for example, the entry at p. 113 of Balfour's *Practicks* 'Of dowrie and tierce, c. XXIX': '17 *Feb.* 1535, *Erle of* Huntlie *contra Lord* Forbes. 6 *Novemb.* 1476, Patrick Wauchope *and his wife* contra George *Lord* Seytoun, 1 *t. c.* 19.

1567) and 1574.[38] One of the specific tasks of the 1574 commission was in fact to 'visite . . . decisionis befoir the sessioun' as well as other sources with a view to a restatement and, if appropriate, amendment of the law. But the commission of 1567 was required to 'mak ane body of the ciuile and Municipale law'. This would also have involved examination of the work of the lords of council and session.

The absence of a simple chronology also seems to point to a trawl of the records rather than a contemporaneous collection or collections subsequently drawn on to produce the Register. While the early pattern does seem to continue after 1503, it is premature to make too positive a statement with regard to the whole Register until the whole Register has been more carefully examined. What can be said is that a trawl of the records would appear best to explain the ordering of the Register so far as the earlier years are concerned. There is nevertheless a good deal to be done to establish as accurately as possible the order of cases in the Register, by correcting the errors where correction seems possible. Some errors may well be beyond correction, as the potential errors include complete omissions detectable only where there happens to be duplication of an entry.[39]

As is observed by McNeill, many of the cases in Balfour can be traced back to the acts and decreets of council so far as these are extant (and some can be traced to the acts of the auditors of causes and complaints in Parliament). When the entry in the acts and decreets is compared with the entry for the same case in Balfour, it is clear that the main difference is that the entry in Balfour states a proposition of law for which the decision or decisions of the council becomes the authority.[40]

---

[38] See *APS*, i, pp. 29ff (Preface, pp. 23ff), iii, 40, c.42 and iii, 89; McNeill, 'Balfour's *Practicks*, introduction, p. xvii; R. Sutherland, *Lord Stair and the Law of Scotland* (Glasgow, 1981), pp. 23–24 (who suggests that, in the light of Balfour's circumstances, the *Practicks* were more likely to have been the fruits of the 1567 commission than the 1574 one, as commonly held).

[39] An interesting example appears in Balfour at pp. 277–78, where the same set of cases is quoted for two different propositions. The one list reads: '18 *Novemb.* 1502, Johne Semple *contra Lord* Drummond. 24 *Jan.* 1535. 16 *Feb.* 1561, Robert Cairncorse *contra the Erle of* Mortoun, 1 *t. c.* 249'. The other reads: '18 *Novemb.* 1502, Johne Sempill *contra L.* Drummond. 24 *Jan.* 1535. 16 *Feb.* 1539. 28 *Feb.* 1561, Robert Cairncorse *contra the Erle of* Mortoun, 1 *t. c.* 249'.

Such omissions may be suspected where very general propositions are vouched by several cases, as where it is said (at p. 148) that clandestine possession does not interrupt true, real or natural possession and two cases are cited, without names of parties, dated in 1546 and 1547. These cases are ascribed to c. 70 of volume one of the Register which would suggest a date in 1491. The cases numbered cc. 69 and 71 in volume one of the Register from 1491 are both to be found in the *Acts of the Auditors*, at pp. 153 and 154 and there is a case, *Countess of Menteith* v. *Lord Drummond* also at p. 154 and dated 17 May 1491 which could have raised a question of clandestine possession.

[40] See Appendix.

Little if anything is added by way of explanation of why the law should be as stated. This is some further argument for the view that the Register is essentially an extract from the records; or from a collection which used the records as a source of propositions of law. It is not an expansion of the material to be found in the records which helps to explain the decision. Nevertheless, as Goodal remarked,[41] the entries give a clear view of what the law on the basis of which the facts were decided was taken to be. They are, therefore, law reports in embryo, even if they may be retrospective rather than contemporary reports. They are not simply records and their collection implies that the lords had authority to settle the law by their decisions.

---

[41] Preface, p. x: 'The Stile in which these Decisions are entred, is both concise and perspicuous, and the *ratio decidendi* for the most Part extremely plain and satisfactory'.

Appendix

ADC, ii, p. 85

10 November 1497, *post meridiem.*

Sederunt: Archiepiscopus Glasguensis; Episcopi Abirdonensis, Moraviensis; Comites de Huntle, Ergile, Levenax; Domini Drummond, Gray; Abbates de Dunfermlyng, Cambuskinneth; Secretarius; Duncanus Campbell; et Magister Ricardus Lausone.

'Anent the complaynt* made be Patrik of Cokburne, ane of the bailyeis of Hadingtone, and Patrik of Douglas, quhilk marit ane of the dochteris and airis of umquhile Archibald Lowdoun, that quhare our soverane Lordis letters war direct to the bailyeis of Hadingtone be synister informacione, as thai understude, at the instance of Schir Alexander Ramsay of Cokpen, knicht, schawand that ane land and tenement biggit be umquhile the sade Archibald within the sade burgh of Hadingtone suld be biggit apone the commone streit and suld thairthrow pertene to the Kingis hienes as his eschete throw purprusione, chargeing thame tharefore to gif stait and saising of the sade land to the sade Alexander or ellis to compere before the Kingis hienes within thre dais til schew quhy thai differrit the sammyn, the quilkis letters the sade bailyes ressavit reverently and war redy til obey and fulfill the command thareof, and than comperit before thame the sade Patrik Douglas and producit divers evidentis of heretable possession of the sade land, with ane instrument of the deliverance of the inqueist takin now of lait in the sade mater be command of the sadis letters schawand that the sade land was na way biggit upone the Kingis common strete, like as is at mare lenth contenit in the complaynt thairuppone: The saidis partiis being personaly present, thare richtis, evidentis, instrumentis and ressons and allegacions being herd, sene and understand, the Lordis of Consale forsaid understandis that this mater is nocht ordourly past to the confiscacione of this tenement albeit that it war biggit on the Kingis strete, as is allegit, tharefore the Lordis referris this mater to the Kingis Justice because it pertenis to the justice are; and ordanis him in the next justice aire to be haldin in the burgh of Hadingtone to mak this party be summond to underly the law apone the pruprisione done to the King be the bigging of this tenement apone the Kingis strete allegit be this parti, and til underly ane assise hereapone; and gif it beis found be the sade assise that this parti has purprisit, as sade is, that it be decernit to pertene to the King and that dome be gevin thareapoun; and the instrumentis producit by baith thir partiis in this mater, quhilkis war twa, war deliverit in keping to the Justice Clerc in presens of the saidis Lordis agane the sade justice aire.'

* This appears to be the case cited in Balfour's Practicks, 'anent purpresture.'
The relevant entries in Balfour are as follows:
Balfour's *Practicks*, pp. 442–43
Anent purpresture.
C. I. Purpresture aganis the King, and pane thairof.

Item, Gif ony persoun biggis ony housis or tenementis upon the commoun streit, within ony of the King's burghis, the samin aucht and sould pertene to the King's Hienes, as eschete throw purpresture, and may be gevin and disponit be him to ony persoun as he pleisis. 10 *Novemb.* 1497, Patrik Cockburne *contra* Alexander Ramsay, 1 *t. c. 95.*

. . .

C. V. Judge competent in purpresture.

All clamis, contraversies, and questiounis concerning purpresture, aucht and sould be decydit and determinat be deliverance of ane inquest, takin, be command of our soverane Lord's letteris, befoir the Justice-general, or his deputis: And gif ony sic actioun be intentit befoir the Lordis of counsal, thay aucht and sould remit the samin to the said Justice; because the samin pertenis to him allanerlie. 10 Novemb. 1497, Patrik Cokburn *contra* Alexander Ramsay, 1 *t. c.* 96.

5

Law Reporting in the 1590s

David Ibbetson

Legal literature was undoubtedly in something of a crisis by the end of the sixteenth century. From the point of view of those studying law, there were hardly any didactic treatises; apart from Littleton's *Tenures*, already well over a century old, and St German's discursive *Doctor and Student*, the few texts which did exist were little more than collections of relevant statutes and cases. There had been no attempt to reduce the law to anything like order, so that even the best-equipped student might be well-advised simply to digest anything he had read under alphabetical headings, in the hope that genuine understanding might eventually flow from this garnering of information.[1]

The absence of recent reports of cases was an even greater problem.[2] As is well known, the Year Books had finally spluttered to a halt towards the end of the reign of Henry VIII, with the publication in the early 1540s of reports of cases from 1535.[3] While the old Year Books continued to be produced in many editions during the rest of the century, there was very little modern material in print. Plowden's *Commentaries* had appeared in 1571 and Dyer's *Reports* in 1585,[4] but although these were welcome additions to the canon they merely scratched the surface. The absence of recent reports must – at the least – have inconvenienced practitioners who would have been forced to place greater reliance on the fickleness of memory,[5] although the collegiality of the Inns of Court did at least provide an atmosphere imbued through and through with legal learning and legal

---

[1] See generally P. Winfield, *Chief Sources of English Legal History* (Cambridge, Mass., 1925); J.H. Beale, *Bibliography of Early English Law Books* (Cambridge, Mass, 1926) pp. 131–74, and *Supplement* (Cambridge, 1943), pp. 17–24; W.R. Prest, *The Inns of Court, 1590–1640* (London, 1972), pp. 143–49.

[2] Fundamental to our knowledge of sixteenth-century reporting is L.W. Abbott, *Law Reporting in England, 1485–1585* (London, 1973).

[3] J.H. Baker, *The Reports of Sir John Spelman*, SS, 94 (1977) ii, pp. *164–78*.

[4] Beale, *Bibliography* pp. 108–10 (Plowden), p. 108 (Dyer). A modern edition of Dyer has been prepared for the Selden Society by Professor Baker.

[5] Coke, *First Report*, i–ii. We must, of course, be careful not to impose our own model of law on the sixteenth century; when there was no strong doctrine of precedent, up-to-date knowledge would not have been so essential as it is today.

discussion. The problem was far greater for those coming to the common law for the first time. The diligent student, recommended to study the Year Books beginning with those of Henry VIII and working backwards, would certainly learn a great deal; but much of this would have been of very limited practical utility. The decades after 1535 had marked a period of consolidation and development of the rapid changes which the common law had undergone at the beginning of the sixteenth century; inevitably these developments were wholly absent from the Year Books.[6]

By contrast with the paucity of printed materials, by the end of the sixteenth century there was a huge number of manuscript reports of cases; the existence of these must have gone some way towards compensating for the lack of printed materials.[7] It is less clear, however, whether these manuscripts should be seen primarily as satisfying the need of practitioners or as filling in the gaps in the provision of materials for legal education. In order to answer this question, it is necessary first to discover the type (or types) of person who wrote the manuscripts and then to examine the use which appears to have been made of them.

It is as well to begin with the brute facts. Leaving aside commonplace books, most of which contain notes on printed sources collected under headings after the manner of the Abridgements, and copies of set-piece arguments which circulated independently, we are still left with over 200 volumes containing cases from the last years of Elizabeth's reign, from 1590 to 1603. Occasionally only a few folios contain such cases, but far more frequently we find volumes of several hundred folios covering this period. Such brute figures do not in themselves show very much: to make sense of them we need to know not merely how many manuscripts there are, but how many *independent* texts. While this will not give us absolute numbers – for no doubt many texts will have been lost – it will give us some idea of how many people were making reports of cases at any one time; we can then go on to ask what sort of people they were and why they were doing it. Moreover, the isolation of individual source-texts enables us to reach some conclusions about the ways in which these were copied and the extent to which they might have circulated within the legal profession.

The first problem in estimating the number of independent texts is that nearly every manuscript is unique in its precise contents, so that a cursory examination is of little real help. The most practicable solution is to examine very carefully the reports of a particular term in a particular court, and to compare these one against another. As well as short-circuiting the vagaries of later copyists, this examination also gives more a more precise indication of the number of individuals reporting at any particular time, rather than the number represented at some time in the decade.

---

[6] J.H. Baker, 'English Law and the Renaissance' *Cambridge Law Journal (1985)* p. 46.

[7] There is no comprehensive list of these manuscripts, but some idea of the size of the surviving corpus can be gleaned from Abbott, *Law Reporting*, appendix 1.

Such examination of the reports of Michaelmas term 1595 in the court of King's Bench reveals somewhere around twenty distinct surviving sets of reports. Of these some contain only a very small number of cases: Coke has only two King's Bench cases this term, Popham only four, for example. Others, however, are more substantial. We can reconstruct the reports of Edmund Escourt of Lincoln's Inn from the surviving copies to produce a total of seventy-five King's Bench cases in this term.[8] A set associated with two figures identified only as W.C. and H.G. has around seventy cases in it.[9] The reports associated with Humphrey Were of the Inner Temple, surviving in more than a dozen copies, contain about 120 separate reports.[10] A set probably made by John Harris has sixty entries.[11] All in all we can identify reports of over 250 cases, many of them with a range of variant versions.

One striking feature of these sets is that the order in which cases are reported is in general remarkably consistent. As well as allowing the production of a fairly reliable calendar of the business of the court, against which we can test the ordering of material in any particular manuscript, it also strongly suggests that reporting was a consistent exercise rather than a random jotting of notes.

Leaving aside the range of the manuscripts, we should turn to their authorship. Some, like those of Anderson and Popham, were the work of judges. Of the King's Bench judges of the last decade of the century, for example, we have reports more or less reliably attributed to both chief justices and to Clench and Fenner of the puisnes, and a reference to reports of a third, Gawdy.[12] Some of these, at least, extend into the time

---

[8] BL, MS Harley 4552, fol. 14v; BL, MS Add. 35947, fol. 3; Inner Temple, MS Barr 13, fol. 174v; BL, MS Lansdowne 1076, fol. 155.

[9] The attribution is found in CUL MS Ii 5.24, fol. 158. Other related manuscripts include: BL, MS Hargrave 50, fol. 167v; BL, MSS Harley 1631, fol. 141; 6745, fol. 139; Harvard Law School, MS 105d, fol. 79v; CUL, MSS Ee 6.17, fol. 141; Gg 2.5, fol. 418; Inner Temple, MS Barr 76(2), fol. 224; CUL, MS Dd 10.51, fol. 24.

[10] BL, MS Hargrave 7, fol. 106; BL, MS Lansdowne 1068, fol. 156v; Lincoln's Inn, MS Misc. 490, fol. 464; John Rylands Library, Manchester, MS French 118, fol. 130; BL, MS Hargrave 14, fol. 89v; BL, MS Harley, 4998, fol. 108; Yale Law School, MS G R 29.9, fol. 132; BL, MSS Add. 25211, fol. 114; 25222, fol. 152; Yale Law School, MS G R 29.7, pp. 25, 377, 535; CUL, MS Ee 6.12, fol. 110v.

[11] BL, MS Add. 25201; see below, n.15

[12] The reports of Anderson and Popham circulated in manuscript and were printed in the seventeenth century. Reports attributed to Wray CJ are found in BL, MS Lansdowne 1084, fos 38v–42v, though Abbott (*Law Reporting*, p. 262) doubts the attribution; Abbott himself suggests (*Law Reporting*, p. 263) that part of Harvard Law School MS 16 may constitute reports taken by Wray, but I can see no overpowering grounds for so thinking. Clench's Reports are found in Yale Law School MS G R 29.5 and BL MS Harley 4556; extracts from those of Fenner are in John Rylands Library, Manchester, MS French 118, fol. 252 and BL, MS Add. 35946 fol. 255; a reference to Gawdy's notes of a case in which he was sitting as a judge is found in BL, MS Lansdowne 1076, fol. 49v.

that their authors were sitting on the bench. But whatever we think of their quality, in terms of quantity of reports these volumes are insignificant.

Some were produced by the leading practitioners. Edward Coke's are of course the most notable, though by the 1590s these were clearly being collected with a view to publication and are in many other respects hardly typical.[13] More substantial, and somewhat closer to the mainstream, are the Common Pleas reports of Peter Warburton, who became a judge of that court in 1600. These begin in Trinity term 1594, immediately after he had been created serjeant at law, continuing long after his elevation to the bench.[14] Another set of reports, clearly the notebook of a practitioner, is in a volume which appears to be the work of John Harris, who entered the Inner Temple in 1580, was called to the bar in 1590 and created bencher in 1603. Beginning in 1591, the reports extend to the end of 1602, and obviously cover the period at the start of his career in the King's Bench.[15] Unlike practically every other book of reports, we can tell by the slight shifts in orthography and ink after each case that these were made up day by day. In a few cases he reports that he was counsel in the case – it is this that enables us to guess at his identity – but it seems clear that in the majority he played no part. In one case, for example, he must be writing at second hand, for he carefully notes that he did not himself attend or hear the arguments in the case.[16] Interestingly, we find a few notes of a similar type, apparently written by Serjeant Drew in the 1590s, in a volume which later came into the possession of Serjeant Thomas Harris and which was given away by him towards the end of his life.[17]

Although these practitioners' books are perhaps the most interesting because of the glimpse that they give us of the lawyer at work, they are overshadowed by the mass of volumes which can be loosely attributed to 'students' or 'apprentices'. This designation is notoriously ambiguous,[18] though, and it is necessary to look more closely at the type of people responsible for them. Richard Lydall is probably fairly typical. Having studied law at Oxford,[19] he was admitted to the Middle Temple in 1598

---

[13] J.H. Baker, 'Coke's Notebooks and the Sources of his Reports' *Cambridge Law Journal* (1972) pp. 59, 70.

[14] Copies (or extracts) are found in BL, MS Harley 4817; CUL, MS Ii 5.25; BL, MS Hargreaves 5, fol. 96; Harvard Law School, MSS 1051, fol. 249; 5070; BL, MS Add. 25200, fol. 177.

[15] BL, MS Add. 25201.

[16] BL, MS Add. 25201, fol. 27.

[17] CUL, MS Dd 11.64, fol. 165v et seq.; the attribution to Serjeant Drew is based on comparison of *Cotton's Case* at fol. 170v with the report in 1 Leon 211.

[18] For its earlier usage, see J.H. Baker, 'Records, Reports and the Origins of Case-Law in England', in Baker, ed., *Judicial Records, Law Reports and the Growth of Case-Law* (Berlin, 1989) pp. 15, 25–26.

[19] He took his BCL at St John's College, where he was a contemporary of James Whitelocke whose own reports are described below.

and called to the bar in 1603. At the beginning of Easter term 1601, he notes, at the age of twenty-two he began attending at Westminster for the purpose of collecting reports. At this time, he tells us, he went on a daily basis to the Common Pleas. His reports in the Common Pleas continue to 1603, but from Michaelmas term 1601 we also have reports from the King's Bench, and these continue until 1607, shortly after he gave up his first chambers in the Middle Temple.[20] The picture is reasonably clear of the young lawyer first frequenting one court on a regular basis, then moving between courts, finally settling down with cases in the King's Bench in preparation for practice there.

James Whitelocke, the future judge of the King's Bench, provides another example, but this time the volume which we can identify as his covers only the days before he was called to the bar. Born in 1570, he went up to St John's College, Oxford, in 1588 as a scholar, and was made a fellow in law there one year later. In his autobiography he tells us that it was always his intention to practise common law, so at the same time as he was studying the civil law at Oxford he joined one of the Inns of Chancery, moving to the Middle Temple in 1593. He spent as much time as his College would allow him in London; on the face of it, they seem to have been more than generous in this after he had taken his Bachelor of Civil Law degree in 1594, but since he was often involved in the furtherance of the college's business the arrangement presumably had benefits for both sides. He did not in fact vacate his fellowship until 1598, two years before he was called to the bar, though by this time he can hardly have been spending a great deal of time in Oxford.[21] Already by this time he had begun to collect reports.[22] The first one in the volume dates from Michaelmas term 1597, and in the course of the next two years, until his call to the bar, he filled 130 folios with case reports.

Other volumes reflect this pattern of reports taken by young men who had been at the Inns of Court for a few years, either side of their call to the bar. The reports collected by Humphrey Were, for example, contain reports by John Bridgman taken five years after his entry to the Inner Temple, by Jonas Waterhouse eight years after entry; by John Penniman between seven and ten years after entry; and by Were himself up to nine years after entry. Another manuscript with a strong Lincoln's Inn bias contains reports by Edmund Escourt taken six years after his entry to the Inn; by Hugh Cressey seven to eight years after

[20] Lincoln's Inn, MS Mayn 66, fol. 135v. For his career in the Middle Temple, see *Middle Temple Admissions Records*, i, p. 73, *Minutes of Parliament*, i, p. 380; ii, pp. 440, 442, 469, 625, 690.

[21] The details of his early biography are best gleaned from his *Liber Famelicus* ed. J. Bruce, Camden Society, (1858). See too R. Spalding, *Contemporaries of Bulstrode Whitelocke* (Oxford, 1990) pp. 425–29.

[22] CUL, MS Dd 8.48.

entry; by Rowland Wandesforde six years after entry; by Edmund Hadde eight years after entry; and by Thomas Tyrwhitt five years after entry.[23] Other named attributions produce similar results. Since call to the bar did not give an immediate right of audience even in the King's Bench,[24] it is not unreasonable to think of these as preparation for practice there.

Internal evidence from the reports similarly points towards the work of 'students'. Just as in the earlier period of the Year Books, the judges seem to have taken cognisance of the gallery and to have directed comments at them. On one occasion an attorney made a not particularly witty aside, whereupon we are told that there was much laughter in court. Popham CJ restored order, remarking that there was much sense in what the attorney had said.[25] On another occasion Fenner J clearly disapproved of counsel's argument. 'Don't put that case in your books', he is reported to have said. With a certain degree of wilfulness the case was duly recorded, together with Fenner's injunction.[26] Senior counsel, such as Edward Coke or Lawrence Tanfield, were not above putting hypothetical cases to the judges 'for learning's sake'.[27] Such questions may have been aimed at the discovery of a judicial point of view towards some hypothetical legal problem, but it is not easy to imagine Coke having an attack of humility and enquiring politely of the bench their opinion on a knotty point of law just to cure his ignorance. Such case-putting may well have had the function of instructing the bystanders as well as the questioner.[28]

Students standing in the wings of the court could hardly have taken contemporaneous notes, and must have trusted to memory. James Whitelocke, we may surmise, used the skills he had developed while studying Hebrew with a Mr Hopkinson of Grub Street before going up to Oxford. While attending court he would listen to what was said, then write up a precis of it later on. One of the early cases he heard was the first of the arguments in the great contract case of *Slade* v *Morley*. John Dodderidge's argument is elegantly and accurately summarised, though he was obviously less impressed with Edward Coke: 'Attorney General Coke argued to the

[23] Yale Law School, MS G R 29.29.

[24] Prest, *Inns of Court*, pp. 50–51.

[25] CUL, MS Ff 2.14, fol. 58.

[26] E.g., BL, MS Harley 4552, fol. 40. The report in CUL, MS Gg 6.29, fol. 16, describes Fenner's remark as having been made to one Carlton; this presumably refers to either Robert or Thomas, both of whom were called to the Bar in 1595.

[27] E.g., BL MS Harley 4552, fol. 38v: 'Cooke Attorney mitt ceo case al court de scavoir lour opinion' (BL, MS Hargrave 50, fol. 178v is quite explicit that the query was not raised in the course of an actual case: 'Mes la fuit nul case dependant en Courte'); CUL, MS Mm 6.58, fol. 39 (Tanfield demanding opinion of court 'for learning's sake'). Another example may be Exeter College, Oxford, MS 152, fol. 109, where Serjeant Spurling is reported to have asked the opinion of the court.

[28] It might happen that there was no work for the court when it was assembled. cf Bodleian Library, MS Rawlinson, C 341, fol. 79: 'Nota 20 counsellors al barre et null case destre moved'.

affirmative, but was so confused through lack of method that I could retain nothing firmly in my memory'.[29] Others – presumably those who had been called to the bar and who were hence able to escape from the crowd of student observers – would have taken brief contemporaneous notes and expanded them later when writing them up in their report-books,[30] very much in the manner of their counterparts in the universities.[31]

There is a consistent picture easily visible behind these manuscripts, a picture of students attending courts to learn law by observing just as their predecessors had been doing for centuries. In the early 1600s Simonds d'Ewes talks of going two mornings a week to the Star Chamber to report cases; slightly later we hear of his resolve to go every morning to report in the Common Pleas, a regime which he seems to have been proud to keep up for the whole of one term.[32] No doubt there were many like him, jostling each other for a position from which they could see and hear what was going on in Westminster Hall. In one manuscript of a case in 1587, for example, Serjeant Walmsley's argument is noted only briefly on the grounds that the reporter had been disturbed from his place and hence could not hear properly.[33] One revealing report describes a case being moved after the 'student observers' had left the King's Bench,[34] which if nothing else suggests that their presence there was at least as regular a feature as their absence.

[29] CUL, MS Dd 8.48, fol. 1.

[30] BL, MS Lansdowne 1087 may reveal the process at work. The volume has bound in to it as fol. 261v a brief scrawled note of *Lord Zouche's Case* which is reported in a more orthodox style at length at fol. 262. Such a method was recommended by Roger North in his late seventeenth-century *Discourse on the Study of Laws* (1824), p. 37.

[31] W.A. Pantin, 'The Halls and Schools of Medieval Oxford: An Attempt at Reconstruction', in *Oxford Studies Presented to Daniel Callus*, Oxford Historical Society, new series, 16 (1964), p. 92; M.B. Parkes, 'The Provision of Books', in J.I. Catto and T.A.R. Evans (eds), *The History of the University of Oxford*, ii (Oxford, 1992), pp. 424–25.
The fair copies transcribed from these lecture notes were known, perhaps significantly, as *reportationes*.

[32] *The Autobiography and Correspondence of Sir Simonds d'Ewes*, ed. J.O. Halliwell (1845), i, pp. 220, 243. cf. the 'Directions to a Student in the University' written by d'Ewes' tutor at Cambridge, Richard Holdsworth, transcribed by H.F. Fletcher, *The Intellectual Development of John Milton* (Illinois, 1961), ii. pp. 623–55, at 652), recommending the development of the skill of remembering lectures, sermons, and disputations, and then writing up a summary of them afterwards. This advice would probably have been of more use to d'Ewes than Holdsworth's suggestion that his students should skim Justinian's *Institutes*: 'The smattering tast of these studies will be of great use and if you gott but only the termes and method it is more then a perfect Scholar can well want' Ibid., p. 646.

[33] BL, MS Lansdowne 1087, fol. 231. Similar remarks about inaudibility are frequent.

[34] *Nicholas* v *Badger* (1594) BL, MS Hargrave, 7 fol. 26v.

The situation revealed by the manuscript reports of the 1590s is remarkably close to that described by Roger North some half a century later:

> It is usual after a year or two's residence in the Inns of Court for all students to crowd for places in the King's Bench Court, when they are raw and scarce capable of observing anything materially, for that requires some competent knowledge ... For this reason I would not have any lose time from their studies after this manner till after four or five years' study, and two years afore they come to the bar, which should not be before seven of study, is more than enough, especially when to get a place they must be very early, and idle about, or worse, till the court sits ... It will be found for some years after calling to the bar their best employment will be that of sitting there and reporting, as I know full well, without more of refreshment than a motion or two in the term.[35]

Identification of the type of people who wrote the late sixteenth-century reports enables us to place them in the framework of legal education and legal practice. Particular care is necessary not to be too rigid in classification: the vast bulk of the surviving corpus of reports seems to straddle the two categories, though perhaps not surprisingly so when legal education was little (if anything at all) more than training for practice.

At the one extreme, reporting might have had a purely (or at least predominantly) educational function, in that the taking of the report – rather than any subsequent use of it – was the purpose of the exercise. William Fulbeck, for example, recommended the keeping of a digest of cases that had been read or heard, not so much with a view to the ease of subsequent reference but rather for the purpose of ensuring that it was properly committed to memory.[36] In the same way, we have references to 'reporting' from memory and without the use of notes in the Inns of Chancery.[37] At least one aim of attending court (and reporting cases) might have been more the mastery of legal practice than the assimilation of legal doctrine: such was the view of Roger North rather later in the seventeenth century.[38]

At the other extreme, reports could have been collected specifically with a view to publication, aiming at the dissemination of legal knowledge. Coke's volumes of reports were clearly intended to be printed and

---

[35] *Discourse on the Study of Laws*, 34 (compared with BL, MS Hargrave 394, fol. 14v). He further recommends beginning with the taking of reports in the Common Pleas on the grounds that it is sufficiently sparsely attended that there is no need to arrive early to be sure of getting a good position from which to hear and observe the court.

[36] W. Fulbeck, *Direction, or Preparative to the Study of the Law* (2nd edn, 1829), p. 116.

[37] A.W.B. Simpson, 'The Source and Function of the Later Year Books' *Law Quarterly Review* 87 (1971) pp. 94, 104.

[38] *Discourse on the Study of Laws*, 32.

designed with the legal practitioner in mind;[39] in this they were probably unique. If we may take him at his word, Plowden collected his *Commentaries* for his private instruction and only caused them to be printed in order to forestall the publication of a pirated edition;[40] and Dyer's *Reports* were published only posthumously, and then only as a selection from the original notebooks.[41] Of the texts remaining in manuscript there is only one series which we suspect may perhaps have been designed to be circulated with a view to its practical utility. This set, known as *Errores in Camera Scaccarii* ('Errors in the Exchequer Chamber'), is a collection of seventy-nine cases determined on writ of error from the King's Bench to the court of Exchequer Chamber (set up by statute in 1585) which survives in a number of near-identical copies.[42] The reports in this collection are concise and sharply focused on the central points in issue, and not in chronological order; in addition, they lack the individuality and marks of personality which are so often found in manuscript reports. They are evidently not the product of the common form of 'student' reporting, and their concentration on what were effectively authoritative decisions would undoubtedly have enhanced their practical value.

The remainder of the texts – the vast majority – fall between these two extremes, displaying some of the characteristics of both types. Like the reports intended to be read by a wider public, we may be reasonably confident that the primary aim of these notebooks was to record legal doctrine. This seems to be so even in the case of the 'practitioner's diary' type of reports, such as those of John Harris[43] which may have functioned mainly as an aide-memoire; it is a yet more obvious feature of the 'students' reports' taken as a preparation for legal practice. The common inclusion of reports said to have been taken by others in the absence of the principal author of the volume points unequivocally in this direction,[44] as does the frequent citation of cases or remarks mentioned in passing by judges or senior practitioners.[45] An aspirant lawyer, such as William Cowdrey, might include a selection of reports copied from

[39] J.H. Baker, 'Coke's Notebooks and the Sources of his Reports' *Cambridge Law Journal* (1972), p. 59.

[40] *Commentaries*, ii, iii. See G. de C. Parmenter, *Edmund Plowden* (1987), pp. 111–19.

[41] *Reports*, preface. See Abbott, *Law Reporting* pp. 158–60.

[42] Copies are found in Harvard Law School, MSS 118b, 1180(2); Lincoln's Inn, MS Hale 80; BL, MSS Lansdowne 1112; Harley 4998; Yale Law School, MS G R 29.9; Yale Law School, MS G R 29.17; CUL, MSS Gg 4.9, Mm 4.31; Inner Temple, MS Barr 7. No doubt there are others which have escaped attention.

[43] See above, n. 15.

[44] For examples see below, nn. 49, 72.

[45] For example: BL, MS Lansdowne 1095, fol. 18 (Wray); John Rylands Library, Manchester, MS French 118, fol. 81v (Gawdy); BL, MS Hargrave 373, fol. 213v (Coke); BL, MS Lansdowne 1106, fol. 115v; CUL, MS Ff 5.4; fol. 286v (Clerke).

elsewhere before progressing to the making of reports from his own observations.[46]

Another pointer in the same direction is the frequency of attempts to check the accuracy of reports. One volume, for example, contains repeated reference to the opinions of an older colleague.[47] A reporter of *Radford v Spurling* (1591) notes that although judgment had been given for the plaintiff in the case, the attorneys told him that it had not been entered on the roll; the defendant had satisfied it and the successful plaintiff was thereby able to avoid the fee which would have been charged for making the entry. The careful reporter adds that he had himself seen the plea roll.[48] A no less painstaking reporter records that he had taken the arguments in another case in part from the notes of William Jones, in part from the notes of Edmund Hadde, in part from elsewhere; and his note of the argument of Glanvill J. had been corrected by reference to Glanvill's own note of the case.[49] Another reporter, suspicious of a case that had been cited in court, 'conferred' it with Serjeant Wray, who confirmed the writer's suspicions by saying that the case had been decided in the opposite way.[50]

A similar concern for the accuracy of the legal doctrine recorded in (or inferred from) the cases can be seen in the occasional annotations of reporters. In one report of the leading case of *Vicary v Farthing* (1595–6) Thomas Walmsley, the assize judge, is recorded as having said to 'us'[51] that judgment should never have been given on the verdict returned by the jury in the case;[52] another report in the same volume notes in passing the chance remark of the defendant in the case that seven of the judges gathered together at Serjeant's Inn seemed to be on his side.[53] Another writer might add some pertinent information given afterwards by the attorney in the cause,[54] or by a fellow-barrister;[55] or the private opinion of one of the judges might be noted down.[56] Annotations might not simply record relevant information gleaned outside the courtroom; a writer might as easily cross-refer to a case which seems to him to be

---

[46] See below, n. 70.

[47] See below, n. 73.

[48] CUL, MS Ii 5.16, fol. 97v.

[49] CUL, MS Add. 8080, fol. 94; cf. BL, MS Lansdowne 1076, fol. 49v (reference to argument of Gawdy J collected out of his own notes).

[50] BL, MS Lansdowne, 1106, fol. 54 (another copy in Harvard Law School, MS 5048).

[51] The student observers?

[52] BL, MS Harley 4998, fol. 124v (and many other copies).

[53] BL, MS Harley 4998, fol. 113v (and many other copies).

[54] BL, MSS Lansdowne, 1087, fol. 190; Add. 35946, fol. 125.

[55] BL, MS Lansdowne 1087, fol. 127.

[56] *Atkinson* v. *Terringham*, BL, MS Hargrave 50, fol. 173v.

analogous to the case reported,[57] or query whether the case reported is consistent with received doctrine.[58]

While these notebooks share the characteristics of the public reports in their concern for legal doctrine, they remain none the less private works hardly intended for wide circulation. Some lawyers, perhaps most, collected cases from observation or hearsay simply for their own use; for them, reporting was indistinguishable from private note-taking, one aspect of the individual's self-education. Other lawyers, though, seem to have collaborated more or less by design: sometimes reports of a single term are attributed to more than one author,[59] sometimes a group of lawyers of approximately the same degree of seniority at the same Inn appear to have reported consecutively, or simultaneously in different courts.[60] While we cannot be certain that the latter reports represent more than the chance concatenation of individuals' notes, the uniformity of style and the neat dovetailing of terms and courts suggests something altogether more deliberate.[61] Yet even if these endeavours tell of a degree of reporting cases with a view to their being used by other lawyers, they should still be seen more as exercises in self-education – albeit collaborative self-education – than as the taking of reports with a view to publication in the manner of Coke's *Reports* or (perhaps) the *Errores in Camera Scaccarii*.

It is more difficult to determine the purpose of this essentially private note-taking. Were these reports intended by their authors to be used by themselves or their collaborators in the course of legal practice, or merely to be read in preparation for it? *A priori* one would expect them to have been intended for continued use: a considerable amount of labour was expended in their preparation; effort was clearly taken to verify that the information which they contained was accurate; many cases are identified not simply by their names but also by the reference to the record of the case in the Plea Rolls of the court, information which would be of little use unless it was envisaged that doubt might at some stage be cast either on the existence of the case or the accuracy of some detail in the report of it. There was no rule that unprinted reports could not be cited. A practitioner who was able to support his arguments by a wealth of precedents would presumably have had some advantage over a less well-equipped opponent, even at a period when there was no established doctrine of *stare decisis*.

[57] Lincoln's Inn, MS Mayn 55, fol. 230v.

[58] BL, MSS Lansdowne 1087, fol. 134; 1101, fol. 59.

[59] For example, the shadowy WC and HG: see above, n. 9.

[60] See in particular the Inner Temple collection of Humphrey Were (see above, n. 10); the Lincoln's Inn collection associated with Edmund Escourt (see above, n. 8) is perhaps another example, although here there is less uniformity than in Were's collection.

[61] Contrast, for example, the far more random collection of Inner Temple material (put together perhaps by Nicholas Jordan) in BL, MS Hargrave 373; or the 'Liber Gastrell' in Leeds Public Library, SR 942.74 P726.

On the other hand, the manuscripts themselves do not give the appearance of having been prepared in a way which would easily lend to their practical utility. Most obviously, only a relatively small number have even a rudimentary index; and those that are indexed normally contain no more than a list of case names, frequently not even in alphabetical order. Of course, the owner of a chronological series of reports might sometimes have indexed or commonplaced them under subject headings in another book. There are many such books; but most of them are insubstantial or contain references only to Year Books and printed reports. Those that do incorporate cases from manuscripts seem often to date from rather later than the period with which we are concerned.[62] A second problem is that a manuscript would commonly contain reports of the same case at different stages of argument, without any indication as to whether or when the case was argued again. There is no good reason to believe that the sixteenth-century lawyers who wrote these reports had any intention of using them systematically in the course of their legal practice.

Not merely were the manuscripts not designed to be used in the course of legal practice; on the whole, they were not so used. This is not to say that cases from manuscript reports were never cited; but such citations are relatively infrequent, sufficiently unusual for a reporter sometimes specifically to note that a 'private' report was being cited,[63] and the use of such precedents was very definitely haphazard rather than systematic. This is not merely an impression created by the nature of the surviving evidence. Careful examination of the arguments in some of the leading cases in the period, arguments prepared and apparently circulated *in extenso* (often, perhaps, initially by counsel in the case) reveals an enormous preponderance of reliance on printed materials. We may reconstruct the arguments of Coke and Dodderidge in *Slade's Case* (1597) with some confidence; both counsel relied on distant analogies drawn from old cases reported in Year Books, none of which was directly in point, while not a single one of the dozens of relevant recent manuscript reports was cited.[64] The arguments in *Chudleigh's Case* (1595) show an identical reliance on printed sources; the majority of citations are to Year Book cases, a minority

---

[62] Thus CUL, MSS Ll 3.8 and Ll 3.9 are commonplaced in CUL, MS Dd 5.22; but both the manuscripts of the reports and the commonplace clearly date from well into the seventeenth century. In the same way, BL, MS Add. 25206 contains Oliver St John's index to Elizabethan and Jacobean reports in his possession, which similarly dates from a considerable time after the reports were taken. An earlier attempt may be CUL, MS Gg 6.29, which seems to consist of cases taken from another set of reports subdivided into rough subject headings.

[63] BL, MS Harley 4812, fol.1.

[64] J.H. Baker, 'New Light on Slade's Case', *Cambridge Law Journal*, 51 (1971) pp. 213; cf. D.J. Ibbetson, 'Sixteenth-Century Contract Law: Slade's Case in Context' *Oxford Journal of Legal Studies*, 4 (1984), pp. 295, 308–10.

to cases in Plowden, Dyer and Brooke's Abridgement.[65] The ballast of Year Book authority in these two cases is particularly noteworthy: both were regarded at the time as highly significant cases, so we might reasonably expect that the arguments were carefully prepared; and both raised points which could not have arisen directly before 1535, but which had been important throughout the second half of the sixteenth century.

In part, no doubt, the marked infrequency of citations from unprinted reports is attributable to the relative awkwardness of finding cases in manuscripts as compared to the printed books, which could be used in conjunction with easily manageable abridgements and indexes.[66] In part, though, it must be attributed to the fact that manuscript reports were inherently less persuasive than those which were in print. Lawrence Tanfield, for example, might have thought that he was on fairly safe ground in 1591 when he cited a case of 1576 from Plowden's unpublished notes. Coke countered, however by citing a contrary case of 1545 from a manuscript in his possession and dismissing Tanfield's case by saying that Plowden would not have put it in his reports since it had clearly been adjudged to the contrary.[67] Robert Clerke's citation of a case from a set of manuscript reports in 1586 similarly backfired: Coke countered with an alternative report pointing in the opposite direction; a third version, a 'good report', in the possession of Tobias Wood of Lincoln's Inn was then produced. Afterwards, the reporter notes that Wood's version was the most accurate, and that Clerke amended his own book accordingly.[68]

If observing cases and reporting them was principally a facet of legal education, then it is easier for us to make sense of some of the surviving manuscripts in which different types of material are seemingly haphazardly juxtaposed. One nice composite volume is that which seems to have been written by William Cowdrey, a Wiltshire man who was admitted to Lincoln's Inn in 1577.[69] The volume begins with various notes on statutes and other legal topics, together with reports of cases dating from the 1560s. This is followed by a few cases from the mid 1580s which seem

[65] I have taken the long report in BL, MS Lansdowne 1073, fos. 18–45v as the basis of my analysis. Coke's printed report (1 Co Rep 113) does contain odd references to materials which were not in print when the case was argued, but all the evidence points to these being interpolated by Coke himself (who, in fairness, does not claim to be giving an accurate transcription of the arguments). Even a cursory reading of the printed version, however, gives a clear impression of the preponderance of Year Book citations.

[66] Although the printed reports, Plowden (1571) and Dyer (1585), were not indexed, tables were printed shorly afterwards: in 1578 in the case of Plowden, 1588 in the case of Dyer. These might be bound in with the Reports. Coke's *Reports* were similarly not published with indexes, but the small number of cases reported in each volume would have made this less important.

[67] CUL, MS Ii 5.16, fol.90v.

[68] BL, MS Lansdowne 1073, fol. 30v; Clerke's come-uppance is also reported by William Cowdrey in CUL, MS Ff 5.4, fol. 291.

[69] CUL, MS Ff 5.4.

to have been copied from elsewhere, but might conceivably be of his own taking, and then by ten or so folios which can be identified as coming from Coke's notebook, although in one case Cowdrey was guilty of a lack of respect when he doctored Coke's text by the tacit interpolation of a none-too-intelligent joke.[70] After another fifty folios of other peoples' reports, we finally come to a case marked almost triumphantly 'One Chudleigh's Case in the King's Bench, of my own reporting'.[71] This is not, in fact, the well-known Chudleigh's Case reported at length by Coke, but an earlier one arising out of the same settlement and heard in the King's Bench in 1585, just eight years after Cowdrey had first entered the Inn. His own reports fill only some thirty folios in this volume, extending over two years, until 1587. He seems to have been following a routine of reporting, not simply dropping into Westminster Hall from time to time, for in one case he notes a judgment to have been reported by Thomas Harris the younger in his absence.[72] His reports are marked by a certain tentativeness, though what they lack in legal sharpness they make up for in useful asides. Particularly interesting is the deference he shows throughout to one Durdant, repeatedly citing his opinions and noting where his reports of cases differ from Cowdrey's own.[73] Thomas Durdant was his junior by two years as a member of Lincoln's Inn, but several years older and a man of considerable mettle. He had been a fellow of Magdalen College, Oxford, and praelector in Logic, but was expelled with a number of other fellows in 1578 for having refused to confirm in his fellowship a nominee of the queen's whom they believed to be insufficiently qualified; he ended up in decent obscurity as Member of Parliament for New Windsor and its town clerk in the early seventeenth century.[74] After completing his own reports, Cowdrey transcribed extracts from Durdant's reports, referring in his turn to Cowdrey, into his book.[75] What we see in this volume is the physical remnant of a course of self-instruction – it might be a bit generous to talk of self-*education* – and of collaboration between men attempting to set out on the road to legal practice.

The prevalence of these students' reports no doubt indicates that they were in some measure a response to the relative lack of printed reports from the second half of the sixteenth century, but this can only be a partial explanation. While the practitioners' book might be seen as a

[70] Compare his report of Mutton's Case at fol. 210 with Coke's autograph in BL, MS Harley 6687B, fos. 332–332v

[71] CUL, MS Ff 5.4, fol. 234v.

[72] CUL, MS Ff 5.4, fol. 270.

[73] CUL, MS Ff 5.4 fos 286, 286v, 289, 291, 292, 292v, 293, 294.

[74] J.R. Bloxam, *Magdalen College Register* (1873), 4.170–171; W.D. Macray, *Magdalen College Register*, new series, (1901), 3.62. The details of the expulsion appear from BL, MSS Harley 416, fol. 194 and Add. 12507, fol. 44, discussed in C.M. Dent, *Protestant Reformers in Elizabethan Oxford* (Oxford, 1983), pp. 55–57.

[75] CUL, MS Ff 5.4, fos. 295–304.

sort of professional diary, the context into which these student books belong is that of the progressive decline of the learning exercises.[76] It is not necessary to assert that there was a decline in attendance at readings or moots, but simply to recognise that the old learning exercises, often raising fiendishly complex points of property law, was becoming ever less useful as a means of preparation for practice in the increasingly important world of the King's Bench where issues of contract, tort and crime predominated. The information, and forensic skills, which would be of value to the newly-called barrister could only be obtained by direct observation.

Law reporting may have been primarily an exercise in self-education, but already by the end of the sixteenth century there may have been a shift in attitude towards these reports, and to law reports in general. The relatively large numbers of surviving copies of certain reports perhaps suggests that there was some idea of a canon of reliable texts:[77] over a dozen copies of Were's collection have come to light, for example, and more than twenty of the late Elizabethan series of reports which may have been taken by Thomas Coventry.[78] To judge by the regularity of the handwriting and by the errors of transcription which could hardly have escaped tacit emendation by a copyist with any legal knowledge but which are repeated in several manuscripts,[79] some at least of these copies must have been made by scribes rather than by lawyers themselves; presumably an individual might obtain a copy of a set of manuscript reports in exactly the same way as he would purchase a volume of printed reports. In addition, these copies might be put together in a way in which they would be more useful in practice: sometimes a copyist will concatenate reports of the different stages of a case into a single report;[80] sometimes a marginal note will indicate that the case was argued again in a later term.

If such a shift did indeed occur, it can perhaps be associated with the change in the common law mentality which occurred in the first half of

[76] Prest, *Inns of Court*, ch. 6.

[77] The similarly wide circulation of the earlier series of reports attributed to Harper, Bendlowes and Dalison (for which see Abbott, *Law Reporting*, pp. 62–149) may indicate that such an idea had earlier roots; but the extreme difficulty of dating individual copies of reports with any degree of precision must incline us towards considerable hesitancy in reaching any conclusions.

[78] For these reports see Baker, New Light on *Slade's Case*, pp. 51, 53 n. 14; idem, *English Legal Manuscripts*, i, p. 55.

[79] A good example is the report of the defendant's words in *Harbin* v. *Barton* in Were's collections (see above, n. 10). The original statement that 'Barton dit a moy ...' e.g. BL, MS Harley 4998, fol. 113v) is transmuted into the bizarrely implausible 'Bracton dit a moy ...' in some (not especially late) copies of the report (e.g. Lincoln's Inn, MS Misc. 490, fol. 481).

[80] See, for example, *Vicary* v. *Farthing* in Were's collections: one version (typified by BL, MS Hargrave 7) reports three arguments in Michaelmas 1595; another version (typified by BL, MS Hargrave 14) unifies them into a single text.

the seventeenth century. As the political theorists' picture of the common law as a system grounded in reason mediated through custom came under attack in the first half of the seventeenth century,[81] so too did common law practice move away from arguments based on reason to arguments based on authority.[82] The publication of Coke's *Reports* was of paramount importance here;[83] no sooner had his report of *Slade's Case* been printed than it – Coke's report of the case rather than the decision itself, it should be noted – was being cited in the court of Common Pleas as a reason why they should depart from their long-standing practice.[84] But the granting of authority to case reports carried with it a need to oversee, if not to regulate, the production of reports. In 1617 Francis Bacon, then lord keeper, introduced a system of official reporters charged with producing reliable reports of important cases.[85] By the middle of the seventeenth century printed law reports carried what amounted to a judicial *imprimatur*.[86] Individuals might continue to take their own notes, but doing so became ever more distinct from the increasingly institutionalised practice of Law Reporting.

[81] On the problems of the political ideology of the common law, see most recently G. Burgess, *The Politics of the Ancient Constitution* (London, 1992), which contains a full discussion of the earlier literature.

[82] Put explicitly by Coke: Co Litt 254a: 'Argumentum ab authoritate est fortissimum in lege'.

[83] It may be worth noting in passing that Coke encapsulates in large measure the three ideal types of 'authority' analysed by Max Weber: *Economy and Society*, ed. G. Roth and C. Wittich (Berkeley, Ca. 1978), pp. 217–54.

[84] *Wright* v. *Swanerton* (1604), BL, MS Hargrave 29, fol. 94, printed in J.H. Baker and S.F.C. Milsom, *Sources of English Legal History* (London, 1986), p. 442.

[85] J. Spedding, R.L. Ellis and D.D. Heath, *Works of Francis Bacon* (1872), xiii, 264–66, together with Spedding's comments at pp. 266–68; discussed, with further literature, by D.R. Coquillette, *Francis Bacon* (Edinburgh, 1992), p. 214 n. 54.

[86] J.W. Wallace, *The Reporters* (4th ed., Boston, 1882), p. 34 n. 3. There had been, at least in theory, regulation of the printing of law books before this: see E. Arber, *Transcript of the Registers of the Company of Stationers of London* (1875), ii, p. 810 (Star Chamber decree of 1586), iv, p. 530 (Star Chamber decree, 1637), v, pp. liii–liv (Ordinance of Lords and Commons, 1643). It was regulated by statute in 1662: Stat. 13 & 14 Car II, cap. 33, s. 3.

6

Sir Julius Caesar's Notes on Admiralty Cases: An Alternative to Law Reporting?

Alain Wijffels

Sir Julius Caesar (knighted in 1603) was deputy judge in the high court of Admiralty from 1582 onwards, and was appointed as the ordinary judge in 1587. He held the post until 1606, when he became chancellor of the Exchequer. During his years at the court of Admiralty, he also held several other offices, including masterships in the court of Requests and in the court of Chancery.[1] Several volumes of Caesar's Papers at the British Library contain documents relating to his work as Admiralty judge.[2] Some of these volumes include miscellaneous papers which Caesar either received or transcribed in the course of the court of Admiralty business: correspondence with litigants or their representatives, lawyers, councillors, muniments, accounts etc. Partly, these documents have been collected according to the origins of the litigants.[3] In addition, five volumes contain Julius Caesar's personal notes (in his own handwriting) on the legal arguments presented by counsel.[4]

[1] All references to Julius Caesar's biography are borrowed from L.M. Hill, *Bench and Bureaucracy: The Public Career of Sir Julius Caesar, 1580–1636* (Cambridge 1988).
The author is indebted to Mr D.E.C. Yale (Christ's College, Cambridge) and Dr J.D. Ford (Gonville and Caius College, Cambridge) for their kind advice and assistance. Financial support was obtained (at various stages) from: CNRS (France); Churchill College, Cambridge; the Bodossakis Fund; and the Netherlands Organization for Scientific Research (N.W.O.).

[2] BL, MSS Lansdowne 123–74, 706, 768, 784; MSS Add. 4190, 5664, 6038, 9045, 10038, 10113, 11405–6, 11574, 12495–507, 14027, 14313, 15208, 34324, 36111–3, 36767, 36969, 36970, 38170.

[3] BL, MSS Lansdowne 132 (*partim*), 133 (*partim*), 135–6, 139 (Spain and Portugal, Denmark, Hanse-Towns), 140 (Italy), 141–6, 147 (Denmark), 148–9 (France), 150 (Germany, Low Countries), 151, 160 (*partim*), 162 (*partim*), 172 (*partim*); MSS Add. 11405 (*partim*), 12503 (Scotland), 12505, 14027 (*partim*), 15208, 36767.

[4] BL, MSS Lansdowne 129–32 and 135.

1. Caesar's Annotations on Maritime Cases: Technique and Methods

Both types of documents (miscellaneous papers and legal annotations) provide a valuable supplement to the high court of Admiralty records. In Caesar's time, the latter include very little material which may help to shed light on legal considerations or reasonings followed by civil law practitioners in admiralty cases. No reports for the period are extant. Both the series of libels and interrogatories in the court's records include much evidence on the court's fact-finding methods, but no records were kept of pleadings or other forms of argumentation and the formula of the decisions was such that it does not always clearly identify (by itself) the subject of the litigation,[5] while legal considerations are entirely passed under silence. Therefore, Caesar's handwritten notes on counsel's arguments are a unique source of our understanding of forensic legal methods in the high court of Admiralty during the late-Tudor and early-Stuart period.

The annotations in the Lansdowne 129–132 and 135 volumes refer to some 400 different cases, of which approximately 350 are related to maritime cases and probably linked with the court of Admiralty. Some proceedings are clearly not linked with the Admiralty (arguments about marriage and wills),[6] while for some cases, the annotations only reflect procedural questions and are too summary to identify (when no additional information is available) the nature of the litigation.[7] The volumes contain

---

[5] For nearly a century, the only accessible scholarly work providing examples of sixteenth-century court of Admiralty documents (transcribed and translated) was R.G. Marsden, *Select Pleas in the Court of Admiralty* Selden Society 11 (London 1897). Very useful for understanding the records in the context of the Admiralty proceedings is the unpublished typescript of the '*Introduction*' to the index of cases of the high court of Admiralty class in the reference rooms at the PRO. From the transcripts in both Marsden's edition and the PRO typescript it appears that sentences could include an abstract of the case. Sometimes, the formula of the sentence refers to one or more documents (e.g. schedules) attached to the sentence itself. M.J. Prichard and D.E.C. Yale, *Hale and Fleetwood on Admiralty Jurisdiction* Selden Society 108 (London 1992 [=1993]) was not available when the present contribution was written.

[6] E.g. (matrimonial causes) BL, MSS Lansdowne 129, fos 136v–137v; 131, fos 134v–135r and 137v–148r; 132, fos 10v–11r, but the most elaborate notes are to be found in the case *Earl of Hertford* c. *Lord Mounteagle* (BL, MS Lansdowne 131, fos 206r, 228v–234r, 241v–242r, 244v–245r, 246v–247r, 248v–250r, 256v–258r, 262v–263r, 266v–269v, 294v–301v; 132, fos 86v–87v). E.g. (wills) BL, MS Lansdowne 129, fos. 23r–24v and 26r; fos 30r–31v; and 135, fos 139r–146r; 130, fol 198r; fos 136v–138r and 141v–142r; 132, fos 298r–301v; 135, fos 7v–8r; 11v and 12rv, 127v. A litigation before the court of Arches concerning tithes: BL, MS Lansdowne 130, fos 27v, 55v–56r, 67r, 75r–77r, 94v. Other ecclesiastical causes: BL MS Lansdowne 135, fos 59v, 71v–77r.

[7] E.g. *Johnson* c. *Brian*, BL, MS Lansdowne 129, fos 32r and 34r deals, as the notes in several other cases, exclusively with questions of evidence. The shortest note is undoubtedly that in *Bird and Scoble* c. *Morgan*: it consists of a single reference ('L. si quis societatem, D. Pro socio', BL, MS Lansdowne 131, fol 133r)! In some cases where the annotations are

continued

almost exclusively forensic annotations in Caesar's hand, although there are also a few short 'questions' briefly addressed in the civil law tradition, some in connection with maritime or admiralty issues.[8]

Caesar's technique of making annotations is very contracted. Because of the very conciseness of his notes, which often provide practically no information about the circumstances or the main issues of the case, they cannot be used by (legal) historians except in conjunction with other material. They also concentrate almost exclusively on the legal authorities quoted by counsel, and since these authorities belong overwhelmingly to the *ius commune* tradition, it is not surprising that they have received only scant attention from (English) legal historians.

continued

too succinct or concentrate on procedural questions, the name or quality of the litigants may suggest Admiralty proceedings. In some cases, of course, a comparison with the court's records is the only way to establish whether a case was brought before the court of Admiralty, e.g. BL, MS Lansdowne 135, fol. 23r (*Williamson c. Van den Steen*) contains only a few references to *ius commune* authorities regarding the plaintiff's duty to make his claim exactly known to the defendant; however, the case can be followed in HCA 3.19. Even when the nature of the case is established, the jurisdiction is not always clear, as in *Tippen c. Tompson*, a case of *iniuria*, apparently because of an allegation of adultery committed 'on the seas' (BL, MS Lansdowne 130, fos 187r and 238r). The figure given for Admiralty cases includes brief annotations which contain at least some reference to maritime law, e.g. in *Hall c. Poulter*, where Caesar simply noted: 'Tract. de naut. navib. et navigat. Straccha num. 18, dominus non tenetur pro nautis, nisi fuerit in culpa in conducendis et constituendis nautis minus idoneis' (BL, MS Lansdowne 129, fol. 26v).

[8] These set questions (mostly on non-maritime matters) are partly concentrated in BL, MS Lansdowne 132: 'Observations by Doctor Talbot touching the King's prerogative to wreck at sea' (fos. 3r–4v); 'Quousque licet Principi superiorem non recognoscenti prohibere piscationem in mari suae jurisdictionis et districtus?' (fos 92r–93v). Brief arguments regarding questions apparently not related to any specific case occasionally occur in the other volumes, e.g. BL, MS Lansdowne 129, fos. 80r–82vb ('A briefe note of certaine reasons giving occasion to judge that the King's Bench prohibitions and other proceedings against the Admiralty should bee voyde; delivered mee by Duck Lambe etc. 26. febr. 1591'). See also BL, MS Lansdowne 130, fos 61v–64v ('An virtute represaliarum contra Florentinos concessarum, originarii Florentini alibi commorantes capi possint?'); 133v–134v ('In quibus casibus concedi possint represaliae?'); 161r–164v, 174v, 180rv ('Tempore belli, ad hostes an ulla bona deferri possint?'); 178r ('That things done beyond the sea are not triable in any court of common law, but before the L. Admirall or his deputy'); 131, fos 83r ('Whether campesche wood brought into the realme by vertue of letter of reprisall bee confiscable'); 150v–151r ('Whether the sea shore may be prescribed from the King?'); 188r–189r ('Bona amicorum onerata in navi hostium capta in bello una cum navi fiunt capientium'); 197r ('An pax superveniens impediat legitimationem praedae captae tempore belli?'); 236v–239v ('Whether that an English ship may be solde lawfully beyond the seas to any stranger no subiect to our King?'); 253r–256r ('Whether piracies were pardoned by the King's generall pardon at the time of his most happy coronation?'). A few questions on procedural issues would also have been relevant for Admiralty causes, e.g. 'Quae et quando sint causae summarie? et quid important haec verba, summarie et de plano, sine strepitu et figura iudicii, sola rei et facti veritate inspecta?' (BL, MS Lansdowne 129, fol. 113rv). A similar observation can be made regarding questions of public (international) law, e.g. BL, MS Lansdowne 130, fos 35r–39r ('Quousque princeps obligetur ex pacto suo?').

In spite of the great diversity of the annotations from one case to another, some general characteristics can be recognised. The standard annotation on a case consists of a definite set of elements:

1. All cases are entered under a heading mentioning the litigants or at least the plaintiff. Because the annotations on the same case are sometimes spread over different parts of a volume, the heading may be repeated at the top of the page whenever the notes on the case are resumed.
2. Facts are sometimes referred to, but if so only very briefly. In most cases, no mention of any *species facti* is made.
3. The annotations consist mainly of counsel's arguments. For every counsel intervening, Caesar mentions the name of the advocate and the party represented. This is then followed by the main contents of the notes: references to legal authorities, and usually the principles allegedly buttressed by the authority referred to. The notes do not reflect the pleadings as they were worked out: more often, the entries under an advocate's name have the appearance not of a fully recorded argumentation, but of a sequence of separate, more or less related arguments.
4. In a few cases only, the annotations also include the transcript of a document, such as a legal opinion or a letter.[9]

The main component of the annotations is therefore the set of references to legal authorities. The vast majority of these authorities, as it has already been noted, belong to the continental European *ius commune* tradition. They appear according to the standard *modus citandi* of such sources, including the conventional system of abbreviations. These *allegationes* include both references to the fundamental texts of the *ius commune* tradition (the collections of the *corpora iuris civilis* and *canonici*) and the 'ocean' of doctrinal authorities. Among these, the traditional *mos italicus* works (*in utroque jure*) largely predominate and the commentaries of that school prevail. Monographies which belong to either the *mos italicus* approach or to the early *usus modernus* are also well represented. Legal humanism only rarely provides authorities. Comparatively, common law sources, on the other hand, are quoted more regularly.[10] Accordingly, the use of legal authorities in the forensic practice of the English Admiralty lawyers (who were not, on the whole, a specialised branch of the civil law

---

[9] For insertions of *consilia*, see below. Other noteworthy documents transcribed among the notes include foreign decisions (in summary form), e.g. 'th'arrest of ye Parliament of Paris then at Tours' (BL, MS Lansdowne 131, fos 5r–6r).

[10] The civil lawyers frequently refer to English statutes, only exceptionally to (common law) treatises and reports (for the latter, see for instance BL, MS Lansdowne 130, fol. 208v (Dyer); 132, fol. 94rv (Coke). In a matrimonial cause, a 'certificate' is said to be based on several (expressly mentioned) English (civil law) precedents (BL, MS Lansdowne 131, fos. 250r and 256v et seq.).

profession) reflects the findings regarding the contemporary holdings of law books in academic libraries at Oxford and Cambridge.[11]

Whereas the annotations are practically the sole source on the legal reasonings, the other Caesar Papers provide some information on the facts, but more importantly on the (extra-)judicial proceedings, which, particularly in cases where the government considered that public interests were involved, could be subjected to the privy council's direct control and influence. It is also manifest that, all the government's acknowledgements of the respect due to the regular process of law notwithstanding,[12] its interference in the court of Admiralty's business in some cases affected the outcome of the proceedings.

For the court's records, Caesar's annotations and other documents provide, when sufficiently detailed, necessary information for their interpretation. Both Acts and Libels classes contain mainly formal (in particular, procedural) documents concerning the lawsuits, which can be more fully assessed or better exploited in the light of the substantial information offered by the Caesar collection. Even such series as interrogatories, which are a primary source of information on facts, will sometimes benefit from the addition of the judge's papers; especially in the absence of other relevant records, the legal implication of some facts or the importance of some facts for the specific legal argumentation of a litigant, which can be inferred from the insistence on the facts in question during the interrogatories, becomes apparent when compared with the legal arguments.

2. The Purpose of Caesar's Annotations

The very abundance of the Caesar Papers bears witness to the collector's wish to look up, accumulate and keep sources in relation to his various professional activities. As master in the court of Requests, Caesar collected sufficient material for writing and publishing a work on the institution.[13] In other offices, too, both practical and scholarly considerations induced him to compile sources which could be useful for either carrying out

[11] From Caesar's notes, it is clear that the advocates who appeared in Admiralty proceedings also acted as pleading counsel in non-maritime cases. However, the notes also indicate that the number of advocates pleading (frequently) in Admiralty cases was very small, and, perhaps, that many advocates who regularly acted in non-maritime cases would normally not have been involved in the business of the high court of Admiralty. In addition, one notes (in the act books) that the Admiralty advocates also often acted as Caesar's deputies.

[12] E.g. Lord Burghley's letter in the Fugger case or the council's and the judges' comments to the Venetian ambassador (BL, MSS Lansdowne 139, fol. 391r; and 145, fos 310ff).

[13] L.M. Hill (ed.), *The Ancient State, Authoritie, and Proceedings of the Court of Requests by Sir Julius Caesar* (Cambridge 1975).

the tasks or supporting the dignity, the advantages or the justification of the office or its institution. As a judge in the court of Admiralty, Caesar intended to clarify the workings of the court, whether or not with a view to publishing the results of his research and notes. Caesar's ultimate motives for his annotations of advocates' legal arguments remain unclear. At least, the technique he applied in making his notes may give some indication regarding the purpose of the annotations.

A first, obvious hypothesis would be that Caesar wrote down a counsel's arguments for his own use as a judge in the case submitted to his court, as a memorandum of the legal authorities put forward during the trial. The implication would be that these authorities played a significant role in the judge's decision. Moreover, since Caesar took great pains to write down not only (and not always) the legal principles referred to, but specifically the technical references to the learned law, one would have to assume that the authorities themselves influenced to some degree the judge's reasoning and the justification of his decision.

The insistence, in various contemporary sources, on a regular legal foundation of the court of Admiralty judgments confirms that, in effect, the official policy was a respect for the due course of law, which implied also the correct application of substantive law. The doctrinal controversies which characterised the learned law of the *mos italicus* did not prevent that, on the whole, the *ius commune* was still credited (pace its numerous critics, both from the Inns of Court and from the ranks of the civil lawyers) to be a sufficiently coherent and authoritative system. However, the legal context and the procedural system of the high court of Admiralty were not propitious for encouraging the development of a case-law based on legal *rationes decidendi*. The court's records do not seem to have made provisions for the preservation of the advocates' legal arguments, and there are indications that it may not have been common practice to submit such arguments in writing.[14] Nor was a reasoned statement of the grounds

[14] This may perhaps be inferred from Thomas Crompton's reply to Gentili in the Botelho case, (A. Wijffels, *Alberico Gentili and Thomas Crompton: An Encounter between an Academic Jurist and a Legal Practitioner*, Studia Forensia Historica, 1, (Leiden 1992), p. 32, n. 93: 'Multum facessis michi (mi Alberice) negotii, ut qui iam diu in foro non in Academia versatus fuero et in dicendi potius quam in hoc scribendi genere exercitatus quae fusuis apud iudicem dixi eadem contra et fori et gentis nostre morem in hac ... causa cogar iam tandem scriptis mandare' (BL, MS Lansdowne 139, fol. 121r). Occasionally, however, a *consilium* by an English advocate (presumably presented in written form) has been transcribed by Caesar and included among his notes, e.g. BL, MS Lansdowne 130, fos 58r–61r (Dr Lloyd); 131, fos. 263v–265r (Dr Hamond). Sometimes, the annotations do not refer to a formal legal opinion, but the style of the argumentation is reminiscent of that of a *consilium*, e.g. BL, MS Lansdowne 130, fos. 61v–64v (Dr Crompton); 129, fos. 37v–38v (causa criminalis contra Saunders; anonymous); 131, fos 42v and 67v–69v (Dr Lloyd in *Maceron c. Davies*; the advocate's plea for the defendant begins with a brief

continued

of a judgment required when the case was tried in appeal, although a memorandum on the legal arguments put forward during the proceedings could in some circumstances have been useful for the judge *a quo*.[15] The judgements as such follow a set pattern, which is more formal than that of many European courts influenced by the *ius commune* tradition and the Roman-canonical law of procedure, and fail to provide much information about the case itself.

A second, similar supposition would be that Caesar made the annotations in order to keep them as a reference for future cases. On the Continent, sixteenth-century notes made by judges have often been preserved. Their ostensible purpose was to serve as a (mostly) personal documentation for looking up precedents or examples (the rule *non exempli . . .* notwithstanding) when judging other cases. When such notes were made by a member of a collegiate jurisdiction, they often contained information about the sittings of the different judges and the (regularly, diverging) opinions which they had expressed. Such notes, in the early modern tradition of supreme courts, mark the beginnings of case law in a modern sense, as they often represent an attempt to establish the (legal) *ratio decidendi* of a case.

However, the elements of Caesar's annotations do not seem to support this second conjecture. The notes, as it has already been observed, only rarely contain an account or résumé of the facts, and even the legal argumentation is in most cases not systematically recounted. The other sources (whether in the Caesar Papers or in the court of Admiralty records) do not, in that respect, supplement the legal annotations.

A third, perhaps less plausible, hypothesis would be to see in the annotations the unprocessed material for a collection inspired by the

---

continued
summary of the facts, followed by: 'Queritur. Whether Davies bee in that case bound to make satisfaction for the robbery committed by the said capten and master? Pro decisione dubii suprascripti, arguitur pro parte affirmative, scilicet . . .'). For a very brief opinion in a matrimonial cause: BL, MS Lansdowne 130, fos 123v–124r (William Aubrey, Julius Caesar, Richard Cosin, William Lewyn). In an appeal case, the notes include (opposite) opinions by Sir Thomas Walmsley and Sir Edward Coke on the question whether a particular ship was to be considered as a deodand and forfeited (BL, MS Lansdowne 131, fol. 99rv). Foreign *consilia* are also included: BL, MS Lansdowne 130, fos 210r–212r ('consilium Hispani cuiusdam advocati in causa controversa inter Richardum Hawkins Anglum et procuratorem fisci coram presidente et iudicibus domus contractationis in Sevilla anno 1596'); A. Wijffels, *Consilium Facultatis Juridicae Tubingensis: A Legal Opinion on a Case of Maritime Warfare (1593)*. Studia Forensia Historica, 2 (Leiden 1993).
[15] G.I.O. Duncan, *The High Court of Delegates* (Cambridge 1971), p. 106ff, describes the presentation of the process by the judge *a quo* in his account of the appeal procedure. It seems that the process transmitted consisted mostly of a copy of the records of the lower court and sometimes original documents had also to be presented. None of these documents would have contained information on legal reasonings. However, for the period under consideration, no processes have been kept in the Delegates' records and archives, ibid., pp. 216–17.

decisiones literature on the Continent. Perhaps Caesar's long and successful career suggests a greater interest in political patronage and advancement, and in the financial benefits of the offices he held, than in scholarly work. Nevertheless, he could also be, whether or not inspired by his personal pecuniary or career interests, a committed advocate of the institutions in which he held office. One way to enhance the credibility of the court of Admiralty at a time when it was under attack and the object of covetous common law prohibitions might have been a collection of *decisiones* according to the continental model.

Although it should be stressed that such a model was by no means unknown to English civil lawyers, it seems nevertheless that it was not a particularly successful genre of legal literature in England. *Decisiones* collections by Guy Pape, Nicolas Bohier, Matthaeus de Afflictis, Joachim Mynsinger or Andreas Gail were available in English academic libraries and possibly at Doctors' Commons but, when compared with their relative importance in continental *ius commune* literature, they occur comparatively rarely in contemporary English catalogues;[16] correspondingly as it would seem, they also provide comparatively few authorities in the Admiralty pleadings by counsel. The reasons for this relative lack of interest are not clear. However, it fits with a more general disaffection characterising late-Tudor and early-Stuart civil law libraries for one of the most fundamental developments in early modern continental legal literature: the combination of the learned civil law with the substantive law of the emerging national states and territories (or, according to the terminology then in use, the amalgamation of *ius commune* and *iura propria*). Even though the *decisiones* were not at first the most striking type of continental legal literature which expressed this modern legal development – as a genre set off by the collections of the Rota and the *Decisiones Capellae Tholosanae* they had produced works long before *ius commune* works started incorporating *ius proprium* – they would provide a very adequate and practical format, the more so since they were mostly linked with a supreme court within a territory, an institution characteristically instrumental in establishing that territory's particular legal system. However, whereas on the Continent, the *usus modernus* literature ensured the blending of the learned *ius commune* tradition with municipal law (to different degrees depending on the specific developments of each territory), the established (or entrenched) positions held by the different branches of the legal profession in England precluded any large-scale unfolding of the programme outlined by John Cowell's *Institutiones*.

The difficulty of combining *ius commune* with English common and statute law would not, however, have been an obstacle for a *decisiones*

---

[16] A. Wijffels, 'Law Books at Cambridge, 1500–1640', in P. Birks (ed.), *The Life of the Law: Proceedings of the Tenth British Legal History Conference Oxford, 1991* (London and Rio Grande 1993), pp. 59–87.

collection of Admiralty cases, in which English municipal law was only seldom being referred to. Caesar's main and most onerous task would have been to arrange his material according to a coherent format, even by the flexible standards of the *decisiones* literature.[17] Perhaps it would not have been necessary to organise the single *decisiones* according to a general plan. Even so, the internal arrangement of the single *decisiones* would have required some difficult choices.[18] Presumably, a *decisio* would have needed some general reference to the facts, an element which was, as it has been pointed out, often omitted in the annotations. Conversely, it would also have been permissible (and in line with some other *ius commune* works) to omit the facts altogether for the purpose of a published version by simply starting with one or more *quaestiones juris*. Subsequently, Caesar would have had the option (always considering the different formulas applied by continental *decisiones* authors) either to discuss the question in a neutral (i.e. impartial) essay form or to oppose the (authentic or apocryphal) arguments of the different counsel. Even in the first option, he would have had the opportunity, according to the prevailing civil law model of reasoning, of including arguments *pro* and *contra* in his discourse. Either way, the annotations would then have proved useful, especially since they accurately provided an indispensable ingredient for any civil law work: the *allegationes* of the legal authorities. After having thus dealt with the set question or questions, it would have been sufficient to state that the judgment had been in favour of the plaintiff or the defendant. The judge, in the civil law tradition, would not necessarily have been expected, not even in a published version, to express his own reasoning or choice of arguments: a possible model of argumentation to reach the decision (such as the argumentation presented by the counsel of the triumphing litigant) rather than the actual legal reasoning of the court (supposing there had been a conclusive legal argument to decide the case) was sufficient to provide a marketable work. Moreover, specific information about the case (name of the litigants, factual circumstances such as the name of the ship involved, dates) which might have enabled a reader to identify the lawsuit could have been dispensed with altogether without altering the nature or the quality of a *decisiones* collection. Alternatively, the single *decisiones* could also have been presented as purely abstract legal questions and the reasonings presented could have been borrowed from different cases where the same (or similar) question had been raised. Whatever the modality opted for, the main task would have been to formulate clearly recognisable legal problems which were sufficiently versatile so as to generate an interest among practitioners.

[17] See part IV of H. Coing (ed.), *Handbuch der Quellen und Literatur der neueren europäischen Privatrechtsgeschichte*, ii, pt 2 (Munich 1976).
[18] For Italian models, cf. the contribution by M. Ascheri, ibid., pp. 1113–94); also M. Ascheri, *Tribunali: giuristi e istituzioni dal medioevo all'età moderna* (Bologna 1989), ch. 3.

Not all 350 cases would have been considered for a revision with a view to publication. In that sense, the relatively limited number of proceedings where Caesar was more elaborate in writing down his notes (in approximately one tenth of the cases) would (possibly in combination with segments from notes on other cases) have provided sufficient material for a (modest) volume of a conventionally accepted size. Since he also made annotations in cases which were not brought before the court of Admiralty, one would have to presume that the collection would not necessarily have been confined to maritime law. Assembling in one work topics belonging to different or even unrelated areas of the law was not, however, contrary to the prevailing legal methods of that time. In fact, even the argumentations in maritime cases borrowed heavily from other branches of the law, and the civil law literature was only beginning to develop the disciplines of international law and maritime law.

3. The Alternative Work: A. Gentili's Hispanica Advocatio

After 1606, Sir Julius Caesar was called to ever higher offices and his Admiralty annotations remained as they were. However, A. Gentili's involvement, during the last years of his life, in Admiralty litigation, partly overlapping with the last years of Caesar's tenure as Admiralty judge, gave the Regius Professor of Civil Law at Oxford the material and the opportunity to write one of the first works on international maritime law. Although the motives and the format of the book, published posthumously by Alberico's brother Scipio (in 1613), were different from the conjectures expressed regarding the purpose of Caesar's annotations, the end result demonstrates both the potential and the limits of Caesar's notes for a publication according to the contemporary expectations and standards applied to a legal work.

Gentili's motive for preparing his pleadings and opinions for publication, if one is to believe a note he sent to (probably) the Spanish ambassador, was his frustration at reactions to his defence of Iberian interests and at the attitude of Caesar's successor at the high court of Admiralty in 1606. More interesting is that Gentili originally planned to publish his opinions as a collection of *consilia*. However, at a later stage, he decided to rearrange the material by bringing together in a first part questions related to (mostly, substantive) international law (mainly prize-law) and other questions (mainly on procedure and evidence) in a second part. Specifics regarding the individual cases tend to be eliminated, though many more or less explicit references remain, perhaps because Gentili died before he could complete the editing and reorganisation of his material. As a result, Gentili's work appears as an imperfectly systematic treatise, with a large emphasis on maritime law. Although it is entirely based on the author's own opinions, and therefore lacks any account of the forensic controversies, its final format is materially not all that different from what could have been achieved with Caesar's notes in a freely conceived form of *decisiones*.

In his will, Gentili had provided that all his papers should be destroyed, but he made an exception for the manuscript of the *Hispanica advocatio*, the only work in his private collection which he considered worthy of publication.[19] He entrusted his brother Scipio with the edition and the book was first printed in 1613. So far, little research has been directed at the writing of the work, which is generally presented as a sample of (more or less opportunistic) advocacy at the high court of Admiralty during the first decade of the seventeenth century. The confused state of the drafts in MS D'Orville 608 may explain why scholarship has devoted comparatively little attention to that volume of the Gentili Papers at the Bodleian Library.[20]

The final structure of the *Hispanica advocatio* is in itself explicit enough as to the author's main purpose. The division into two books expresses an original attempt to concentrate all the chapters on international, in particular maritime, law in one homogeneous ensemble. By his earlier publications on ambassadors and the law of war, Gentili himself had strongly contributed to the development of the new literature on topics of international law. Maritime law, at the beginning of the seventeenth century, was still a largely neglected subject in legal literature. Gentili's working experience at the court of Admiralty in London would have drawn his attention to this lacuna and to the potential rewards – both academically and financially – of a work which might become a standard authority in international maritime disputes. Neither is the *Hispanica advocatio's* second part a mere repository of miscellaneous questions which did not fit in Book I. The emphasis on procedural questions was probably meant to draw as large an audience of legal practitioners as possible. At the same time, most of the procedural questions dealt with were particularly relevant to international maritime litigation.

If the general division of the work reflects an attempt to establish maritime law as a new scholarly discipline, the sub-division in chapters

---

[19] This is confirmed by Scipio Gentili in his preface to the *Hispanica advocatio*: 'Nam relictis compluribus de iure civili commentariis, cum eos omnes supprimi vel aboleri iussisset, hunc solum excepit, quem, quod minus, quam caeteri, imperfectus, minusque impolitus esset, in lucem a me edi voluit'. It is also consistent with his brother's last will (English version in PRO, PROB 11/128, fol. 442r):' All my bookes written with my hand my said brother shall cause to be burnte bycause they are to much imperfecte, onely the Spanish bookes ad vocationis [sic] which yf they be not verye perfecte he my said brothr maye withowte necessary [read: unnecessary] trouble mende them.'

[20] The description in the *Catalogue of Western Manuscripts at the Bodleian Library* matches K.R. Simmonds' characterisation in his 1959 article on 'The Gentili Manuscripts', pp. 534–35, who confirmed that, in spite of the 'revival' of interest in Gentili since T.E. Holland's inaugural lecture in 1874, the manuscript collection had usually been given no more than a 'passing mention.'

lacks a coherent structure. No attempt, it seems, was made to organise the sequence of the chapters according to a specific plan. Even the chapters dealing with more general, abstract questions often contain particular references to controversies which are not presented as a form of *casus* and are therefore often not entirely intelligible. The uneasy combination of abstract legal issues with specific circumstances is further exacerbated by the inclusion of letters and advices which mix legal reasonings with mere tactical considerations referring to particular, yet unexplained proceedings. These features of the *Hispanica advocatio* (together with the often repeated accusations of contradictory positions depending on the interests of Gentili's clients) are mainly to blame for the legal historians' reluctance to credit the book with doctrinal authority.

The *Hispanica advocatio's* hybrid character – both treatise and partisan advocacy – could be ascribed, Gentili's instructions in his will notwithstanding, to the author's premature death. In an ideal final version, the partly unintelligible references to specific circumstances would then have been omitted altogether. The draft versions in MS D'Orville 608 do not, however, bear out this view. Among the drafts in that collection, two versions stand out:

(a) One draft almost identical to the printed version. It is divided into two books and the sequence of chapters is the same as in the 1613 imprint. It is, however, incomplete, as it ends with chapter 18 of book II.[21] The differences between this manuscript and the printed version do not qualify as variants. In most cases, the manuscript version is the more accurate one, as single words or names have been misprinted or, on a few occasions, small passages have been inadvertently omitted.[22] The handwriting is Gentili's and corrections and minor alterations throughout (which were included in the printed text) prove that this version corresponds to the

---

[21] The reconstructed sequence from MS. D'Orville 608 is fos. 103r–106v, 110r–119v, 63r–75v, 80r–81v, 76r–79r.

[22] For example, on fol. 78v (p. 122 in the 1661 edition): 'privatis' instead of 'piratis'; fol. 80v (= p. 106): 'Peregr[inus]' instead of 'Parerg.'; fol. 87v (= p. 144): 'inidoneos' instead of 'idoneos'; fol. 88v (=p. 148) and passim: 'Barulo' instead of 'Bamlo'; fol. 89v (= p. 152), fol. 97v (= p. 177): 'scientia' instead of 'sententia'; fol. 100[bis]r (= p. 191): 'appellatio' instead of 'applicatio'; fol. 108r (= p. 204):'reparabit' in place of 'separabit'; fol. 116v (= p. 42): 'utro' instead of 'vero'; fol. 68r (= p. 73): 'parque' instead of 'parsque'; fol. 73v (= p. 95): 'iudex' in place of 'juxta'; fol. 80r (= p. 104): 'ergo' instead of 'vero'. Fol. 112v (= p. 28): read 'in auctoritate quadam *Bartoli: et iterum illorum, qui fundabant se in auctoritate quadam* Baldi . . .' (text in italics omitted in the 1661 edition); fol. 118v (= p. 50): 'Qui cum alio contrahit, *presumitur scire condicionem, et omnes qualitates eius, cum quo contrahit,* et rei de qua contrahit.' (text in italics omitted); fol. 68v (= p. 75): 'contra spoliatorem (contra spoliatores, Hispanorum sunt cause fere omnes) *pro spoliato admittitur sine mandato quilibet. Atque cessat (quod et obiectatur)* hic titulus . . .' (text in italics omitted). On fol. 105r, the passage corresponding to p. 9, lines 27–36 and p. 10, lines 1–31 does not appear in the manuscript; part of an addition, it was probably written on a separate (loose) sheet which has been lost.

author's intentions. This, presumably, was the version which Gentili asked his brother to publish.

(b) Another version, which can be reconstructed from MS D'Orville 608, consists of a sequence of 25 'responsa'.[23] This version, also in Gentili's handwriting, contains many corrections and alterations. The original numbering of these *consilia* has sometimes been crossed out and replaced by the heading 'cap.'. The single *responsa* have a title which, in most cases, anticipates that of the chapters in the final version. The *responsa* are mostly different from the corresponding opinions in the Caesar Papers (whether as holographs or in Caesar's notes), which would in some cases suggest that they are the result of an earlier redrafting by Gentili himself. However, a number of these *responsa* are evidently very close to original drafts. Some contain very specific references to the law-suits for which the arguments were worked out, including discussions of individual testimonials.[24] Some opinions and letters also bear Gentili's signature at the end.[25] The amplitude of modifications between these *responsa* and the final version varies considerably. Responsum I contains much of the material of book I, chapters 1–8, but in a much rearranged format. Further *consilia*, which are also considerably shorter, were to a lesser extent edited. The *responsa* provide material for thirty-three of the *Hispanica advocatio's* fifty-nine chapters.

In addition MS D'Orville 608 contains a substantial residuary consisting partly of drafts, some of which may complement the sequence of *responsa*,

---

[23] A summary concordance between this sequence and the printed *Hispanica advocatio* was published by K.R. Simmonds, 'The Gentili Manuscripts', pp. 550–51. The concordance is in so far misleading, as it suggests that the chapters in the printed work correspond as such to the version of the *responsa*. The concordance offered below (pp. 104–10) shows that this is not the case for several *responsa*.

[24] For example, responsum VI, at the beginning (fol. 26r): 'Ecce septem testes, qui de summa paupertate Juncii [= Hendrik de Jong] deponunt . . .', followed by brief references to the depositions of W. Roe, Laurence Davidge, W. Hixon, Bernard Ashwood, John and Arthur Adyn in the Saint Anthony case; see also ibid., fol. 29rv. Responsum VI, fol. 32r and 33r contains detailed references to the depositions in the case of the Sainte Anne. The *responsa* also mention names which have disappeared in the printed version: for example, responsum XIX mentions 'Adrianus Rebellius' (Rebell, Robell) where the *Hispanica advocatio* i, 11 reads 'hostis quidam'; responsum XXI, fol. 38, reveals that 'Petrus' is Peter Withepole, 'Philippus' Philip Bernardo (both names have been crossed out); the mention of 'in domo Sancti Georgii', on the other hand, has been completed by the location: 'Genua'. Another characteristic feature which marks the difference between the *responsa* as early drafts and the printed version is the alteration of particular expressions closely linked to the original context of the argumentations; e.g. in responsum II, fol. 52v, a letter to the Spanish ambassador, the expression 'ut declarat praeses vester Menochius . . .' becomes 'praeses noster . . .' in *Hispanica advocatio*, ii, 24, p. 223; the references to the 'archidux' in responsum III have been replaced in *Hispanica advocatio*, i, 9, by 'hostis'; in ii, 5, p. 144, line 20, 'Hollandum' corresponds in responsum VI, fol. 29r, to 'Juncum'.

[25] Responsum IX, fol. 35r; responsum XI, fol 36v; responsum XXI, fol. 38v; responsum XXII, fol. 57r; responsum XXV, fol. 58v.

although they present no formal connection with that sequence, partly of fragments of mostly later versions of some of the texts already included in that sequence. Pages of a different format contain notes, apparently by Gentili himself, but in a much more hurried handwriting, regarding the witnesses' depositions in the cases of the *San Antonio* and the *Sainte Anne*.[26]

The sequence of *responsa* apparently represents the author's initial concept of the work, probably concomitant with the proceedings. Some of the texts, in particular those which include specific references to testimonials and facts, may even closely correspond to Gentili's original drafts. From Gentili's papers, it is clear that the original aim of the publication was strongly motivated by the will to present a justification, both of the defence of the official Spanish interests and of the legal arguments and doctrines developed in the opinions.[27] At that stage, the traditional format of *consilia* may have appeared the most adequate to express the author's views. However, it must have been clear from the start that Gentili's opinions were not apt to be presented as *consilia* or *responsa* following the conventional standards of the genre. In spite of his protestations to be acting as a *consiliator*, not *advocatus*, Gentili's opinions were in fact much more steeped in advocacy than in the approach of the *consilia* tradition. Even when one looks at the *responsa* as they appear in D'Orville 608, it is clear that the features of a *consilium* are rarely present. For example, when facts are included, they fail to provide a summary of the case which may help to understand the legal issues at stake; references to specific depositions by witnesses, for instance, usually do not make sense in the absence of at least a brief statement of the *species facti*. With respect to Gentili's presumed wish to address not only an English, but also a much wider audience of legal professionals throughout Europe, it may be questionable whether the inclusion of some particular aspects of the English system was desirable. These characteristics suggest that it is unlikely that the publication of the sequence of *responsa* as they appear in D'Orville 608 was seriously considered by the author himself.

To illustrate the differences between the *responsa*, the opinions as they appear in Caesar's notes and the printed version, one – simplified – example may be taken from the case of the *Spanish Ambassador* c. *Sir Richard Hawkins*, more specifically regarding the question of the vice-admiral's duty of care and his responsibility as an official.[28] The

---

[26] MS D'Orville 608, fos. 167r–173v.

[27] This intention appears clearly in one *responsum* which was not included in the printed version: responsum V, now published in Wijffels, *Alberico Gentili and Thomas Crompton*, pp. 37–41.

[28] Early 1605, a French ship, the *Sainte Anne* from Toulon, on her way back from Brazil to Leghorn, laden with brazilwood and sugar, fell victim to the English and was brought to Salcombe under the commandment of a Captain Jolliffe. Shortly after her arrival,

continued

following transcripts give the text of *(a)*, in the left column, Responsum VIII in D'Orville 608, and *(b)*, in the right column, excerpts from Caesar's notes on Gentili's intervention.

continued

Sir Richard Hawkins, vice-admiral of Devon, seized the ship and her cargo and had his own representative and an official of the Customs positioned on board until he should receive instructions from London. Part of the brazilwood was brought ashore in order to secure payment for necessary repairs and victualling of the ship. Hawkins then left Salcombe for Exeter, where he was to attend the assizes as a justice of the peace. During Hawkins' stay in Exeter, Hendrik de Jong, on his way back from London, carried out, with some twenty well-armed fellow countrymen, a raid on the *Sainte Anne* and ousted the English officials. The Dutchmen also made sure that the ship, in spite of her poor state, could sail off at short notice. The Portuguese factor who had been on the *Sainte Anne* at her first taking, and who claimed to be part-owner of the lading and to represent other Iberian part-owners, persuaded some Englishmen (including, possibly, members of the crew who had captured the *Sainte Anne* in the first place) to launch a counter-raid, which was successful. When Hawkins came back to Salcombe, the Portuguese factor and representatives of the Spanish embassy offered the vice-admiral control over the ship. Meanwhile, the English who had recaptured the *Sainte Anne* threatened to deliver the ship back to the Dutch unless they were instantly paid the £600 they had been promised. Hawkins apparently then brought together the French purser, the Portuguese-Spanish representatives and representatives of the Dutch and English sailors, and acted as a 'broker' to negotiate a settlement. The French and Iberian parties were persuaded that, unless they accepted less favourable terms, the *Sainte Anne* and the main part of her cargo would be altogether lost to them.

An agreement was reached and the *Sainte Anne* sailed off under De Jong's command shortly before orders from the privy council and instructions from the Spanish ambassador to sequestrate the *Sainte Anne* and her lading reached Hawkins. The Spanish ambassador, seconded by Iberian merchants claiming an interest in the cargo, sued Sir Richard Hawkins before the high court of Admiralty, accusing him of negligence and holding him liable for the losses due to the inadequacy of the measures he had taken for securing the control over the *Sainte Anne*. It was also alleged that the vice-admiral had gained personal profit from the dealings and had led the negotiations after concluding a secret agreement with the English and Dutch parties. The French ambassador sued Hawkins in a separate procedure. Julius Caesar's notes in this case are in so far exceptional as the reported arguments presented by counsel focus to a large extent on the depositions by witnesses and therefore on facts. The main issue which emerges from this discussion appears to be the question of Hawkins's integrity and that of the effectiveness of the measures he had taken to secure the control of the *Sainte Anne* by English officials. The Iberian witnesses claimed that they had only accepted the terms of the agreement under threat that, if they did not consent, the ship would be carried away and that they 'would loose all'. Hawkins, they intimated, had favoured the Dutchmen and denied the Portuguese factor the protection he had demanded on the pretext of being under obligation to acknowledge the Dutchmen's possession as well.

For the Iberian interests, both Dr Lloyd and Gentili acted as counsel. Lloyd's intervention is characterised by references to principles which are directly applicable to the controversial facts, at least as they were presented by his clients and the witnesses in their favour. Gentili developed two main arguments. The first, on evidence, is similar to the one already used in the *Saint Anthony's* case. It consists of *salvationes*, i.e. arguments aiming to counter objections expressed against the client's witnesses. Gentili here again argued that, under the circumstances, depositions by witnesses who have been paid by one of

continued

MS D'Orville 608, fos. 32r–33v[29]	*MS Lansdowne 132, fos 50v–51r*

Januario.
Responsum VIII

De magistratus culpa punienda.[30]

<table>
<tr>
<td>

Potuit dominus viceadmirallius
intelligere, navim sancte Anne esse
Anglorum, non Junci; quos in ea
vidit omnes, non Juncum. [a: Soc.
in § nihil commune, num. 31] Et ex
possessione presenti quis presumitur
dominus, ubi de dominio alterius
non apparet, et incidenter tantum
queritur de dominio, que est opinio
communis. Etiam hoc probatur ex
eo, quo ait Guilielmus Roe, serviens
admirallitatis, quod Adynus se, et
Randollum rogavit, ut intercederent
apud viceadmirallium, qui daret
eidem Adyno partem suam bonorum
navis. Et quod idem Roe testis scit,
Randollum egisse cum viceadmirallio.
Idem deponit Laurentius Davidge,
actum fuisse domino viceadmirallio,
quod navis pertineret ad Anglos,
nullo modo ad
</td>
<td>

8. Debuit viceadmirallus Hawkins vim
Junii prohibere et potuit, sed non
prohibuit, ergo in culpa fuit, 1. culpa
caret, D. de regul. iur..

9. Ex possessione presenti potest quis
de dominio intelligere sive presumere,
Socyn. in § nihil commune, 1.
naturaliter, num. 31, D. de acquir.
possessio.
</td>
</tr>
</table>

continued

the litigants, or who have received 'instructions' from an interested party, are nonetheless admissible. Similarly, criminals can be accepted as lawful witnesses, in particular when their depositions made for truth's sake include a self-incrimination. Moreover, all such testimonials may be added to presumptions and thus contribute to form a 'full proof'. The second argument touches the essence of the forensic controversy: whether the defendant could be held liable for negligence. Gentili's argumentation refers both to general principles on the duties of someone to whom it is entrusted to keep guard over a thing and to more specific principles governing an official's duty of care. Inevitably, the applicability of these principles depends on the appreciation of the factual circumstances: Gentili's argumentation only establishes that, given the facts as they are presented by the Spanish-Portuguese parties, the vice-admiral's liability is founded on civil law principles. The opponents' arguments confirm at least that counsel on both sides regarded the vice-admiral's responsibility as the central legal issue of the case.

[29] Square brackets indicate that the text occurs in the margin. Minor differences in the printed version (1661 edition) are not mentioned in the notes.

[30] But for a few variants and minor additions, the text corresponds to book I, chapter 19 of the *Hispanica advocatio*. However, the passages at the beginning (from the first sentence to 'de consecutis rerum dissipationibus') and at the end (from 'Pulsi sunt, esto', until the end, except for one sentence) were not included in the printed version.

Juncum. Et idem Johannes Adynus.
Cum quo Randollus, quod iste
Adynus ivit ad viceadmirallium,
hec narravit, iustitiam petierit
contra Juncum. Ergo rem intellexit
viceadmirallius. Neque hic est questio.
Est questio, si idem viceadmirallius
culpam admisit ullam, propter
quam teneatur de consecutis rerum
dissipationibus.

[b: Decia. 1, cons. 29, Ceph. 661]
Atque dicitur quidem, quod non
presumitur culpa, nisi probetur.
Et quod probare eam habet, qui
allegat, claram, et certam; quin
potius, ad evitandam suspitionem
culpe, presumitur quis fecisse, quod
alius verisimiliter faceret. [c: Eug.
cons. 60, Ceph. 359, Decia. 2, lib.
1, Gramm. 24, cons. crim., Menoch.
cons. 622] Et in officialibus quidem
specialiter presumitur diligentia.
Presumuntur officiales diligenter et
fideliter officium suum exercuisse.
Lex presumit pro officialibus, et eis
favet. Contra eos scrupulosa omnis
reicitur inquisitio, etc. Hec vera sunt.
[d: Fulg. ii de probat., Cuma. 1. 1,
de ma con.] Sed et illud, quod imo
ipsi officiales probare habent, gesta
recte in officio. *Non est necesse pupillo
probare, fideiussores pro tutore datos, cum
accipiebantur, idoneos non fuisse. Nam
probatio exigenda est ab his, quorum
officii fuit providere, ut pupillo caveretur*,
inquit lex. Et doctores inquiunt,
sic esse quoniam officiales probare
habent, gesta recte in officio, que
spectant ad officium ipsorum. Aut,
si quid speciale[31] ilic caussaris[32] in
pupillo, qui sibi curare non potuit.
Idem in peregrina navi Lusitanorum
dices magis, que[33] sibi cavere de
idoneis custodibus non potuit. Hoc
de custodibus non idoneis obiicitur
viceadmirallio. Aut si etiam vis cum
aliis doctoribus communiter, onus eius
probationis incumbere magistratibus,
quia ex presenti tempore, quum
apparent fideiussores non idonei,
presumatur, nec fuisse idoneos[34]

10. Ad evitandam suspitionem
culpe presumitur quis fecisse, quod
alius verisimiliter faceret, Decia. 1,
consil. 29, et Cephal. consil. 661, et
in officialibus quidem specialiter
presumitur diligentia, Eugen. consil.
60, Cephal. consil. 359, Menoch.
consil. 622, Decia. 2 consil., lib.
1, vide Fulgosium in 1. 2, D. de
probatio., et Cuman. in 1. 1, de
magistrat. conveniend.

[31] Printed version: officiale.
[32] Printed version: dicas.
[33] Printed version: added, 'sub manum Officialis'.
[34] Printed version: idonei.

tempore dationis. Etiam hoc valde
facit contra viceadmirallium.[35]
Nam eius custodes reperti non sunt
idonei sane.[36]

[e:Gl. c. pe., de reg. iu., Turz.
comm. 385, Alc. 3, presu. 15, Ceph.
cons. 362][37] Dico nunc de custodibus,
quod culpa ipsorum <, qui custodire
debuerunt, > presumitur, etiam
fortuitus casus intervenisse. Ipsis
incumbit probatio casus fortuiti:
cum ipsi ratione officii sui debeant
custodiam habere.[38] Et in quocunque
custode sic est. [f: Jas. 1. 61, de leg.
1, Alex. 1, cons. 50, Alc. 8, cons.
20, Rip. ult. de pes. 2, Menoch.
cons. 118] Culpam etiam levissimam
prestat custos: id est, exactissimam
diligentiam in precavendo. Hanc
probare debet, qui dicit prestitam,
quia nec reperitur communiter tanta
diligentia. [g: Ceph. cons. 640] Nec
absque difficultate vitatur ea culpa.
[h: Menoch. cons. 246, Anch. 121]
Officiales autem publicos etiam erga
privatos lesos teneri proque levissima
culpa civiliter, imo et pro casu,
quem culpa precedit, adhuc leges
tradunt, et interpretes. De qualibet
teneri negligentia, que parti nocet, [i:
Rebuff. 1. 164 de V.S., Menoch. cons.
335] id est etiam de minima. [k: Fulg.
de off. pr. vig. 1. 1, de re. vi., 1. 40,
loca.] Custodes tenentur de robaria,
tenentur de fuga, tenentur de damno
dato ab aliis, aut probent, nullam esse
ipsorum culpam.

11. Culpa eorum, qui custodire
debuerunt, presumitur cum fortuitus
casus intervenerit; ipsis igitur
incumbit probatio casus fortuiti,
cum ipsi ratione officii sui debeant
custodiam habere, et in quolibet
custode sic est, glos. cap. penult.,
de regul. iur., Turz. com. opinio.
385, Alciat. 3, presumpt. 15, et
Cephal. consil. 362. Culpam enim
levissimam prestare debet custos,
id est, exactissimam diligentiam in
precavendo, Jason in 1. 61, D. de
legat. 1, Alexand. 1, consil. 50,
Alciat. 8, consil. 20, Menoch. consil.
118, et eam diligentiam probare
debet, qui dicit prestitam: quia nec
reperitur communiter tanta diligentia,
nec absque difficultate vitatur ea
culpa levissima, Cephal. consil. 640.
Officiales autem publicos teneri etiam
erga privatos lesos, proque levissima
culpa civiliter, immo et pro casu,
quem culpa precedit, adhuc leges
tradunt et interpretes, Menoch. consil.
246, et Rebuffus in 1. 164, D. de
verb. signif. Custodes tenentur de
robaria, tenentur de fuga, tenentur
de damno dato ab aliis, aut probent,
nullam esse ipsorum culpam, Fulgos.
de offic. prefecti. vigil., 1. 21, de rei
vendicat., 1. 40, loca.

Aut nostri isti[39] probent, quomodo
absque ulla ipsorum culpa pulsi de
possessione[40] sunt ab Hollandis. Nulla
narratur pugna. Et defensio fuisset
facilima eo loci: ubi idem Hollandi
negotio nullo facti paullo ante captivi
fuerant. [41]Etiam qui erant in navi

---

[35] Printed version: nostrum Officialem.
[36] Printed version: one sentence added.
[37] Printed version: added, a reference to Corneus's *Consilia*.
[38] Printed version: added, a reference to Menochius.
[39] Printed version: hi custodes.
[40] Printed version: de custodia, et de possessione navis.
[41] Printed version: the following sentence has been omitted.

custodes potuissent soli vim omnem repellere Hollandorum. Aut si ulla fuit facta vis, non viceadmirallius pro suo officio, pro iniuria facta suis, pro iniuria sibi facta, ultus Hollandos fuisse? Non accusasset?[42]

Particeps est, aut fautor criminis, qui negligit punire. Dicerem, non audivisse de vi ista aut ab aliis, aut a suis, si rem absurdissimam non dicerem. Si suos cum isto tacito non vincerem in aperto dolo. [m: Fulg. de off. pret. vig.] Et custodes ipsi quandoque furantur. Unde et ait Satyra, *Quis custodit ipsos custodes?*

Particeps aut fautor criminis est, qui negligit punire, Giacch. addit. Clar., § fin. quest. 73,

[n: 1. 23, pro soc., Jas. 1. 35, si cer. pet., Fulg. 1. 8, manda.] Quorum dein negligentia noceret domino, non dolus solum. Et igitur, si non vi aperta, sed clam irrepserunt Hollandi per noctem, magna fuit negligentia custodum, {phulalontôn phulakas tès nuktos}.

et custodum negligentia nocet domino, non solum dolus, 1. 23, D. pro socio, et Jason in 1. 35, D. si cert. petat., et Fulgos. in 1. 8, D. mandati,

[43]Qui non faciebant quod facere omnes in navibus solent: certe solent, et debent facere custodes omnes. [o: Menoch. cons. 121, 175, Ceph. 265, 388, Bertr. 136, vol. 1, p. 2] Dolus vero arguitur in his, qui omittunt facere, quod facere ex officio debent, quod alii facere passim consueverunt.

et dolus arguitur in hiis, qui omittunt facere, quod facere ex officio debent, Menoch. consil. 121 et 175, et Cephal. consil. 265 et 388.

Et regula hec est, sive sciunt, sive scire debent, se debere facere. [p: c. ult. de reg. iur., Alc. 8, cons. 20] *Non potest esse pastoris excusatio, si lupes oves comedit, et pastor nescit,* inquit lex, *non potest.* [q: Jas. 1. Gallus, prin.[44]] Et denotat necessitatem precisam, et remotionem potentie. Inquit, *nescit.* Et est ratio, [r: Rip. 1. quod te, si cer. pe.] quia nescientia eius, quod

Non potest esse pastoris excusatio, si oves lupus comedit, et pastor nescit, cap. ult., de regul. iur., et Alciat. 8, consil. 20, nam nescientia eius, quod sciri debet, dicitur affectata, et itaque pro scientia habetur, Ripa in 1. quod te, D. si cert. petat., et Bart. consil. 102, et Decia. 2, consil. 46, et Castrensis in 1. 12, D. locati et Cephal. d. consil. 640, et Menoch. consil. 118 et 406.

---

[42] Printed version: the last question replaced by two sentences (including several references).

[43] Printed version: added, a reference to Straccha.

[44] Printed version: added, a reference to Cephalus.

sciri debet, dicitur affectata. Et itaque
pro scientia habetur. [s: Bar. cons.
102] Probatur negligentia varie, et
quum quis tenetur ad factum certum,
limitatum tempore et loco, eo ipso,
quod factum illud non est. Et in tali
facto nos versamur. [t: Decia. 2, cons.
46] Negligentia custodum probatur:
et itaque velut dolus. [u: Castr. 1.
12, loca., Ceph. d. 640] Negligentia
viceadmirallii arguitur, qui discedens
non reliquit, qui bene custodirent.
[x: Menoch. cons. 118, 406] Etiam
dolus probatur eius, qui non facit,
quod facere debet, qui remedia debita
non adhibuit. Quis non notet hic et
custodes, et dominum?[45] Pulsi sunt,
esto. Non accusant Hollandos. Adeon'
vili viri habent iniurias suas? Adeon'
inhonorati sunt, qui honores gerunt
magistratus? Que autem secuta dicitur
post[ea] transactio inter Hollandos, et
Lusitanos, nihil ad vim illatam hanc
Anglis custodibus. De vi agnoscit
ipse viceadmirallius, et dicunt testes
nonnulli.

Ego tamen agnoscere vim nequeo, nisi
simulatam, per hactenus disputata.
Etiam Laurentius Davidge, quod
custodes illi permiserint Hollandis
ingressum navis: nec ullatenus
resisterint. Etiam Johannes Adyn,
ingressos Hollandos permittente
domino viceadmirallio. Quibus
testibus credendum magis sit: qui
verisimilia magis deponunt, ut
ius vulgo notum, et tritum est.
Atque, si vera vis fuisset, cur
(quod omnes homines fecissent) vi
navim non recuperavit? Potuit de
iure magistratus vi rec[u]perare
ablata per vim sibi, et custodibus
suis. Quis homo hoc ius nescit?
Potuit per litteras celtissimorum
consiliariorum: que mandabant ei,
ut navim custodiret. Nam recuperare
ablatum certe est custodire. Potuit,
quum sciret, navim esse a piratis
allatam. De facto potuit. Ecce alii sic
recuperarunt, qui minus poterant,
quam dominus iste, viceadmirallius,
et iusticiarius pacis. Sed noluit
recuperare. Audi Jacobum Mayn,
quod noluit capere in possessionem

---

[45] Printed version: dominum. Followed by the last sentence of the chapter.

viceadmirallius, quia auctoritatem
non haberet. Idem audis Cesarem
Ugonem, idem Prosperum Sergium.
Et quod iste addit ex viceadmirallio,
non ausum eum explodere tormenta
in navim, quia navis Gallorum
esset: adhuc minus aptam habet
viceadmirallii responsionem. An
enim aliter non potuit iste navim
recuperare? Etiam Prosper, quod
rogavit viceadmirallium, ne sineret
ferri commeatum in navim. Et
quod viceadmirallius nec noluit id
impedire, at ferri semper permisit.
Quid tamen disputo, si potuit?
Fecit, recepit navim. Ecce idem
Jacobus Mayn, quod viceadmirallius
procuraverat Anglis libras sexcentas
si navim recuperassent, qui
recuperarunt. Angli isti sunt ipsi
pirate, qui primum cepere navim, et
de navi pulsi a viceadmirallio postea
fuere. Pelluntur, cogniti pirate.
Reducuntur in premia, novi homines
fact . . . Fraus nulla hic facta est.
Johannes Adyn narrat fraudem,
aperit composita viceadmirallii, et
Junci omnia. Et hactenus dixi,
quod per culpam magnam exciderit
viceadmirallius possessione navis.
Item, quod per etiam magnam
culpam non recuperavit possessionem,
per magnam negligentiam ultus
non est [in] vim Hollandorum, sibi,
Lusitanis. Dico,

magnam fuisse viceadmirallii culpam,
quia non exposuit saltem merces de
navi in terram omnes, ut exposuit
sua et potuit omnes, possessor navis
pacificus dies plurimos. Rogavit enim
Pintus institor Lusitanorum in navi,
ut istam compositionem faceret, sed
viceadmirallius respondit, se non
habere auctoritatem. Prosper rogavit,
ut arrestaret, que apud ipsum essent
viceadmirallium, sed viceadmirallius
etiam negavit sibi esse potestatem.

[46][y: Anch. cons. 337] Non caret scrupulo societatis occulte, qui manifesto facinori desiit obviare. Non excusatur si dicit, se non potuisse: cum debuerit, et potuerit satis auxiliis aliunde habere, ab opido iuncto, ab aliis vicinis. [z: Saly. 1. 1, C. de his, qui latro.] Que Salycetus ad legem, notatam meo Floydo. Ad quam et Fulgosius, quod solis literis huius officialis debent alii credere, et auxilium prebere. De quo et facilitatem noto habendi auxilium. Adnoto unum, quod coram et respondi domino iudici non esse satis, si officialis suam, aut aliorum solitam isthic adhibuit diligentiam. Nam leges requirunt (ut dixi) exactissimam et in presenti casu longe exactissima requiritur, quum propter has guerras piraticas est periculum longe maius. [a: Anch. d. cons. 121] Ut sic custodia diligentior solito notatur Anchoranus sane.

Nec caret scrupulo societatis occulte, qui manifesto facinori desiit obviare, Anchora. consil. 337.

12. Metus probatur coniecturis, et per leviorem probationem, Alciat. 3, presumpt. 7, et dolus ex nullis persuasionibus arguitur, et persuadere est plus quam cogere, et actio hinc de dolo est, Menoch. consil. 175, 406.

13. Cautele nimie probant dolum, Cephal. consil. 718 et Menoch. consil. 37 et Cephal. consil. 210. Dolus et presumitur eius, qui transigit cum procuratore, nec curavit videre mandatum, Cephal. consil. 316.

A comparison of both versions and a collation with the printed version brings forward four main characteristics of the *responsum*. First, it is obvious that the references to specific facts presuppose that the reader is already acquainted with the case. In order to understand the opening paragraph of the *responsum* and comments on witnesses' depositions further on in the argumentation, the addressee (or reader) may even be expected to be familiar with the interrogatories. Secondly, in spite of these close associations with presupposed facts, the legal argumentation is more elaborate than in Caesar's notes. Yet, most of the authorities used in the *responsum* also occur in the notes. Perhaps this can be ascribed,

---

[46] The following sentence occurs on p. 79 in the printed version.

in this particular example, to the brevity of Caesar's annotation. The passage following the quotation 'Non potest pastoris esse excusatio . . .' seems to support that view, as both versions contain the same sequence of allegations, but the references in the *responsum* are interspersed with the principles which they are deemed to establish. Yet, in spite of the greater length of the *responsum*, both versions are not, with respect to the legal arguments, substantially different. Thirdly, the date mentioned at the beginning of the *responsum* (January, which must be the first month of the year 1606 n.s.) indicates that the text is probably concomitant to the proceedings and that it is not the result of a later redrafting. This is also confirmed by the inclusion of references to circumstances of the case which are deemed to be known. Both the contents and the style even suggest that the *responsum* may have been the actual version submitted as an opinion or pleading to the judge. Fourthly, compared with the printed version, the editing in this case has been limited; most specific references to facts and all the references to interrogatories have been left out. The few additions including legal arguments do not modify the general purport of the *responsum*. The remaining references to the particular circumstances of the case do not specially enhance the understanding of the chapter.

The editorial changes, which, in some cases, resulted in a complete reshaping of the original opinions, were not accompanied with alterations of the substance of the arguments. Neither did the changes effect a transformation of the opinions into abstract treatises or essays. Considering the amount of meticulous work involved in the rewriting of some opinions and chapters, and even allowing for the fact that the editing may not have been completely finished at the time of Gentili's death, it is unlikely that the author meant to exclude all the references to facts or specific circumstances of the cases. It is more plausible, an hypothesis which would be reinforced by the title of the work, that Gentili, after first considering the possibility of a *consilia* collection, decided on a formula closer to that of the '*plaidoyers*', a successful genre, particularly popular among French legal practitioners. This type of literature, which allowed for a more incisive style and greater emphasis on personal views, and which, at the same time, justified a particular attention to procedural questions, departed from the traditional mould of the *consilia*, but offered a solution to the dilemma between such *consilia* and the shorter treatises. Perhaps, also, Gentili considered that the material he had gathered in his opinions was insufficient for a monograph as those he had written earlier in topics of international law. Nor may it have been very clear what topics he would have had to deal with in such a monograph on maritime law. Admittedly, the questions of prize-law and piracy, the status of neutrals and, to a lesser extent, the law of the sea, would have provided most of the subject-matter. However, even for those comparatively more clearly defined areas, legal reasonings and arguments, in the approach followed by Gentili, were still largely sustained by sources, methods and principles which were not specific for international maritime controversies. As in the *ius commune* tradition at large, the rules governing possession and property command a wide variety of litigation-related legal reasonings. Gentili's inclination to develop his arguments in close connection with traditional doctrinal authorities reinforced the effect of a work steeped in *mos italicus* learning. In some ways, his works on ambassadors and the law of war, less dependent or relying less directly on *mos italicus* literature, were more modern, as was, if only considered by the standards of the sources used, Grotius's *De iure praedae*, written at the same time as some of the earlier opinions or drafts of the *Hispanica advocatio*. Both comparisons – with Gentili's own previous publications on international law and Grotius's work – tend to strengthen the impression that the specific character of the *Hispanica advocatio* was mainly due to Gentili's aim to create a work which would appeal to legal practitioners. Ironically, this regard for the conventions of legal practice may well have been, in retrospect, the principal reason why, in the changing developments affecting the *ius commune* methods during the first half of the seventeenth century, Gentili's last work failed to become a major and lasting authority in early modern international law – and why it was largely disregarded by legal scholars and, latterly, by legal historians.

7

Law Reports in England from 1603 to 1660

W.H. Bryson

In 1972, John Baker referred to the period 1500 to 1700 as 'the Dark Age of English Legal History'.[1] Before that date, most of the legal historians were medievalists, and the modernists rarely reached back to the seventeenth century. Only one set of reports of cases from this period had been published since the nineteenth century. These were Lord Nottingham's reports edited by David Yale.[2] The numerous manuscripts of law reports were poorly catalogued and unused for centuries. No help was to be found in the reading of them as they were in law French, a difficult jargon of the lawyers of long ago.

The bright spot was the availability of a respectable edition of the statutes[3] and some royal proclamations.[4] As to the case reports, the Year Books and the reports of Dyer, Plowden, Croke, Moore, and Coke shed some light on the law up to about 1616, the date of Coke's last printed case. After 1660, the reports appear to be reasonably full and reliable. Holdsworth wrote in 1922 'the sixteenth and early seventeenth centuries are the period of transition from the medieval to the modern law. After the Restoration, this period of transition is over, and the development of the modern law is begun'.[5] The dim period of reports, 1603 to 1660, is the focus of the present essay.

A look at the law reports of the reigns of James I and Charles I and of the Interregnum reveals a somewhat dreary literary scene. The holders

---

[1] J.H. Baker, 'The Dark Age of English Legal History, 1500–1700', in D. Jenkins, ed., *Legal History Studies 1972* (Cardiff, 1975), pp. 1–27; rept. in J.H. Baker, *The Legal Profession and the Common Law* (London, 1986), pp. 435–60.

[2] D.E.C. Yale, ed., *Lord Nottingham's Chancery Cases* (London, 1957, 1961), Selden Society 73, 79.

[3] *The Statutes of the Realm* (London, 1810–1822); C.H. Firth and R.S. Rait, *Acts and Ordinances of the Interregnum, 1642–1660*, 3 vols (London, 1911; rept. Holmes Beach, Fla, 1972).

[4] P.L. Hughes and J.F. Larkin, *Tudor Royal Proclamations*, 3 vols (New Haven, Conn., 1964–1969); J.F. Larkin and P.L. Hughes, *Stuart Royal Proclamations* (Oxford, 1973).

[5] W.S. Holdsworth, 'The History of Remedies Against the Crown,' *Law Quarterly Review*, 38 (1922), p. 280.

of the monopoly for the printing of common law books chose primarily to reprint the older law books and the Year Books.[6] Between 1603 and 1648, the only contemporary law reports to be printed were those of Sir Edward Coke and those of Sir Henry Hobart. Hobart died in 1625, and his reports were published posthumously in 1641. (The other reports circulated in manuscript form if they were available at all.)

With the collapse of the monarchy in the 1640s, the enforcement of the royal patent for printing law books became impossible. The general mood of the country was strongly against censorship of the press and control of printing because of the political and religious restrictions of Charles I and his advisers. The efforts aimed at controlling the publication of books during the Interregnum were directed against political and religious fanatics, not the publishers of law reports. The result was a minor flood of new law reports to satisfy the pent-up demand.

From 1648 to 1660, the following reports appeared in their first editions:

> J. Bridgman (1651 or 1652)
> Brownlow and Goldesborough (1651–52)
> Bulstrode (1657–59)
> Calthrop (1655)
> Clayton (1651)
> Croke, parts 2 and 3 (1657)
> Godbolt (1652)
> 'Hetley' (1657)
> Hutton (1656)
> Lane (1657)
> Leonard, parts 1 and 2 (1658–59)
> Ley (1659)
> March, New Cases (1648)
> Noy (1656)
> Owen (1650)
> Popham (1656)
> Style (1658)
> 'Winch' (1657)

Of these reports, the following were published posthumously and thus saw the light of day without any permission of the supposed author and thus without his editorial assistance and advice:

> John Bridgman (d. 1638)
> Richard Brownlow (d. 1638) and John Goldesborough (d. 1618)
> Sir Henry Calthrop (d. 1637)
> Sir George Croke (d. 1642)

[6] H.S. Bennett, *English Books and Readers 1603 to 1640* (Cambridge, 1970), pp. 118–27.

John Godbolt (d. 1648)
Sir Thomas Hetley (d. 1637)
Sir Richard Hutton (d. 1639)
Sir Richard Lane (d. 1650)
William Leonard
Sir James Ley (d. 1629)
William Noy (d. 1634)
Thomas Owen (d. 1598)
Sir John Popham (d. 1607)
Sir Humphrey Winch (d. 1625)

Of these reports, those attributed to Noy, Owen, and Popham contain cases dating after the deaths of the reporters. They must therefore have been merely the owners and not the authors of the manuscripts upon which the printed books were based.

It is interesting to note that the reports of 'Hetley,' Ley, Style, and 'Winch' were not thought to be worth reprinting until their inclusion in the *English Reports Reprint* at the end of the nineteenth century. These volumes were not inaccessible – John Mercer of Stafford County, Virginia, had copies of all four in his library in 1746.[7]

In consideration of these observations, one should not be surprised at the poor quality of the reports of this era. It was an age of bibliographical darkness even in its own time. This darkness was moderated somewhat by the publication after 1660 of more reports from the period under consideration. They were as follows with the dates of first publication:

Aleyn (1681)
Benloe (1661)
Croke, part 1 (1661)
Dickens (1803)
Duke (1676)
Foley (1739)
Glanvill (1775)
Hardres (1693)
Hawarde (1894)
Jenkins (1661)
W. Jones (1675)
Latch (1661 or 1662)
Leonard parts 3 and 4 (1663–5)
Littleton (1683)
Moore (1663)
Nelson (1717)
Palmer (1675)
Reports in Chancery (1693–94)

---

[7] W.H. Bryson, *Census of Law Books in Colonial Virginia* (Charlottesville, 1978), pp. xviii, 7, 10, 15, 17.

Rolle (1675–76)
Siderfin (1683–89)
Yelverton (1661)

Of these, the following were published posthumously:

William Benloe (Bendlowes) (d. 1584)
Sir George Croke (d. 1642)
John Glanvill (d. 1661)
John Hawarde (d. 1630)
John Latch (d. 1655)
William Leonard
Sir Edward Littleton (d. 1645)
Sir Francis Moore (d. 1616)
Sir Geoffrey Palmer (d. 1670)
Henry Rolle (d. 1656)
Sir Henry Yelverton (d. 1630)

One of the results of the lack of contemporary reports in print was the wide circulation of manuscript reports. Another was the copying of these manuscripts into other manuscript collections of great bibliographical complexity, some of which then came to be the basis of printed reports. Most of the manuscript copies either omitted literary attribution or confused ownership with authorship. Each manuscript report must be carefully examined by comparison with the other manuscripts and with the printed volumes before authorship and accuracy of any of them can be unravelled. When this has been done, then they should be edited, translated and published.

In the course of my research into the history of equity, I have unearthed some bibliographical information about Robert Paynell (d. 1658) and three of his colleagues at Gray's Inn. This adds some interesting details to the research and observations of Edward Umfreville, John W. Wallace and John H. Baker.[8] Judging from the bibliographical evidence of surviving manuscript reports, it appears that in the early years of the reign of Charles I, Robert Paynell, Thomas Widdrington (d. 1664), William or George Allestree, and Humphrey Mackworth entered into a joint reporting venture. Paynell covered the Exchequer, Widdrington the King's Bench,[9] and Allestree and Mackworth the court of Common Pleas.[10] They must have known each other very well. Paynell and Widdrington both matriculated

---

[8] J.H. Baker, 'Dark Age', pp. 453–54; manuscript notes of Edward Umfreville in BL, MS Hargrave 362, fol. 3v; J.W. Wallace, *The Reporters*, (4th edn, Boston, 1882; rept. Buffalo, NY, 1959), pp. 261–62, 266, 270–71.

[9] Manuscripts of Widdrington's reports are listed in J.H. Baker, *English Legal Manuscripts* (Zug, 1978), ii, p. 85.

[10] Manuscripts of Mackworth's reports are listed in Baker, 'Dark Age', p. 453, n. 95.

at Christ's College, Cambridge in 1617. Both were admitted to Gray's Inn in 1619. Mackworth was admitted to Gray's Inn in 1621, William Allestree in 1618 and George Allestree in 1623.[11]

There are numerous manuscript copies of these reports; there are in fact more manuscript copies of Paynell's reports than of any other Exchequer collection. The reports commonly attributed to Winch are only an abbreviation of Allestree's reports; those called Hetley's *Reports* are only a part of Mackworth's reports. Littleton's *Reports* include some cases taken from Mackworth, and one term of Paynell's reports is also printed in *Littleton*, pp. 85–146, 124 *English Reports*, pp. 149–79. Some cases from Widdrington's reports were printed many years later in F.K. Eagle and E. Younge, *Cases Relating to Tithes* (London, 1826).

The reports of Paynell and Mackworth are interspersed by term in BL, MS. Add. 35962. Those of Paynell and Widdrington are interspersed by term in BL, MSS. Add. 35961 and Lansdowne, 1083.

My opinion that these four members of Gray's Inn were acting in concert and for a wider circulation than themselves is based on several grounds. Many of the manuscripts attribute the reports to a specified person; the reports are interspersed by term in several manuscripts;[12] there is no overlapping of cases or competition;[13] and a comparatively large number of copies of these reports have survived considering the few reports from the reign of Charles I. It is also interesting to note that on the title page of 'Hetley' in 1657, the reporter was said to have been Sir Thomas Hetley (d. 1637), one of the two official law reporters appointed in 1617 upon the initiative of Sir Francis Bacon (d. 1626). Hetley was described as a reporter in 1623. We know that the reports ascribed to him were made by Humphrey Mackworth. The other official reporter appointed in 1617 was Edward Writington. Hetley, Writington and Bacon were all members of Gray's Inn.[14] Perhaps further research will show that Paynell, Mackworth, Widdrington and Allestree were the successors, officially or otherwise, of Hetley and Writington.

The best exemplars of Paynell's reports are BL, MSS Add. 35961 (Trinity term 1627 to Hilary term 1629) and Harley 4816, fos. 8–26v (Easter term 1629 to Hilary term 1631). Derivative copies are to be found in the following books:

> CUL, MS Ii.5.22
> BL, MS Add. 35962

[11] J. Peile, *Biographical Register of Christ's College* (Cambridge, 1910), i, pp. 313–14, 321; J. Foster, *Register of Admissions to Gray's Inn* (London, 1889), pp. 152, 153, 154, 164, 170.

[12] Umfreville noted that they 'united their collections'. BL, MS Hargrave 362, fol. 3v.

[13] Turner speculated that Paynell and Widdrington 'may have arranged not to compete with one another, and to make their notes in different courts'. G.J. Turner, *Year Books of 4 Edward II* (London, 1914), Selden Soc. 26, p. xxii.

[14] Baker, 'Dark Age', pp. 453–54; Turner, *Year Books of 4 Edward II*, pp. xix–xxiii.

> BL, MS Add. 25193, fos 79–93
> BL, MS Add. 11764, fos 120–214
> BL, MS Hargrave 41
> BL, MS Lansdowne 1083
> LI, MS Maynard 21, fos 367–402
> Exeter College, Oxford, MS 179, fos 1–96
> HLS, MS 5051
> YLS, MS G.R. 29.3, fos 404–21 [8 cases only]
> YLS, MS G.R. 29.23, fos 254–72 [2 cases only]
> BL, MS Add. 36081, fos 78–84 [4 cases only]

Only from a close comparison of the texts of these manuscript reports could the identity of the reporter be discovered.

In addition, the following identifiable reporters have been discovered by John Baker.[15] These manuscript reports, along with the many anonymous ones, await close investigation and publication:

> George Beare (d. 1662)
>   HLS, MS 1166
>   HLS, MS 5071
>   YLS, MS G.R.29.25
> Thomas Cory (d. 1656)
>   BL, MS Hargrave 23
>   LI, MS Misc. 586
> Charles Cremer
>   Gray's Inn, MSS. 33, 34
> Henry Denne (d. 1640)
>   HLS, MS 5058
> Sir Heneage Finch (d. 1631)
>   Georgetown University Law MS B88.6
> John Glanvill (d. 1661)
>   LI, MS Maynard 21, fos 254–323
>   LI, MS Misc. 716
> Sir Nicholas Hyde (d. 1631)
>   BL, MS Hargrave 27
> R. Levinge and T. Levinge
>   BL, MS Lansdowne 1077
> Richard Lydall
>   LI, MS Maynard 66, fos 136–395
>   CUL, MS Ee.6.12
> John Merefield (d. 1666)
>   Folger, MS V.b.48, fos 101–24
> Antony Mills
>   BL, MS Hargrave 19

---

[15] J.H. Baker, *English Legal Manuscripts*, 2 vols (Zug, 1975, 1978); idem *English Legal Manuscripts in the United States of America* (London, 1990), ii, *1558–1902*.

Francis North (d. 1685)
  Kansas University MS A40
  LI, MS Hill 82
  Bodl. MS North, fol. 16
Thomas Powys (d. 1671)
  HLS, MS 5052
Thomas South (d. 1636)
  HLS, MS 5052
Francis Tate (d. 1616)
  HLS, MS 5067
Sir Peter Warburton (d. 1621)
  BL, MS Harley 4817
  HLS, MS 1051
  HLS, MS 5070
  CUL, MS Ii.5.25
Bulstrode Whitelocke (d. 1675)
  LI, MS Maynard 79, fos 89–327v
  LI, MS [unnumbered]
George Wither
  Huntington Library, MS HM 103

Until this work has been done, we will not know what is there in manuscript form. Perhaps there are some surprises, but certainly there are case reports worth reading. My own research has unearthed several interesting cases.

In the field of trusts, several unknown reports of well-known cases have been found; they involved the issue of forfeiture for treason of leases held in trust where the traitor was the beneficiary.[16] In another line of cases, lands devised to superstitious uses were forfeited to the Crown,[17] but there was no forfeiture if the use was void *ab initio*.[18] The Statute *De Donis Conditionalibus*[19] applied to lands held in Wales.[20]

The dispute between Lord Chancellor Ellesmere and Sir Edward Coke over injunctions after final judgments at common law is well known.[21]

---

[16] *Attorney General* v. *Raleigh* (Ex. 1609), LI, MS Maynard 21, fol. 127, pl. 1 (settlor-beneficiary was attainted); *Attorney General* v. *Carr* (Ex. 1618), BL, MS Hargrave 386, fol. 358, pl. 28, Cro. Jac. 512, 79 Eng. Rep. 437, Hobart 214, 80 Eng. Rep. 361, Jenkins 293, 145 Eng. Rep. 213 (beneficiary was attainted); *Attorney General* v. *Abington* (Ex. 1613–1619), BL, MSS Hargrave 33, fol. 77; 385, fos. 130, 387v.

[17] E.g. *Hotham* v. *Eynus* (Ex. 1583), BL, MS Hargrave 573, fol. 212v, pl. 2; *Hampden* v. *Dyott* (Ex. c. 1589), BL, MS Harley 4998, fol. 21, pl. 1.

[18] *Anonymous* (Ch. 1597), BL, MS Harley 4998, fol. 246, pl. 2.

[19] Stat. 13 Edw. I, c. 1, *Stat. Realm*, i, pp. 71–72.

[20] *Anonymous*, Gray's Inn, MS 27, fol. 31v.

[21] J.H. Baker, 'The Common Lawyers and the Chancery, 1616' in *The Legal Profession and the Common Law* (London, 1986), pp. 205–29; J.P. Dawson, 'Coke and Ellesmere Disinterred: The Attack on the Chancery in 1616', *Illinois Law Review*, 36 (1941), pp. 127–52; C.M. Gray, 'The Boundaries of the Equitable Function', *American Journal of Legal History*, 20 (1976), pp. 192–226.

However, the best reports of one of the leading cases, *Russwell's Case*, remain in manuscript,[22] the printed one having been poorly prepared for the press.[23] In addition, the arguments of counsel in *Glanville's Case* and *Allen's Case* have not been printed in any form.[24]

It has been thought that the lack of reports of equity cases reflects the lack in equity courts of the doctrine of precedent. But numerous equity case reports have been found for the late Elizabethan and early seventeenth century periods. Two collections are exclusively notes of Chancery cases,[25] and Robert Paynell and Arthur Turnour reported numerous equity exchequer cases. The reports were clearly made for future use as precedents in the same manner as the reports of common law cases.

It is certainly true that many more common law cases were reported than equity ones. Perhaps this resulted from the tradition of the law students' attending regularly the court of common pleas instead of either the court of chancery or the court of exchequer. However, the equity reports show that counsel in their arguments cited precedents to the equity courts regularly, and this suggests that equity judges, as others, decided like cases in like ways and were guided by prior case law as a general rule of fairness. In the case of *Swinerton* v. *Wolstenholm* (Ex. 1627),[26] Baron Trevor considers the cases cited in argument, and he cannot resist citing the *Case of Customs*,[27] noting smugly that counsel had overlooked it in their arguments.

The future appears dreary as to the dispersing of the darkness covering the subject of English legal history from 1603 to 1660.

In the last twenty-one years, we have seen the sixteenth century brought to life. The reports of Sir John Spelman and those of Sir John Port have been published by John Baker.[28] Richard Helmholz has published a collection of sixteenth-century defamation cases.[29] In addition to monographs, bibliographical studies and law French dictionaries have appeared

---

[22] BL, MS Add. 35957, fol. 2v, pl. 1; Bodleian Library, MS Rawlinson C. 382, fos 56v, 63; HLS, MS 109, fol. 65.

[23] 1 Rolle Rep. 192, 218, 219, 81 Eng. Rep. 425, 443, 445.

[24] BL, MS Stowe 298, fos 210 and 212. The other manuscript copies of these arguments are too numerous to list here.

[25] Those of Richard Powle, Oxford, Bodleian Library, MS Rawlinson C. 647, and the collections of the time of Chancellor Ellesmere; CUL, MS Gg. 2.31, fos 437–79v; and Hertfordshire Record Office, MS Verulam XII.A.50, fos 59–76.

[26] BL, MS Add. 35961.

[27] Davis 7, 80 Eng. Rep. 496 (KB 1607)

[28] J.H. Baker, ed., *The Reports of Sir John Spelman* (London, 1977, 1978), Selden Soc. 93, 94; idem, ed., *The Notebook of Sir John Port* (London, 1986), Selden Soc. 102.

[29] R.H. Helmholz, ed., *Select Cases on Defamation to 1600* (London, 1985), Selden Soc. 101.

to illuminate the Tudor period of legal history.[30] The Restoration Era at the end of the seventeenth century has been well served by the publication of tracts by Sir Matthew Hale.[31]

But the middle period of John Baker's dark age remains obscure. There have been several monographs on the early seventeenth century civil law published since 1972,[32] and there has been some work on the criminal law. However, comprehensive scholarship awaits new editions of the law reports, the major source of information as to what the courts were doing at the time.

When will these reports be edited and printed? The Selden Society in 1903 began to edit and print the medieval Year Books; ninety years later, they have produced only thirty-three volumes of Year Books and eyres, which is a very small percentage of the task. If one considers that the rate of publishing Year Books has been steadily declining, it is regrettably clear that very few modern editions will ever be made.[33]

If the seventeenth century manuscript law reports are to be published, different techniques from those of publishing the Year Books will have to be employed. The most obvious issue to be dealt with is that of publishing the original law French. There are good reasons for not doing so, but for printing the English translations only. The law French of the seventeenth century was a totally artificial language; the writers were thinking in English, and the quirks of their French were matters of legal jargon, not of linguistics.[34] Thus, the true original language is English. This is clear from the vocabulary and grammatical structure of the texts. The reporters regularly used the English word when they did not know the French one. The 'Brickbat Case' is only the most famous

---

[30] E.g. L.W. Abbott, *Law Reporting in England, 1485–1585* (London, 1973); J.H. Baker, *English Legal Manuscripts* (Zug, 1975, 1978), 2 vols; idem, *English Legal Manuscripts in the United States of America* (London, 1990), part ii [1558–1902]; idem, ed. *The Reports of Sir John Spelman* (London, 1978), vol. 2, Selden Soc. 1978, vol. 94, pp. 164–78; idem, *Manual of Law French* (2d edn, Aldershot, 1990).

[31] D.E.C. Yale, ed., *Sir Matthew Hale's Prerogatives of the King* (London, 1976), Selden Soc. 92; D.E.C. Yale and M.J. Pritchard, eds., *Hale and Fleetwood on Admiralty Jurisdiction* (London, 1993), Selden Soc. 108.

[32] L.A. Knafla, ed., *Law and Politics in Elizabethan England: The Tracts of Lord Chancellor Ellesmere* (Cambridge, 1977); W.H. Bryson, *The Equity Side of the Exchequer* (Cambridge, 1975); L.M. Hill, *The Ancient State, Authoritie and Proceedings of the Court of Requests by Sir Julius Caesar* (Cambridge, 1975); L. Bonfield, *Marriage Settlements, 1601–1740: The Adoption of the Strict Settlement* (Cambridge, 1983); N.L. Matthews, *William Sheppard: Cromwell's Law Reformer* (Cambridge, 1984); C.W. Brooks, *Pettyfoggers and Vipers of the Commonwealth: The 'Lower Branch' of the Legal Profession in Early Modern England* (Cambridge, 1986).

[33] This pessimism is shared by the general editors of the Selden Society itself. D.E.C. Yale and J.H. Baker, *A Centenary Guide to the Publications of the Selden Society* (London, 1987), p. 30.

[34] See generally J.H. Baker, *Manual of Law French* (2nd edn, Aldershot, 1990), pp. 1–6.

of many examples.³⁵ In the case of any doubt, the modern reader can resort to the microfiche copy of the original manuscript, which is readily available in many cases. The difficulties of translation come from the law and not the language, from elliptical writing, from poor handwriting, poor copying, and the bad physical state of the manuscripts. If these economies of time, space, and expense are not taken, the seventeenth-century reports, like the medieval Year Books, will never be edited and published.³⁶

There is much to be done with the seventeenth-century legal sources. This time was a period of legal and constitutional crisis and growth; it is a broad field awaiting cultivation. If the next twenty-one years could produce for seventeenth-century English legal history what the past twenty-one years did for the sixteenth century, it would be a good and lasting achievement.

³⁵ Anonymous (1631), Dyer 188b: 'ject un brickbat a le dit Justice que narrowly mist, & pur ceo immediately fuit indictment drawn per Noy envers le prisoner . . . ' quoted from D. Mellinkoff, *The Language of the Law* (Boston, 1963), p. 125.

³⁶ Baker, 'Dark Age', p. 460.

8

The Nature and Function of the Early Chancery Reports

Michael Macnair

The purpose of this essay is to explore some peculiarities of the early Chancery reports. In the first place I should say what I mean by 'Chancery reports'. For present purposes, this is specialist Chancery series of reports, before the 1660s. The reason for this limitation is that Chancery cases are not infrequently reported in general 'common law' series, and when found there are in the same style as the rest of the reports; secondly, specialist Chancery series, roughly from the Restoration, begin to be generally much the same as the contemporary 'common law' series. In the earlier Chancery series, however, there are some specific features which may be of interest for what they tell us about the use of precedent in Chancery in this period.

What is distinct about the nature of these reports, and what does this tell us about their function? Broadly speaking, the early Chancery reports fall into three classes. The first class is reports *stricto sensu*, i.e. notes of what was said in court which are comparable to contemporary common law reports. The second is extracts from or notes of decrees and orders in the Register's Books (the Chancery decree and order books in the Public Record Office). From the 1630s some of these series include some notes of what was said in court together with extracts from the decree or order, and some simple reports mixed in with precedents and report/precedents. The third is indexes, which are probably indexes to precedents in the Register's Books.

The 'reports *stricto sensu*' in print include:

1. Cary, 'Reports or Causes in Chancery', in *English Reports* xxi (London, 1902), pp. 20–33; and 'Choyce Cases' (i.e. the Carew part of Cary), ibid., pp. 103–9.[1]

---

[1] *Reports or Causes in Chancery: Collected by Sir George Cary, out of the Labours of Mr William Lambert* (London, 1650), reprint, *English Reports*, xxi (London, 1902); and *Choyce Cases in Chancery* bound with *The Practice of the High Court of Chancery Unfolded* (London, 1650), the reports reprinted in *English Reports*, 21; cf. Ward, 'William Lambarde's Collections on Chancery', *Harvard Library Bulletin*, 7 (1953), p. 270, for the common origin of these two sets of reports.

2. The reports of Egerton *dicta* in *The Proceedings of the High Court of Chancery*[2] and *The Practice of the High Court of Chancery Unfolded*.[3]
3. Some (not all) of the reports from the 1630s to 1660s in Nelson, *Reports of Speciall Cases*, in *English Reports*, xxi, pp. 1–152;[4] Freeman, *Reports of Cases Argued and Determined in the High Court of Chancery*, in *English Reports*, xxi, pp. 146–50[5] and a few cases at the beginning of Dickens,[6] *Reports and Cases*, pp. 5–7.[7]

In manuscript there are:

4. The reports made by Richard Powle, a six clerk, in the 1580s and 1590s, the earliest example of the type.[8]
5. Several copies of Cary/ 'Choyce Cases'.[9]
6. An unprinted collection from the 1590s, represented by BL, MS Harley 1576, fos 149–154v; and CUL, MS Gg 2.31, fos 221–232 and (another copy) fos 402v–410v.

---

[2] *The Proceedings of the High Court of Chancery* (London, 1649), bound with Tothill, *The Transactions of the High Court of Chancery*.

[3] *The Practice of the High Court of Chancery*.

[4] [Nelson], *Reports of Speciall Cases Argued and Decreed in the Court of Chancery in the Reigns of King Charles I, King Charles II and King William III*, (London, 1717) in *English Reports*, xxi, pp. 1–152.

[5] [Freeman] London, 1742. *Reports of Cases Argued and Determined in the High Court of Chancery, principally between the years 1660 and 1706*, in *English Reports*, xxi, pp. 146–50.

[6] [Dickens] *Reports and Cases Argued and Determined in the High Court of Chancery: Collected by John Dickens, Esq., Late Senior Register of that Court* (London, 1803), pp. 5–7.

[7] Chapter 6 of Duke, *Charitable Uses* (London, 1676), 'Cases Adjudged upon Appeals', though given as a Chancery Reporter by Wallace, is focused on extracting relevant 'resolutions' in the style of Coke and is probably some distance from the original reports on which it was based.

[8] Bodleian Library, MS Rawlinson C 647, fos 62–65, 125–147v, 163–68, Chancery reports from 1581–88, 1579–80 and 1588–98, and 1599–1600. This is strikingly different from the later Chancery reports in that it displays no interest at all in the English bill procedure and little in the scope of substantive equity, though it is distinct from contemporary common law reports in the emphasis given to uses, wills and administrations, and copyhold, and the extreme rarity of criminal and tortious matters. It appears to be mostly notes of the opinions of Chancery judges on points which could have arisen at common law, so that it is less helpful than it might at first appear on the early development of the reporting of Chancery equity.

[9] J.H. Baker, 'A Catalogue of Law Manuscripts in Cambridge University Library' (unpublished, held in Cambridge University Library), cites as examples of Cary, CUL, MSS Dd 9.92, fos 1r–80v; Gg 2.26; BL, MS Stowe 415; Harvard Law School, MSS 1036, fos 190v–326v and 1090; Lincoln's Inn, MS Misc 51; Bodleian Library, MS Rawlinson C 694; National Library of Wales, MS 765D; Hertfordshire Record Office, MS Verulam XII A 40. Baker, *English Legal Manuscripts in the USA*, ii (London, 1992) also gives Harvard Law School, MS 1034, fos 136 et. seq., Cf. also BL, MS Hargrave 281; MS Lansdowne 599. See also Ward, 'William Lambarde's Collections on Chancery', p. 270, on BL, MS Stowe 415 and Harvard Law School, MS 1034.

7. Some collections of Egerton *dicta* included in Chancery treatises, some of which have some relation to (2) above.[10]

8. Some reports from the 1630s to 1650s which mix notes of what was said in court with reliance on extracts from the Register's books.[11]

These reports are not radically different from the thinner of the contemporary 'common law' reports. They do, however, have two features which make them slightly distinct. The first is that they are almost wholly uninterested in the identity or arguments of counsel; they are in substance simply collections of judicial comments and observations. The second is that they seem only to be interested in the comments and observations of some judges. There are several collections of 'What Egerton said' from the 1590s and 1600s; then silence until the appointment of Coventry as lord keeper in 1625.

A possible indication of the meaning of this silence is to be found in a report in 1 Chan. Cas. that Lord Nottingham 'asked if any [precedents] could be shown in the Lord Ellesmere's or Coventry's time'; these judges evidently stood out as oracles of equity, as opposed not only to the older authorities but also to those who went between.[12] It is no doubt not very surprising that Bishop Williams, lord keeper, 1621–25, should not be regarded as an oracle of the law, but slightly more so that Francis Bacon should not.

There may be a connection with the circumstances of Bacon's chancellorship, his appointment in the immediate aftermath of the Chancery

[10] BL, MS Add. 20700, fos 10–13v, dicta and orders of Egerton from the 1590s–1600s included in a more general Chancery treatise based on medieval record sources; CUL, MS Gg 2.31, fos 346v–381v, 'English Suits in Chancerie, The Proces Therein', a practice book containing some Egertoniana (also in some places supported by references to the Register's Books), fos 437r–480v, 'Observations in Course of Chancery Practice', Egertoniana mostly without case-names or other references; BL, MS Lansdowne 1125, fos 67–75, a treatise called 'Cancellariae processus' also including Egertoniana. (The main body of this MS, though bound as *Equity Cases Abridged*, is not in fact the Abridgement published under that name but an earlier Abridgement of equity materials completed in 1702 (p 1).

[11] Two relevant MSS are catalogued in Baker, *English Legal Manuscripts in the USA*, ii: Folger Shakespeare Library, MS V a. 462, a printed copy of Littleton's *Tenures* with MS annotations including (at end, fos 20–24v) reports in Chancery 24 Eliz. (1581–82) and Mich. 37 and 39 Eliz (1594 and 1596); and Kansas University, MS D 87, John Lisle's Chancery commonplace book from his period as commissioner of the great seal including reports of cases from this period, 1649–59.

[12] *Pratt* v. *Taylor* (1674) 1 Ch Cas 237. The report of the case in Lord Nottingham's own reports, as *Pruett* v. *Masters*, Selden Society 73, nos 128, 139, makes clear that what was really going on was an attempt by Serjeant Maynard to bounce the court into ignoring a decision of 1663 by producing Elizabethan precedents. It does not contain the particular form of words quoted here; but there is no reason to doubt the Chan. Cas. report as at least an indication of how the bar understood the point. Yale Introduction to Selden Society 73, pp. l–li, takes the point to be simply that older precedents are to be preferred; but putting it together with the pattern of the reports it seems to be more than that.

controversy of the years around 1615 and his dismissal under charges of corruption. There is some evidence for the view that Bacon was seen as having made undesirable innovations in the equity practice established by Ellesmere.[13] At any rate, the silence of the reports suggests that contemporaries' view of Bacon's importance was less high than that of modern historians.[14]

The second class of early Chancery reports is collections of extracts or notes from the Register's Books. Into this class, among printed works, fall: (1) the larger part of Cary/ 'Choyce Cases', i.e. the 'Labours of Master Lambard', cases from the 1550s to the 1580s; and (2) the first half of 1 Reports in Chancery (*English Reports*, xxi),[15] cases from the 1620s to the 1650s. In manuscript are: (3) possibly the earliest example of this or any type, CUL, MS Gg 2.31, fos 520–542, which seems to be a collection of decrees and orders from the 1540s mixed with Year Book cases; from fol. 542 this shifts, in the same hand, into a discussion of proof based on civilian authors; (4) BL, MS Harley 1576, fos 146–149, contains decrees and orders from earlier in the reign of Elizabeth before shifting into reports from the 1590s; and (5) Professor Baker's catalogue of *English Legal Manuscripts in the USA* gives (no. 562) Harvard Law School, MS 1035(2) as 'Penniman's Cases in Chancery', cases from the records 1558–1603 collected by Penniman, a six clerk, in 1616.[16]

As already indicated, there is a variant form in which substantial reliance on the Register's Books is combined with elements of a report of what was said in court. This form is characteristic of the reports from the 1630s to the 1660s in 3 Chan.Rep. and 2 Freeman, and of the reports of the 1660s and 70s in the later part of 1 Chan.Rep. and 2 Chan.Rep. BL, Hargrave MS 174, which contains reports from the 1630s on, begins by telling us that 'All the parts relate to docquettes of decrees in the office of John Wilkinson Esqr one of the Six Clerks', but does include reported as well as recorded material; BL, MS Harley 1576, fos 229 et seq.,

[13] Williams' arrival was marked by the production of treatises dedicated to him on the Chancery: Norbury's 'Abuses and Remedies of the Chancery', in Francis Hargrave (ed.), *A Collection of Tracts Relative to the Law of England* (London, 1787); and on Star Chamber, Hudson, 'A Treatise of the Court of Star Chamber', in Francis Hargrave (ed.) *Collectanea juridica* (London, 1791–92), ii, p. 1. T.G. Barnes has established that the latter was in part aimed to persuade Williams to abandon the dubious practices of Bacon in favour of the 'good old ways' of Egerton: 'Mr Hudson's Star Chamber', in Guth and McKenna (ed.), *Tudor Rule and Revolution: Essays for G.R. Elton from his American Friends* (Cambridge, 1982), pp. 298–304.

[14] E.g. W.S. Holdsworth, *A History of English Law* (London, 1922–66), v, pp. 238–54.

[15] *Reports and Cases Taken and Adjudged in the Court of Chancery, in the Reign of Kings Charles I, Charles II, James II, William III and Queen Anne*, i (London, 1693; reprint, London, 1902), originally a separate volume; Wallace, *The Reporters Arranged and Characterised* (Boston, 1882), pp. 478–79.

[16] J.H. Baker, *English Legal Manuscripts in the USA*, ii, (London, 1991).

similarly has report and decree mixtures from the 1640s; and Lincoln's Inn MS Maynard 23, which is attributed to Maynard, has decrees and orders from pre-1660 mixed with conventional reports from post-1660 in a different hand.

As already indicated, this type of 'report' which relies heavily on the records did not immediately disappear in the Restoration, though from that time simple reports of what was said in court tend to become the dominant form (as can be seen in *English Reports*, xxii and xxiii: Chan.Cas, the later parts of 2 Freeman and Vernon). 2 Chan.Rep. retains the 'mixed' form down to 1688. As late as 1725 Nelson thought it worthwhile to put on the market Rep. t. Finch, a simple collection of precedents from the Register's Books from the time of Lord Nottingham.

Before considering the significance of this form of reporting it is convenient to consider the third type, the subject index. Only one example of this species is in print, Tothill.[17] However, there are several manuscript examples. Precursors to the printed Tothill containing some of the earlier cases are found bound with Cary/Choyce Cases in several MSS,[18] in BL, Hargrave MS 281, fol. 110, described as 'Presidentiall and Speciall Orders made in Extraordinary Cases in Chancery which are to be Found in the Register's Books'. The set of reports from the 1590s found in BL, MS Harley 1576 and CUL, MS Gg 2.31 is similarly accompanied by what appears to be an index in the style of Tothill, though the content varies in the three different copies of this set.[19]

What distinguishes these indexes from the ordinary case of Abridgments or reports made in the form of alphabetical commonplaces is primarily the presence of cross-references to the Register's Books in some cases, and (less significantly) the extremely skeletal character of some of the notes – most clearly in Tothill. It seems clear that this form is a subject index to materials in the Register's Book. An intermediate form is represented by Lincoln's Inn, MS Misc. 576, an alphabetical digest of Chancery materials from the 1650s, by several hands; under some heads ('Demurrer', 'Discovery', 'Forfeiture', 'Outlawry') pre-1650 material is included, and some of this material is supported by references to the Register's Books; but the text overall is closer to an Abridgment or commonplace. It includes references to Tothill, *Proceedings* and *The Practice . . . Unfolded*, and many of the cases reported are undated and unsupported by any references at all.[20]

Besides 'true reports', then, we have two forms which are specific to Chancery: collections taken from the Register's Books (or from other

---

[17] *The Transactions of the High Court of Chancery* (London, 1649; bound with *The Proceedings* (above n. 2); the reports are reprinted in English Reports, xxi.

[18] E.g., BL, MS Stowe 415; MS Hargrave 281.

[19] BL, MS Harley 1576, fos 159–172; CUL, MSS Gg 2.31, fos 217–220, 394–402v.

[20] As indicated, above n.10, BL, MS Lansdowne 1125 (1700) is a genuine Abridgement.

copies of decrees and orders),[21] and indexes to the Register's Books. Why were Chancery lawyers making collections of this type?

The explanation is, in fact, fairly simple and has been known for some time. From the time of Egerton at the latest, precedents were used in argument and judicial decision-making in Chancery. In this activity the approach of the Chancery was considerably more formal than the use of precedent in argument at common law: the precedents which counted were decisions recorded in the Register's Books, not reports of what was said in court, and there was a regular procedure of the adjournment of proceedings for a search for and production of relevant precedents. The procedure was certainly in existence in the 1590s and 1600s, when it is attested by references in Monro[22] and in the reports,[23] and by two cases which show a certain caution on Egerton's part about decrees and orders which might make precedents: in *Charnock* v. *Worsley* (1593) a rehearing on the ground of fresh evidence was specifically ordered not to be a precedent;[24] and in *Mynn* v. *Cobb* (1604)[25] the danger of making a precedent is given as a ground for not making a decree on less than full proof.[26] Another example, which I owe to Mr N.G. Jones, is *Golding* v. *Tuffin* (1612):[27] in this case, after both a search for precedents and a reference to the judges, Ellesmere 'thought not then fit to give order ... but would be better advised thereof in respect this case might be a leading case in the like cases'.[28]

This procedure in relation to precedents in Chancery has been known about for quite some time: W.H.L. Winder drew attention to it in an article in the *Law Quarterly Review* in 1941.[29] The connection between it and the form of some at least of the early Chancery reports was made

[21] Cf. BL, MS Hargrave 174, from dockets held by a six clerk (above).

[22] (1600) Monro, *Acta cancellariae* (London, 1847), i, pp. 744–45, 758–59, cited by Holdsworth, *History of English Law*, v, p. 276.

[23] BL, MS Harley, 1576, fos 147r–147v.

[24] Monro, *Acta cancellariae*, i, 687, cited by W.J. Jones, *The Elizabethan Court of Chancery* (Oxford, 1967), p. 294 n. 3.

[25] Cary, English Reports, xxi, p. 25; cited by Holdsworth, *A History of English Law*, v, p. 276.

[26] The requirement of full proof to make a decree was a rule independent of the rules about precedent: see my 'The Law of Proof in Early Modern Equity' (unpublished Ph.D thesis, University of Oxford, 1992), pp. 293–95 and ch. 9. The point here is that making a decree without full proof in this case would be used as a precedent to allow decrees without full proof in other cases.

[27] Tothill, *Transactions*, p. 124. Mr N.G. Jones, of Corpus Christi College, Cambridge, kindly sent me a transcript of the MS reports of this case: BL, MS Hargrave 281, fol. 185, MS Lansdowne 640, fol. 21 (which are MS antecedents of the 'Tothill' index); and CUL, MS Gg 2.5, fol. 169v (a report of a point of law referred to Croke and Warburton JJ) and of the relevant parts of the record.

[28] PRO, C 33/123, fol. 413, order of 11 Feb. 1612/13, from Mr Jones' transcript.

[29] W.H.L. Winder, *Law Quarterly Review*, 57 (1941), p. 245.

by both Sir William Holdsworth[30] and by David Yale, in his introduction to Lord Nottingham's reports in the Selden Society series.[31] What do I have to add to these observations, besides the addition of a number of manuscript instances?

First, it is commonly said that precedent and fixity in Chancery equity start with procedure before moving to substantive rules.[32] In the light of the early reports this view may be questioned. The topics covered even in the earliest printed collection, that of Lambarde contained in Cary, 'Choyce Cases', cover substantive as well as procedural rules. The book begins with a list of substantive rules from various sources (Year Books, *Doctor and Student* and reports) before moving on first to reports, then to precedents; while most of the precedents are procedural, they include, for example, one on rights of common from 1559/60, and one on parol leases from 1561/2.[33] There is, to be sure, a considerable bias towards procedural rules; but then, a similar bias will be found in common law collections. While there may be a prehistory of procedural stabilisation before the reports, there is no really hard evidence for it. The series of orders printed by Sanders start at much the same time as the reports,[34] and the earliest practice books rest on precedents from the time of Egerton.[35]

Conversely, Metzger has argued that the Chancery at the time of Wolsey and down to the 1540s was still the fluid and precedent-free affair of the later middle ages.[36] The space this leaves for a period of stabilisation of procedure without the development of substantive rules is about fifty years, from the 1540s to the 1590s (by which time there are definitely reports, use of precedents, and substantive rules revealed in the reports). It is not impossible, but it seems simpler to abandon the idea of a phase of procedural stabilisation combined with substantive flexibility and instead see the stabilisation of both procedural and substantive equity as proceeding hand in hand.[37]

---

[30] Holdsworth, *History of English Law*, v, p. 276.

[31] Selden Society, 73, p. xliv.

[32] E.g. Jones, *Elizabethan Chancery*, pp. 2–3.

[33] *Fielding* v. *Wren*, p. 46; *Harrison* v. *Chomeley*, p. 51.

[34] *Orders of the High Court of Chancery*, i, pt 1 (London, 1845). There are orders dealing with various administrative matters and in relation to procedure with the examination of witnesses, particularly examination *in perpetuam memoriam*, from the 1540s on; but systematic general orders for the regulation of various aspects of procedure seem to start with the orders promulgated by Puckering and Egerton in 1596, Sanders, i, p. 69.

[35] *The Proceedings of the High Court of Chancery* and *The Practice of the High Court of Chancery Unfolded* above nn. 2–3 and text there.

[36] Metzger, 'The Last phase of the Mediaeval Chancery', in Harding (ed.), *Law Making and Law Makers in British History* (London, 1980), p. 87, suggesting that the change begins with the beginning of decree rolls in 1543.

[37] Cf. also the character of the earliest 'true reports', the Powle series in Bodleian Library, MS Rawlinson C647, which are wholly uninterested in procedure.

Secondly, both Yale[38] and Jones[39] suggest that the procedure of search
for precedents was carried out by officers of the court and that the
collections and indexes were, therefore, made by them. There are two
issues involved here. One is the strictly technical question of who made
the early Chancery reports. The second is what this tells us about the
procedure of search for precedents. In support of the view that officers
of the court made the reports, it may be said: (1) that Cary, 'Choyce
Cases', was certainly made by Masters (Lambarde and Carew); (2) that
Tothill, a six clerk, had attributed to him both a practice book and an
index;[40]; (3) that the collection in BL, MS Hargrave 174 is said, as I
have already stated, to relate to 'docquettes of decrees in the office of
John Wilkinson Esquire one of the Six Clerks'; and (4) the existence of
the Penniman collection catalogued by John Baker, again by a six clerk.
In particular, the strongest association seems to be with the six clerks, since
Lambarde's personal history as a writer on the courts explains his collection
of precedents. Carew merely added reports to this collection. Though the
procedure of search for precedents was used in the Exchequer, the sworn
clerks there do not seem to have made collections of precedents.[41]

One might draw a stronger conclusion from this idea about authorship;
that is, it might be (and was by Yale and Jones) inferred from the
involvement of the Chancery's officers that the procedure of search for
precedents was in some sense inquisitorial – the court was informing itself.
I do not think this conclusion can be properly drawn.

Taking the cases cited by Winder as a starting point, three of them do
show chancellors asking officers to examine precedents and certify the
result; but all these turn on narrow issues of *clerical* practice, and in none
was a six clerk – the possible producers of the collections and indexes –
called on.[42] On the other hand, five of Winder's cases, and four others

---

[38] 73 Selden Society, p. xliv.

[39] Jones, *Elizabethan Chancery*, p. 4.

[40] Tothill was certainly a six clerk in 1606: HMC, 9 Salisbury (Cecil), xviii, p. 44. This is
early enough to have been involved in the production of the early versions of the collection
which goes by his name, though it is not clear if he was wholly responsible for it.

[41] *Gray.* v. *Alport* (H 1610/11), BL, MS Add. 25207, fol. 13b, '& non obstante presidents
were moved'; *AG* v. *Mico* (H1658/9, Hardres 137, adjournments for the parties to deliver
precedents, PRO, E 125/39 f 35v; E 125/38 f 268r. This may be due to the fact that the
Exchequer decree and order books are much smaller and hence easier to search in than
those for the Chancery.

[42] *Price* v. *The Hundred of Chewton* (1718), 1 P. Wms 437, an issue as to the dating of
common-law writs, referred to the cursitors to examine precedents and certify; *ex parte
Jephson* (1720), Pre Ch 549, a complaint by the serjeant at arms that the practice in relation
to arrests for contempt had recently altered so that he lost fees; the register to examine
precedents and certify whether the old practice was as alleged by the serjeant at arms;
Sellon v. *Lewen* (1533), 3 P Wms 239, issue as to the normal drafting and effect of an order
that a plea should stand for an answer, reserving its benefit as a plea; the Register, again,
to examine precedents and certify.

picked up without a full search, show indications that the procedure of search for precedents was in general adversarial.[43] A good example is *AG* v. *Mico* in the Exchequer in Hilary term 1658/9. The order in the Decree and Order Book is 'that either side shall mutually deliver noates of the presidents which they intend to insiste uppon unto the Attorneys in court on either side respectively . . .' Hardres' draft argument, which he naturally includes *in extenso* in his report of the case,[44] shows the precedents culled from this search integrated in the form of arguments not radically different from common law arguments; the difference is not in the way the precedents are used but in their nature and source.

This brings me on to my final point, which is the extent to which the particular features of the early Chancery reports suggest a conception of precedent distinct from that at common law at the same period. In this respect there is, I think, one primary point to be made, and a couple of caveats.

The primary point is that the use of the Register's Books as a source of precedent involves a concept of precedent which is in one sense more like the conception reflected in modern law reports than that shown in most contemporary law reports. The modern law report characteristically gives you an account of the facts, or at least the material facts alleged, and of the decision of the court; the Incorporated Council series give you the arguments of counsel as well, but this is fairly clearly a secondary requirement. Seventeenth-century common law reports, in contrast, are pretty erratic about giving either facts, or the eventual decision of the court; a lot of attention is paid to what we would now call *dicta*, and the better series devote quite a lot of attention to what counsel said.

In this respect the Chancery's use of the Register's Books as a source of precedents, and the later reporting which grew on the basis of the

---

[43] Winder's cases: *Goodfellow* v. *Morris* (1618), Ritchie, *Reports of Cases Decided by Francis Bacon* (London, 1932), p. 133, P's counsel alleged precedents; *Jackson* v. *Barrow* (1626) Nels 2, 'a precedent was produced'; *Miller* v. *Kendrick* (1667/8) Nels 113, 'a precedent was produced for the plaintiff'; *Howel* v. *Price* (1715), Gilb. Rep 106, 'my Lord made no decree, but ordered them to search for precedents'; *Babington* v. *Greenwood* (1718), Pre. Ch. 505, 509, 'it being urged that there were abundance of precedents to the contrary . . .'; other cases: *Gray* v. *Alport* (H 1610/11) above n. 36, 'presidents were moved'; *Golding* v. *Tuffin* (1612), above PRO, C 33/121, fol. 1088, order of 15 June 1612, from Mr Jones' transcript, 'This court wisheth that the said plaintiff should search for some precedents in like cases . . .'; *AG* v. *Mico*, above n. 40, and below; *Pruett* v. *Masters* (1674), above n. 12.

It should be noted that in seven of Winder's cases the reports give no indication about how precedents were collected and used: *Atkins* v. *Temple* (1625/6), 1 Ch Rep 13, 14; *Mayor of London* v. *Bennet* (1630/1), 1 Ch Rep 44, 45; *Arundel* v. *Trevilian* (1634/5), 1 Ch Rep 87; *Basset* v. *Nosworthy* (1673), Rep t Finch 102; *Herne* v. *Myrick* (1712), 1 P Wms 201; *Napier* v. *Howard* (1726), Mosely 66n.; *Duke of Chandos* v. *Talbot* (1731), 2 P Wms, 610, 612. (This last case is noteworthy for the lord chancellor doing his own research into the significance of a couple of cases in the reports.)

[44] *AG* v. *Mico* at Hardres, pp. 139–47.

use of collections of precedents from the 1630s on, is more like modern law reports: what is interesting is the facts and the decision, to a much lesser extent what the judge said, and even further down the list the arguments of counsel. This distinction should not be overstated: in either case, precedents are authority for propositions of law. But the form of the common law reports assumes some survival of the older view that the common opinion of the profession was a source of law: it is this which may be expressed in the way in which the precedents were used. In the collections and indexes of Chancery precedents, it is brutally clear that the source of law which is being relied on is the prior similar action of the (particular) court. It may be this clarity which leads to the appearance in the reports of a marked difference between the authority, and therefore reportability, of individual chancellors.

There are two caveats to this observation. The first is that there does not appear to be any period after reporting started for which there is *only* collections and indexes of precedents, apart from the collections from the earlier part of the reign of Elizabeth which were probably themselves made in the later part of that reign. There is a gap in reporting between Ellesmere and Coventry, but it is a complete gap. *Dicta* of the chancellors, keepers and commissioners were reported, and to this extent Chancery lawyers were not exclusively interested in formal precedents. The second is that, as indicated above, what I have been discussing are peculiarities of the *early* Chancery reports, peculiarities which evaporated in the 1660s and after. The seemingly modernity of the early use of precedent in Chancery may, therefore, be merely a curious anachronism.

9

Detecting Non-Fiction: Sleuthing among Manuscript Case Reports for What was Really Said

James Oldham

While serving with Lord Mansfield on King's Bench, Francis Buller remarked on a case in William Blackstone's *Reports*, observing that subsequent to the phase of the case reported in *Blackstone*, the court had decided the case 'quite the other way'. This prompted Mansfield to exclaim, 'What a terrible thing it is that such loose notes are published.'[1] Another time, Mansfield scolded Serjeant Glynn for relying on a case from Bunbury's *Reports*, observing: 'Mr *Bunbury* never meant that those cases should have been published, they are very loose notes'.[2]

Having spent the better part of a dozen years transcribing, editing and arranging for the publication of Lord Mansfield's trial notes in hundreds of cases,[3] perhaps I have inflicted on Mansfield the same injury that Serjeant Glynn gave Bunbury. Regardless, along the way I have travelled through quantities of manuscript case notes. What I present here is an extension of a study begun some years ago at the Conference on British Legal Manuscripts held at the Newberry Library in Chicago.[4] There I gave particular attention to comparing Lord Mansfield's trial notes in selected cases with printed reports of those cases. Today I will expand the inquiry to sample surviving manuscript notes from the seventeenth and eighteenth centuries of post-trial proceedings – notes kept sometimes by sitting judges, sometimes by attorneys, sometimes by unknown hands. Like the printed reports, manuscript notes are widely variable in quality. What makes the exercise worth doing is the occasional jackpot – when

---

[1] *R.* v. *Atkinson*, 'Copy (from Mr Gurney's short hand Notes) of the proceedings on a motion for arresting the judgment in the Court of King's Bench April 29, 1784', PRO, TS 11/927, fol. 11.

[2] *Tinkler* v. *Poole*, 5 Burr. 2657, 2658 (1770).

[3] *See* J. Oldham, *The Mansfield Manuscripts and the Growth of English Law in the Eighteenth Century*, 2 vols (Chapel Hill and London, 1992).

[4] The conference was held in April 1986. My paper was published subsequently as 'Eighteenth-Century Judges' Notes: How They Explain, Correct and Enhance the Reports', *American Journal of Legal History*, 31 (1987), p. 9.

detailed manuscripts turn up for cases that became influential despite poor or abbreviated printed reports.[5]

Part of the fun, of course, is playing the detective, and naturally the search does not always succeed. Take, for example, the well-known case of *Miller* v. *Race*.[6] There, Sir Richard Lloyd, counsel for defendant, invoked the turn-of-the-century case of *Ford* v. *Hopkins*,[7] in which Chief Justice Holt is reported as equating lottery tickets with bank notes in terms of negotiability. Lord Mansfield, who came down strongly in *Miller* in favour of negotiability of stolen bank notes, was reported to have said of Salkeld's report of *Ford* v. *Hopkins*: 'But this must be a very incorrect report of that case: it is impossible that it can be a true representation of what Ld. Ch. J. Holt said. It represents him as speaking of bank-notes, Exchequer-notes, and million lottery tickets, as like to each other and a bank-note. Now no two things can be more unlike to each other, than a lottery-ticket and a bank-note'.[8] In fact, a manuscript report of *Miller* v. *Race* puts the Mansfield observation more colourfully, quoting Mansfield as explaining that the report of *Ford* v. *Hopkins* 'turns on the Reporter flinging in Bank notes with the Tickets'.[9]

The reports in question – Salkeld's – have a sound reputation. The first two volumes, according to J.W. Wallace, 'were published under the supervision of Lord Hardwicke, and their general accuracy . . . has not been questioned, except in a single instance'.[10] Also, lottery tickets appear in the second printed report of *Ford* v. *Hopkins* as well.[11] What one suspects, indeed what one must be on guard about, is that Mansfield in *Miller* v. *Race* was playing the 'blame the reporter' game, dismissing an adverse or inconvenient precedent by merely asserting that it was wrongly reported.[12] The answer to whether or not this was so, of course, might be discovered in manuscript reports of *Ford* v. *Hopkins*, perhaps revealing what Chief Justice Holt *really* said. Unfortunately, I have been unable to find any.

Sometimes, however, the detective work does pay off. I will give five examples. The first will illustrate how our understanding of a case can be altered by learning about phases of the litigation that post-date the

[5] Luckily this proved possible with one of Mansfield's most famous decisions, the *Somerset* case, as I related in 'New Light on Mansfield and Slavery', *Journal of British Studies*, 27 (1988), p. 45.

[6] *Miller* v. *Race*, 1 Burr. 452 (1758).

[7] *Ford* v. *Hopkins*, 1 Salk. 283, Holt K.B. 119 (1701).

[8] 1 Burr. at 459.

[9] Lincoln's Inn Library, MS Misc. 552, fol. 126.

[10] J.W. Wallace, *The Reporters Arranged and Characterized* (Boston, 1882), p. 399. The 'single instance' was not Mansfield's comment in *Miller*, but was a case reported at 5 Taunton 190 referring to Salkeld as a book that, 'in general, was of no authority'.

[11] Holt KB 119.

[12] In fairness, Mansfield pointed out, as reported by Burrow, that Holt had expressed views but two years previous to *Ford* that opposed the idea of equating lottery tickets with bank notes. 1 Burr. at 459.

phase presented in the printed report. The second will show how poor-quality reports have created entrenched misinterpretations that have taken decades – indeed, centuries – to undo. Thirdly, I will show how case manuscripts can reveal an internal court procedure that in turn helps solve a notorious factual puzzle. Fourthly, I will demonstrate how full manuscript case notes and pleadings can alter our understanding and evaluation of a case as given in an abbreviated printed report. Finally, I will mention the insight that manuscript casenotes can yield into the interplay among judges in reaching consensus on a case, especially in an era in which opinions were announced verbally, often without collegial deliberation.

I referred above to an example in William Blackstone's reports in which the result shown was opposite to the ultimate outcome because of a later reversal. Not quite as dramatic, but interesting nevertheless, is the late seventeenth-century case of *Gibbon* v. *Pepper*.[13] This case survives to the present as an example of the tort doctrine of unavoidable accident. According to the printed reports, and also according to the plea roll,[14] defendant was riding his horse down Drury Lane in London when his horse took sudden fright and bolted; defendant yelled to plaintiff to get out of the way; plaintiff did not move and was injured. The court of King's Bench remarked that defendant would have been found not guilty if he had not botched his pleading, since defendant evidently did not act with tortious intent or cause the accident. But since defendant mistakenly confessed the battery and argued the facts as a justification, instead of pleading not guilty on the general issue, he lost. John Baker points out this case as one of several early decisions which 'were by no means as sweeping as some of the language suggests', since 'none of the pleas had put the defendant's fault at issue'.[15] This is true, but perhaps the *Gibbon* decision should be given at least a little more weight, once we take into account a later phase of the case. From a manuscript report of proceedings during the term following that reflected in the printed reports, we learn that the plaintiff lost one of his eyes and nearly his life, that he recovered a verdict of £20, but because of affidavits for the defendant setting out the facts of the unavoidable accident (plus what in a later era would be called contributory negligence), 'the Court would not allow the Damages'.[16]

My second illustration pertains to arbitration. Both in England and America, a nineteenth-century notion took hold that, in Lord Campbell's

[13] 1 Ld. Raym. 38, 4 Mod. 404 (1695).

[14] The record from the plea roll is given at J.H. Baker and S.F.C. Milsom, *Sources of English Legal History* (London, 1986), pp. 335–36.

[15] J.H. Baker, *An Introduction to English Legal History* (3rd edn, London, 1990), pp. 458–59.

[16] Harvard Law School, MS 1071, fol. 119.

words, 'the courts of law had, in former times, acquired a horror of arbitration'.[17]

The eighteenth-century cases that were taken to have fixed the doctrine of revocability of arbitration agreements, and to have established its rationale as an unwillingness of the courts to have their jurisdiction ousted by private arbitrators, were *Wellington* v. *MacIntosh*[18] and *Kill* v. *Hollister*.[19] Both cases were victims of incomplete or inadequate reporting. In *Wellington*, according to Atkyns's report, a Bill in Chancery was brought by one partner against another 'to discover and be relieved against frauds, impositions and concealment'. Defendant's plea averred that the partnership agreement contained an arbitration clause covering all differences that might arise concerning the business, and that defendant had offered and stood ready to submit to arbitration, but plaintiff refused. Atkyns's report of Lord Chancellor Hardwicke's opinion is brief; in it, Hardwicke disallowed the plea invoking arbitration because an arbitrator would not have had the power to grant the relief requested in the Bill. Hardwicke did state, nevertheless, that 'Persons might certainly have made such an agreement as would have ousted this court of jurisdiction'.[20]

Later interpreters of *Wellington* considered Hardwicke's opinion to have been misreported. For example, Lord Chancellor Loughborough in *Mitchell* v. *Harris*[21] observed, 'There is no doubt, that the reporter has mistaken Lord *Hardwicke's* reasons in that case', and, despite Hardwicke's disclaimer that parties 'might certainly have made such an agreement as would have ousted this court of jurisdiction', Lord Loughborough in *Harris* concluded that 'still the case [*Wellington*] stands as a clear authority that the plea was overruled'.[22]

A full manuscript version of *Wellington* is at Lincoln's Inn Library. In the manuscript report, we learn that the Bill prayed for a general accounting and a satisfaction of what should appear due to the plaintiff, as well as a discovery concerning several transactions alleged to be tainted by fraud. The defendant pleaded that the partnership agreement contained a provision 'that they the plaintiff and defendant would submit all matters that should arise in difference between them concerning or anyway relating to the said co-partnership to the award and the determination of two indifferent persons as arbitrators of the same, the one to be chose by the plaintiff and the other by the defendant' – further, 'that the defendant had offered to the plaintiff to name an arbitrator on his part but that the plaintiff has absolutely refused to name any arbitrator for him and refused

[17] *Russell* v. *Pelligrini*, 6 E. & B. 1020, 1026 (1856).
[18] 2 Atk. 569 (Chancery 1743).
[19] 1 Wils. 129 (KB 1746).
[20] 2 Atk. 570.
[21] 2 Ves. Jun. 129 (Chancery 1793).
[22] 2 Ves. Jun. 135.
[23] Lincoln's Inn Library, MS Coxe 46, fol. 166.

to submit the matter in controversy between them to such arbitration'.[23] Counsel for defendant insisted upon the reasonableness of submitting such matters to arbitration, 'where the parties might choose proper judges for themselves versed and knowing in the matters of their controversy, and the statute of King William[24] was urged to show the great encouragement which the Legislature gives to such submissions'.[25]

In response, plaintiff's counsel insisted, among other things, that 'such agreement of the parties ought not to be permitted to oust the jurisdiction of the court, and it was said that there had been a case where upon this foundation such a plea as is now pleaded was overruled, but the name of this case or the time when it was so determined was forgot'. The manuscript report of *Wellington* gives Lord Hardwicke's disposition of this argument as follows: 'As to the covenant tending to oust the jurisdiction of the court, he thought that an objection of no weight, for most certainly men may submit their differences to the arbitration of persons chose by them without applying to the courts of public justice'.[26] Thus we can confirm that the report of *Wellington* v. *MacIntosh* as given by Atkyns was ambiguous and was fairly open to criticism. Lord Hardwicke's opinion was straightforward, and was strongly supportive of the arbitration process.

The main eighteenth-century case standing for the doctrine of revocability of agreements to arbitrate was not Hardwicke's 1743 opinion in *Wellington* but was the decision of the court of King's Bench three years later in *Kill* v. *Hollister*. The entire report of that case, as given by Wilson, is but twelve lines, as follows:

> This is a cause of action upon a policy of insurance, wherein a clause was inserted, that in case of any loss or dispute about the policy it should be referred to arbitration; and the plaintiff avers in his declaration that there has been no reference; upon the trial at Guildhall the point was reserved for the consideration of the court, whether this action well laid before a reference had been, and by the whole court if there had been a reference depending, or made and determined, it might have been a bar, but the agreement of the parties cannot oust this court, and as no reference has been, nor any is depending, the action is well brought, and the plaintiff must have judgment.[27]

---

[24] The reference is to a 1698 statute drafted by John Locke, which encouraged private arbitration by endorsing a scheme that would make the contempt power of the courts available for enforcement purposes. For the background and effect of this statute, see H. Horwitz and J. Oldham, 'John Locke, Lord Mansfield, and Arbitration During the Eighteenth Century', *Historical Journal* 36 (1993), p. 36.

[25] Lincoln's Inn Library, MS Coxe 46, fos 168–69.

[26] Lincoln's Inn Library, MS Coxe 46, fos 170–71.

[27] 1 Wils. 129.

For *Kill* v. *Hollister*, there are at least four manuscript reports, each of which has details not given by Wilson.[28] The manuscript reports show that the principle for which the case came to stand was a secondary point. The action was on a Bristol insurance policy containing a clause that, if any dispute should arise it should be referred to two persons, one chosen by the insured, the other by the insurer, and the two named persons were to choose a third arbitrator. According to Justice Foster, 'all the Bristol policies are in that manner'.[29] The question of ousting the court of jurisdiction was a by-product of a contract interpretation question. All the judges agreed that the language in the Bristol insurance policy did not make arbitration a condition precedent, and this interpretation resolved the case. Some of the judges did remark that the parties did not have it in their power to make arbitration a condition precedent because that would take away the court's jurisdiction. But this point was not fully debated or well argued, and no one mentioned *Wellington* v. *MacIntosh*.[30]

As was often true, therefore, Lord Campbell was guilty of gross over-statement in saying that 'somehow the courts of law had, in former times, acquired a horror of arbitration'.[31] Indeed, as Henry Horwitz and I have documented,[32] references to arbitration by the central courts steadily increased throughout the eighteenth century, accelerating in the last few decades and carrying over into the nineteenth century.

My third example concerns one of the so-called 'fixed stars' of the jurisprudential firmament of contracts – the case of *Hadley* v. *Baxendale*.[33] One would have supposed that there would be nothing left to say about this case after Richard Danzig's much-admired study in volume four of the *Journal of Legal Studies*.[34] Yet, to the present day, law teachers still draw students' attention to the discrepancy between the reporter's version of the facts and that stated in Baron Alderson's opinion. According to

---

[28] Two of the manuscript reports are among the Denison MSS at the Harvard Law School – Long Notebook 83 (with a notation in the report that the case was determined in Easter Term 1746), fol. 48b; Long Notebook 150, fol. 110. The two additional reports are at Lincoln's Inn Library. One is at MS Misc. 136, fol. 1317; the other is among the Hill MSS, and it is unique in that it reports an intermediate phase of the case in Hilary Term 1746. MS Hill 26, fol. 149.

[29] Lincoln's Inn Library, MS Misc 136, fol. 1317.

[30] The validity of an arbitration clause as a condition precedent was accepted in later cases. *See* E.S. Wolaver, 'The Historical Background of Commercial Arbitration', *University of Pennsylvania Law Review*, 83 (1934), pp. 132, 143.

[31] *Russell* v. *Pellegrini*, 6 E. & B. 1020, 1026 (1856).

[32] H. Horwitz and J. Oldham, 'John Locke, Lord Mansfield, and Arbitration during the Eighteenth Century', *Historical Journal*, 36 (1993), p. 137.

[33] 9 Exch. 341 (1854). The 'fixed star' description of *Hadley* was that of Grant Gilmore in *The Death of Contract* (Columbus, Ohio, 1974), p. 83, and is quoted by Richard Danzig in his study of the *Hadley* case, cited below.

[34] R. Danzig, '*Hadley* v. *Baxendale*: A Study in the Industrialization of the Law', *Journal of Legal Studies*, 4 (1975), p. 249.

the reporters,[35] the agent from Pickford & Co., the carrier which was taking away the mill shaft to be repaired, was told by plaintiff's clerk that the mill was stopped and that the shaft must be sent immediately. But Baron Alderson said that the only facts communicated by plaintiffs to defendants at the time the contract was made was that the article to be carried was a broken shaft of a mill, and that the plaintiffs were millers of that mill. The reporters' version would have justified what have come to be called special damages in the form of profits lost while the mill was idle. Baron Alderson's version supported the outcome in the case – the denial of such profits. Most modern law teachers – in America, at least – advise students that the reporters probably got it wrong, and certainly the reporters are not to be trusted over Baron Alderson.

I argue that the reporters' version is the more trustworthy, which, if true, undermines the special damages outcome in the case. My argument derives from assize procedures with which I became acquainted while examining the Dampier Manuscripts in Lincoln's Inn Library.[36] When a question of law arose in an assize case that did not originate in the assize judge's own court, the judge would not be present when the case came on for argument in London, and thus could not read out the facts from his trial notes, which was the normal procedure. Consequently, the assize judge in such cases wrote out a careful statement of the facts of the case as well as the question reserved for argument, forwarding these to the proper court in London.[37]

This is what I think happened in *Hadley* v. *Baxendale*. The case originated in the court of Exchequer, but it was tried at the Gloucester assizes by Sir Charles Crompton,[38] a junior justice of the court of Common Pleas. When the case came back to the court of Exchequer in London for argument, Crompton was not there, not being a judge on that court. Unless procedures had changed by the mid nineteenth century (and I have no reason to think that they did), Crompton would have sent to the court of Exchequer his written report of the facts of the case and the question reserved. In such event, the facts would have been read out from Crompton's report; perhaps each of the Exchequer judges had a copy – possibly even the court reporter.

The degree of factual detail in the reports from the assize judges varied of course from judge to judge, according to personal habit and

[35] The printed report of *Hadley* appears in the Exchequer reports compiled by Welsby, Hurlstone and Gordon. No assessment of the individual reporters or of the quality of their work product appears in any of the standard works on the law reports.

[36] See, E. Heward, 'The Dampier Manuscripts at Lincoln's Inn', *The Journal of Legal History*, 9 (1988), p. 357.

[37] For a fuller description of this procedure, see Oldham, 'Eighteenth-Century Judges' Notes', pp. 29–31.

[38] Not Sir *Roger* Crompton, as mistakenly stated by Danzig, '*Hadley* v. *Baxendale*: A Study in the Industrialization of the Law', *Journal of Legal Studies*, 4, p. 252.

inclination. Crompton, however, was reputedly a meticulous judge who took painstaking care with the facts in his cases.[39] All of this leads to my supposition that the version of the facts of *Hadley* given by the reporter derives from Justice Crompton, giving it a higher pedigree than the version stated by Baron Alderson.

Comparatively few pre-nineteenth-century cases in the field of contract law still make an appearance in modern casebooks and textbooks. Two such cases are *Kingston* v. *Preston*[40] and *Boone* v. *Eyre*,[41] both decided by Lord Mansfield. The cases are doctrinally related, both dealing with operational features of the executory bilateral contract. Both cases are celebrated as major evolutionary steps in contract law – *Kingston* for the proposition that, unless specific language or context dictates otherwise, mutual promises in a bilateral contract are constructively conditional upon each other; *Boone* for the proposition that where mutual promises in a bilateral contract do not, by language or context, indicate that they go to the whole of the reciprocal performance, then only substantial performance by one party is needed to allow that party to demand the return performance. Both cases gained their influential status despite sketchy, abbreviated printed reports.

In Douglas's report of *Kingston*, Mansfield is quoted as giving a taxonomy of covenants: (1) those that are mutual and independent; (2) those that are dependent conditions; and (3) those that are mutual conditions to be performed at the same time. The lasting fame of *Kingston* pertains to the third of these and the idea that mutual covenants to be performed at the same time are constructively conditional upon each other. The facts involved contractual arrangements for Preston to retire and transfer his silk mercer business to two young men – Kingston and Preston's nephew. Mansfield ruled that a promise by Preston to give up his business to Kingston was conditional upon Kingston's first supplying security for the payment of a specific sum of money. Mansfield said:

> In the case before the court, it would be the greatest injustice if the plaintiff should prevail: The essence of the agreement was, that the defendant should not trust to the personal security of the plaintiff, but, before he delivered up his stock and business, should have good security for the payment of the money. The giving such security, therefore, must necessarily be a condition precedent.[42]

---

[39] Danzig quotes the following observation by a contemporary of Crompton's: 'Crompton, J., was remarkable for learning, depth and acuteness and was painfully conscientious about speaking accurately when he spoke judicially.' Danzig, '*Hadley* v. *Baxendale*', pp. 249, 252 n. 10, citing Sir W. Erle, *Memorandum on the Law relating to the United States*, pp. 38–39 (1869).

[40] 2 Doug. 689 (1773), quoted within the case of *Jones* v. *Barkley* (1781).

[41] 1 H.Bl. 273n (1777).

[42] 2 Doug. at 691.

The first interesting point about *Kingston* is that there is a second printed report of the case in Lofft's reports that is often overlooked, perhaps because it appears there anonymously.[43] In that report, we get a strong hint that the court was deciding the case not so much on the language of the contract as on what Mansfield thought any right-thinking businessman who was selling his partnership to a young stripling would have *meant* to do. According to Lofft's version, Mansfield said:

> It would be the most monstrous case in the world if the argument on the side of Mr Buller's client [plaintiff] was to prevail. It's of the very essence of the agreement, that the defendant will not trust the personal security of the plaintiff. A court of justice is to say, that by operation of law he shall, against his teeth? He is to let him into his house to squander every thing there, without any thing to rely on but what he has absolutely refused to trust? This payment, therefore, was a precedent condition before the covenant of putting into possession was to be performed on the part of the defendant.[44]

Further, Lofft reports Justice Aston as remarking that there was a transposition of the articles (that is, the provisions) in the agreement 'which are ill marshalled', and since this went against the evident intent of the defendant, 'the law will so marshal the words, as to give it this effect'.[45] Justice Ashurst is shown as emphasising the intent from the nature of the transaction and the meaning of the parties, noting that the result reached by the court could not hurt Kingston since he could never have been held liable for the payment if the stock of the business were not assigned or possession delivered.

A lengthy manuscript report of *Kingston* v. *Preston* is among the Hill Manuscripts at Lincoln's Inn Library.[46] It contains none of the judges' opinions, but both the facts and the arguments of counsel appear in fuller detail than in either printed report. First the facts: the terms of the agreement show that Kingston was to work for a year and a quarter as a covenant servant in the trade of a silk mercer and, in consideration of the premises *and of the said service*,[47] Preston would pay Kingston £200,

---

[43] Lofft 194 under 'Covenant'. The Lofft report neither appears in nor is referred to in most of the standard contracts casebooks or textbooks in the USA. An exception is F. Kessler, G. Gilmore and A. Kronman, *Contracts* (3rd edn, Boston, 1986), p. 981, in which a portion of the Lofft report is quoted. The report is cited in other works, e.g., E.A. Farnsworth, *Contracts*, 2 vols (Boston 1990), ii, p. 399n.; E.W. Patterson, 'Constructive Conditions in Contracts', *Columbia Law Review*, 42 (1942), pp. 903, 908n.

[44] Lofft, at 198 (emphasis deleted). In the quoted language, I have supplied the two question marks, which are called for in context.

[45] Ibid. (emphasis deleted).

[46] See the Appendix for the full transcription.

[47] The underscored words are missing from Douglas's report, as Serjeant Hill observed in a margin note in his MS.

and also after the year and a quarter Preston 'should and would' yield up and surrender his trade and business of silk mercer 'unto the plaintiff and Jonathan Preston (the nephew of the defendant) or unto the plaintiff and some other person to be nominated by the defendant in the stead of the said nephew'.[48] Kingston and Preston (or his substitute) were then to accept the stock in trade, execute articles of partnership, 'and at and before the ensealing and delivery of the said articles cause and procure good and sufficient security to be given unto the defendant to be approved of by the defendant'. Kingston in his declaration averred that he had done all that the agreement called for, having served the year and a quarter, at the end of which he *'was ready and willing*[49] to take with said John Preston [or his substitute] as his copartner in the said trade', and 'he was also ready and did offer at or before the ensealing and delivery of the said articles to cause and procure good and sufficient security to be given unto the defendant'. Nevertheless, defendant would not surrender the business to Kingston and Jonathan Preston or his substitute.

Francis Buller argued strongly on plaintiff's behalf. He carefully distinguished precedents that had been presented by defendant, and emphasised that 'The subject matter of the plaintiff's covenant is such as could not be performed before defendant's covenant was performed and therefore if they had been dependent still it would have been no bar to this action to say plaintiff had not performed his covenant'. Furthermore:

> The plaintiff therefore had time to give this security till the time of executing the articles of partnership and two acts were to be done by defendant before articles could be executed. First he was to name a person to be plaintiff's partner. Secondly, he was to quit his trade and yield it up to plaintiff and such person. He never did quit his trade and it is for not doing that, that this action is brought. Therefore it is no plea to an action for that breach to say that the plaintiff has not done an act which in bides of time and from the nature and circumstances of the case was not to be done till the defendant had performed this covenant on which the present action is brought. This would have been the case if the whole matter of the deed had been contained in one clause or the defendant's covenant had been dependent on the plaintiff's, but here covenants are totally distinct and independent. Each party's covenants are dressed up in the modern stately garb of conveyancing. They do not even squint at each other . . ., and each covenant is distinctly ushered in by the conveyancer's three graces – covenant, promise and agree. The two covenants are as distinct and independent as any two covenants in any one deed can be.

For the defendant, Nash Grose (both Grose and Buller were later to join Lord Mansfield as judges of King's Bench) hammered at the practicalities of the business deal. It was not for defendant 'to trust a man not worth

48 Lincoln's Inn Library, MS Hill 4, fol. 176.
49 Underscoring again by Serjeant Hill.

a farthing and therefore he insists on it as a condition precedent to what he was to do that the plaintiff should find responsible security, and if the court was to determine he need not, it would be obliging the defendant to rely on the plaintiff's personal security contrary to the agreement'.

Grose's argument made perfect sense to Mansfield, himself a shrewd man of business. But on the language of the agreement Buller's argument was forceful, as Justice Aston apparently acknowledged, according to Lofft's report. Further, the case takes a new shape altogether upon examining Justice Ashurst's copy of the Demurrer Book, found among the Dampier Manuscripts at Lincoln's Inn.[50] An edited transcription of this document is given in the appendix to this essay, for those who may wish the full flavour of the opposing positions. From the Demurrer Book, we learn surprising things about the case. First, the phase of the case reflected in the printed reports took up only two of defendant's seven pleas responding to plaintiff's declaration; the other five pleas raised flatly conflicting factual disputes, as to which the parties 'put themselves on the country', that is, requested a jury trial. Secondly, the claims made by Preston in the five pleas sent to jury trial reflect a position that is sharply different from that constructed by Nash Grose in arguing Preston's case on demurrer before the court of King's Bench.

Grose, again, said it made no sense for defendant 'to trust a man not worth a farthing' – or, as put in Ashurst's notes of Grose's argument: 'Defendant [is] a mercer. [He] has a very large stock. [He] had in view the taking his nephew into partnership & securing the payment for his stock. Defendant [was] worth nothing. His covenant [was] worth nothing . . . . [It would be] absurd to say that though the Plaintiff stipulates previously to give security, the Law should say Defendant shall do the act & trust to his personal security'. But if we are to believe Preston's own claims, as given in his answers to Kingston's declaration, Grose's characterisations of Preston's plight are completely wrong. Preston says that he named his brother, William, as Kingston's partner, and that he notified Kingston about this, but Kingston would not accept William. Had William been made partner, this without more ado would have gone a long way to providing the security that Richard Preston was seeking. Further, Preston appears to have been anxious to unload the business – by his own claims, he waited around the shop until late in the day on 24 June 1771 (the day ending the year and a quarter), and as well for three more days, hoping that Kingston would turn up, but to no avail. Preston represented that he stood ready and willing to hand over the trade and business to John and his partner-designate, William Preston, and in none of Richard Preston's

---

[50] Lincoln's Inn Library, MSS Dampier, Ashurst Paper Book 17.

pleas was this willingness described as conditional on prior receipt of the specified security.[51]

Whether the five pleas raising factual disputes went before a jury I have been unable to determine.[52] In the event, the case is a striking illustration of Sir Henry Maine's admonition that the growth of the substantive law can be found secreted in the interstices of procedure.[53] The case presented on demurrer to the court of King's Bench was narrowly circumscribed by the points of law being argued, and only within these narrow confines were the fame and influence of *Kingston* forged.

As others have pointed out,[54] the ideas Mansfield expressed in *Kingston* about the interrelationships of covenants were not new. Yet, as has also been noted,[55] the old law of independence of executory promises persisted, prompting Justice Willes of the court of Common Pleas to state in 1744:

> But I expressed my dislike of those cases, though they are too many to be now over-ruled, where it is determined that the breach of one covenant, though plainly relative to the other, cannot be pleaded in bar to an action brought for the breach of the other, but the other party must be left to bring his action for the breach of the other; ... this notion plainly tending to make two actions instead of one, and to a circuity of action and multiplying actions, both which the law ahbors.[56]

Justice Willes's lament is the more interesting because twenty-eight years earlier, his own court – Common Pleas – had squarely anticipated Lord Mansfield's taxonomy of covenants as given in *Kingston*. The occasion

[51] Further, by the terms of the agreement, only part of the security called for by the agreement was to be provided at the time of the formation of the partnership; another part was to come later, when the value of the stock had been reduced to £4000.

[52] The Demurrer was joined in Hilary term 1773 with argument before the court of King's Bench following at Easter. Had the disputed pleas gone to trial, it could have occurred during the sittings as early as Hilary 1773 or as late as Michaelmas of that year. The case would probably have been tried before Mansfield, but no trial notes for Lord Mansfield survive for 1773 except for Hilary term, and the case does not appear there. See J. Oldham, *The Mansfield Manuscripts and the Growth of English Law in the Eighteenth Century*, 2 vols (Chapel Hill, NC, and London, 1992), p. 163. Furthermore, no entry for any such trial appears in the Entry Book of Final Judgments from Michaelmas 1772 through Hilary 1774 (PRO, KB 139/99). (I am grateful to Henry Horwitz for the latter fact.)

[53] See F.W. Maitland, *The Forms of Action at Common Law* (Cambridge, 1968), p. 1, quoting Maine's *Early Law and Custom*.

[54] See, e.g., W.M. McGovern Jr, 'Dependent Promises in the History of Leases and Other Contracts', *Tulane Law Review*, 52 (1978), p. 659.

[55] Ibid.; see also J. Dawson, W.B. Harvey and S.D. Henderson, *Contracts* (6th ed, Westbury, NY, 1993), pp. 787–88.

[56] *Thomas v. Cadwallader*, Willes 496, 499–500 (1744).

was the unreported case of *Oddin* v. *Duffield*, decided in 1716.[57] The *Oddin* manuscript is part of Chief Justice Peter King's own casenotes. The dispute concerned an agreement for the sale of freehold and copyhold for £170, to be paid in specified installments, and: 'The plaintiff covenants upon payment of the said sum of £170 in manner aforesaid to give unto the defendant a good conveyance & assurance of the premises, and the defendant covenants upon receiving a good assurance of the premises to pay to the plaintiff the said £170 in manner aforesaid'. The final payment of £120 was the subject of litigation, and the difficulty, according to Chief Justice King,

> arose on the seeming contradictoriness of the mutual covenants, the plaintiff covenanting to make an assurance upon payment, and the defendant covenanting to pay upon making assurance. In which case it was agreed, that if these mutual covenants were entirely insensible, then the words in the former part of the Articles mentioning six score pounds *agreed* to be paid would be an express covenant for payment of the money to the plaintiff and then the plaintiff could maintain this action without averring that he had made assurance.

But the court held 'that this explication ought not to be admitted without an utter impossibility of putting any sense in the subsequent covenants'. The court found it possible to construe the contract to interpret the general words at the beginning as 'only a recital in part of the subsequent covenants'. Thus the meaning of the subsequent covenants was,

> that at the day it should be at the election or choice of either party to have a performance. If the plaintiff was willing to have the money he might at the day make the assurance and tender it and so be entitled to the money; if the defendant was willing to have the assurance he might at the day pay or tender the money and so be entitled to the assurance. It was at the day in the power of the one to tender a conveyance and in the power of the other to tender the money. If neither of them did either they then both elected to let the covenants drop. Neither of them is entitled to a performance from the other but on the performance of his covenant first, and therefore the plaintiff not making the assurance at the day is not entitled to have the £120 from the defendant.[58]

Boone v. *Eyre* raises the question of whether Mansfield was consciously articulating the doctrine of substantial performance, for which the case

---

[57] Harvard Law School, MS 1113, fol. 45. At the time, there was very little reporting going on in Common Pleas. Cooke's and Strange's reports span 1716, but neither contains the case.

[58] Why Justice Willes would not have been aware of this case is a puzzle. One would suppose that manuscript copies of earlier decisions from the same court would be sought by a chief justice, especially casenotes kept by an earlier, respected chief justice such as Peter King.

came to stand. In many ways the case seems a gloss on *Kingston* v. *Preston*. The facts of *Boone*, as given by Henry Blackstone, were simple:

> Covenant on a deed, whereby plaintiff conveyed to the defendant the equity of redemption of a plantation in the West Indies, together with the stock of negroes upon it, in consideration of £500 and an annuity of £160 per annum for his life; and covenanted that he had a good title to the plantation, was lawfully possessed of the negroes, and that the defendant should quietly enjoy. The defendant covenanted that the plaintiff well and truly performing every thing therein contained on his part to be performed, he the defendant would pay the annuity.[59]

Boone sued Eyre for non-payment of the annuity, and Eyre pleaded that, at the time of making the deed, Boone had not been legally possessed of the slaves on the plantation, and so did not have good title to convey. On a general demurrer, Lord Mansfield ruled for the plaintiff; his reported opinion was as follows:

> The distinction is very clear, where mutual covenants go to the whole of the consideration on both sides, they are mutual conditions, the one precedent to the other. But where they go only to a part, where a breach may be paid for in damages, there the defendant has a remedy on his covenant, and shall not plead it as a condition precedent. If this plea were to be allowed, any one negro not being the property of the plaintiff would bar the action.[60]

The Hill MSS at Lincoln's Inn contain notes of *Boone* v. *Eyre*, and two details appear that are not in the printed report of the case. Mansfield is shown as giving an example of a contract where mutual covenants go to the whole of the consideration – 'as where a man buys an estate at such a price, the paying the money and the conveying the estate are mutual conditions'. Secondly, Justice Aston is shown citing the King's Bench case of *Martindale* v. *Fisher*, 16 Geo. 2.[61] The latter case circles back to the *Kingston* problem, in that it dealt with the question of dependent versus independent covenants and what had to be averred.

In *Martindale*, the dispute was over a bet on a horse race. Plaintiff agreed to deliver to defendant a certain amount of cloth, for which defendant was to pay an agreed sum if Sir Marmaduke Wyvill's horse should beat the plaintiff's horse, but if plaintiff's horse won, defendant was to pay nothing. Plaintiff sued, claiming that Sir M.W.'s horse had won, and gained a jury verdict. Defendant moved to arrest the judgment on the ground that plaintiff had not averred in his declaration that the cloth had been

[59] 1 H. Bl. 273 (1777).
[60] Ibid.
[61] 1 Wils. 88 (1745).

delivered, citing the 1615 case of *Nichols* v. *Raynbred*.[62] Justice Denison rejected the motion, stating, according to Wilson's Reports:

> Where a plaintiff declares that in consideration he the said plaintiff would deliver to the defendant a piece of cloth, that the defendant should pay such a sum of money for it, in that case an averment of the delivery of the cloth is necessary; but if plaintiff states an agreement, and then lays it that in consideration of such a promise or agreement, &c. there is no need of an averment.

This could be read to suggest that the averment is needed where the promise sued upon is dependent on the promise to deliver the cloth, but not where the promises are independent. A manuscript version of *Martindale*, however, reveals that Denison was differentiating between what today would be called unilateral and bilateral contracts and, in doing so, he was following *Nichols* v. *Raynbred*. Denison's opinion in the manuscript report is as follows: 'If it had been thus, that in consideration that the plaintiff would *deliver* the cloth, the defendant promised to pay, there the delivery must be averred. So if it had been upon the agreement that in consideration that the plaintiff *would perform* his part of the agreement, the defendant would perform his part, there it would be necessary to aver the performance; but here it is in consideration the plaintiff had *promised* to perform the said agreement, the defendant *promised* to perform the said agreement. So that the performance is not the consideration, but the plaintiff's *promise* to perform, & therefore the performance is not necessary to be averred'.[63] Similarly, in *Nichols* v. *Raynbred*, where Nichols had agreed to sell Raynbred a cow for which Raynbred promised to pay 50 shillings, the court held 'that the plaintiff need not aver the delivery of the cow, because it is promise for promise'.[64]

In *Boone* v. *Eyre*, Lord Mansfield took a very different approach. Typically, he disregarded form to reach substance, and he would not allow a partial breach by the plaintiff that could be compensated in damages to bar plaintiff's action, when the defendant had received the essential thing he had bargained for – the plantation.

We can learn a good deal more about the circumstances of the *Boone* case from Justice Ashurst's copy of the Demurrer Book, which survives among

---

[62] 1 Hob. 88. This case is yet today paired with *Kingston* v. *Preston* to illustrate the old and new views of independency and dependency of covenants in bilateral contracts. See e.g., J. Dawson et al. *Contracts*, pp. 786–90.

[63] Lincoln's Inn Library, MS Misc. 136, fol. 1181. Separate, brief opinions in accord are also given for Chief Justice Lee and for Justice Wright. According to the chief justice: 'It is laid here as a mutual agreement, not like the case where the delivery is the foundation of the promise, but here were mutual agreements. Where there is a mutual promise, the *promise* is the consideration & there is no need of any averment of performance'.

[64] Hob. 88 (1615).

the Dampier Manuscripts at Lincoln's Inn. Laid out in the document is the Declaration (reciting the terms of the agreement in full), the Plea, the Demurrer and the Joinder. On the backside of the Demurrer Book are Justice Ashurst's notes of the arguments of counsel and of the court's opinion.[65]

The transaction involved in *Boone* was the sale of a working plantation named Capuchin in the Dominican Islands. The transfer was to include not only the land but also the buildings, plant and equipment used for working the land (all specified in the agreement), plus 112 slaves. Approximately ninety of the slaves residing on the plantation were identified in the agreement by name,[66] 'together with the said Negro called Pompey at New York and the said Negro called Antonia at Mary Gallant[67] and all other the Negroes and slaves of the said John Boone and Diana his wife . . . [including] the issue of the females above mentioned'. Boone and his wife Diana conveyed the plantation 'with general warranty of all the premises except of Negroes said to be dead'.[68]

Substantively, there are two interesting points revealed by the documentation of *Boone* in the Dampier Manuscripts. The first derives from Ashurst's notes of the arguments of counsel about whether conveyance of the slaves was a condition precedent to the defendant's obligation to pay the annuity. For the plaintiff, Francis Buller argued that defendant's plea (claiming such a condition precedent) was bad 'because the *land* is conveyed', and, 'Shall he keep that & pay nothing because plaintiff had not title to the *Negroes*?' Buller added, 'Supposing that were true, the words *performing, &ca* can't amount to *condition precedent*'.[69] For the defendant, William Baldwin argued that Eyre's obligation to pay the annuity (rent) was 'to arise from the profits of the plantation', yet 'the Negroes had been removed'. Without the slaves to work the land, there would be no profits; thus, even if the agreement did not explicitly label the obligation

---

[65] See the Appendix for the full transcription.

[66] The number is approximate because the recitation of names is unpunctuated, and although most are first names only, some appear to be full names.

[67] Marie Galante, an island in the French West Indies, discovered by Columbus in 1493, and said to have acquired its name from the ship Columbus was then sailing. *Encyclopaedia Britannica* (11th edn, New York 1911).

[68] Pompey of New York and Antonia of Marie Galante were added, apparently to compensate for those slaves 'said to be dead'.

[69] Buller's reference is to the following language in the agreement (see Appendix for context): 'And the said Francis Eyre did . . . covenant, promise, grant & agree to & with the said John Boone & Diana his wife, that he the said John Boone well, truly & faithfully doing, fulfilling & performing all & singular the covenants, clauses, recitals & agreements in the said Indenture contained, that he the said Francis Eyre . . . should & would well & truly pay or cause to be paid in London unto the said John Boone . . . from thenceforth & by half yearly payments during all the natural life of him the said John Boone the annuity or clear yearly rent of £160'.

to supply the slaves a condition precedent to Eyre's obligation to pay rent, it implicitly did so.

The second interesting aspect of *Boone* raised by the manuscript reports is the question whether, despite the principle enunciated by Mansfield in the plaintiff's favour, the defendant should have won on the merits. Since the case came forward on demurrer, the parties agreed to let the outcome abide the question put to the court. Plaintiff lost because the agreement to provide the slaves was held not to be a condition precedent. The principle for which the case came to stand was that, absent a true condition, only a *material* breach of contract justifies withholding the promised return performance. Clearly, as Lord Mansfield said, the plaintiff should not be barred from his action merely because a single slave was dead or was not the plaintiff's property[70] or, as Justice Ashurst apparently remarked, the defendant 'ought not to keep the estate because the plaintiff had not a title to a few negroes'.[71]

But what were the facts? As noted earlier, the agreement recited approximately ninety slaves by name and warranted that the plaintiff had good title to them, the land, the plant and equipment on the land, and to the unnamed additional slaves making up the total of 112 (plus any issue of named female slaves). The warranty excepted 'Negroes said to be dead', in exchange for Pompey of New York and Antonia of Marie Galante. If Baldwin, defendant's counsel, was correct and defendant was unable to generate profits from the land because 'the Negroes had been removed', and if the parties understood that the promised annuity was rent that was 'to arise from the profits of the plantation', it is easy to consider the breach by plaintiff as material. Had that question been left to a jury, the defendant might well have prevailed.

The *Boone* case served as an important precedent during the late 1700s and early 1800s. The importance of *Boone* was the point that, unless contract context or language dictated otherwise, a small deficiency in plaintiff's performance would not disqualify him from being able to demand the return performance. That is, defendant's performance was not expressly conditional upon the whole of plaintiff's performance. How one decided when the language or the nature of the transaction required

---

[70] In the printed report of *Boone*, Mansfield is quoted as saying, 'If this plea were to be allowed, any one negro not being the property of the plaintiff would bar the action'. 1 H.Bl. 273. But the version in Serjeant Hill's manuscript of *Boone* is, 'If there were but one Negro dead, the Plaintiff would be barred his remedy for his rent'.

[71] The Ashurst remark does not appear in the printed report of *Boone*, or in either the Hill or Dampier manuscript version. It was quoted by Lord Kenyon in a later case, *Campbell* v. *Jones*, 6 T.R. 570, 573 (1796). The full quote by Kenyon was: 'And Mr J. Ashurst added, "There is a difference between executed and executory covenants; here the covenants are executed in part, and the defendant ought not keep the estate because the plaintiff has not a title to a few negroes"'. Kenyon must have been reading from another manuscript copy of *Boone*, perhaps his own notes.

an expressly conditional relationship was the uncertain part – as in paying money at a stated price for the conveyance of an estate.

The later cases in which *Boone* figured influentially are too numerous to review here, but several are worth mentioning. In one of them, for example, we learn how *Kingston* v. *Preston* was propelled into prominence. Also we can see how difficult it was consistently to apply the *Boone* principle.

In *Campbell* v. *Jones*,[72] plaintiff agreed to sell to defendant plaintiff's patent for purifying linen, rags and other materials used in paper-making. The sale price was £500. Plaintiff promised to convey the patent, and expeditiously to instruct defendant in bleaching and preparing the materials for paper-making, in accordance with the patent specification. Half of the purchase price was paid down, the other half to be paid 'on or before the 25th of February or sooner, in case the plaintiff should before that time have instructed the defendant'.[73] Defendant refused to pay the £250 by 25 February, claiming that he had not been instructed by plaintiff and that the obligation to pay the further £250 was dependent on his having received the promised instruction. This claim did not succeed before the court of King's Bench. The court thought the claim unsupported by the language of the agreement. Further, relying on *Boone* v. *Eyre*, Lord Kenyon stated: 'Under this agreement the defendant has a perfect title to use the patent, and the instruction of the defendant cannot be taken to be the most material part of the consideration, as the specification must be supposed to contain full instruction for that purpose, though some advantage might arise from the assistance of the inventor'.[74] As in *Boone*, the agreement was partially executed, the plaintiff's breach could be recompensed by damages, and the defendant should not be allowed to keep the patent right without paying the other half of the purchase price merely 'because he may have sustained some damage by the plaintiff's not having instructed him'.[75]

[72] 6 T.R. 570 (1796).

[73] 6 T.R. at 572.

[74] Ibid., at 573. The 'specification' was the essential description of the invention contained in the patent, and by law, it had to be such as would permit one other than the inventor to figure out how to make the invention. In practice, many specifications were difficult to follow, and Kenyon's remark that 'some advantage might arise from the assistance of the inventor' was a definite understatement. Nevertheless, because the law conclusively presumed that the specification was capable of being followed unassisted by the inventor, it was difficult for the court in *Campbell* to designate the failure of the inventor to instruct the defendant a material breach. For a discussion of the law dealing with patent specification, see Oldham, *The Mansfield Manuscripts and the Growth of English Law*, pp. 730–33.

[75] Ibid. The Demurrer Book in *Campbell* v. *Jones* is in the Dampier Manuscripts at Lincoln's Inn – in this case, the copy belonging to Justice Lawrence. Folded in with the Demurrer Book are separate sheets containing notes by Lawrence. One of these turns out

continued

Three years later, the *Boone* issue came again before the court of King's Bench, this time involving a contract for the sale of a grammar school. In *Glazebrook* v. *Woodrow*,[76] the agreement called for the transfer by the plaintiff to the defendant of not only the land and buildings but also the right to take over the pupils then enrolled in the school. For the first year, the defendant was entitled to teach the pupils, to receive the profits, and to try to persuade the parents and guardians of the children to let them continue with the defendant. Then, after that year, defendant was to pay plaintiff £120 and plaintiff was to convey the buildings and land (both events were called for 'on or before the 1st of August 1797'). Defendant took over and ran the school for a year, but did not pay the £120 on 1 August 1797 because, he claimed, plaintiff had not conveyed title to the land and buildings. Plaintiff sued, and the question referred to the court of King's Bench on demurrer was whether the covenant to pay and the covenant to convey were dependent or independent. Relying on *Campbell* v. *Jones* and distinguishing *Boone* v. *Eyre*, counsel for plaintiff argued that the covenants were independent. The court was not impressed. Chief Justice Kenyon stated: 'If these be not dependent covenants, it is difficult to conceive what covenants are so. The very substance of the consideration to entitle the plaintiff to receive the money, was the making of the conveyance required'.[77] The other justices agreed. Justice Lawrence gave the clearest analysis. He observed: 'If the agreement appear to be that the whole of what the plaintiff engaged for, was to be done before the money was to be paid, it will not follow that, because a part only has been performed, he can recover the money, and leave the defendant to his remedy upon the agreement for the breach of the other part'.[78] He added that the question 'depends entirely upon, the words and nature of the agreement', and that 'part execution is only a circumstance from whence the intention of the parties is to be collected'.[79] Lawrence then discussed *Boone* v. *Eyre*,[80] noting that 'in the form the breaches were assigned, the plea did not necessarily go to the whole of the consideration', but 'if the plea had been that the plaintiff had no title at all to the plantation itself, I

continued
to be a draft opinion for the court, which Kenyon, for the most part, adopted. Much of Kenyon's opinion is taken verbatim from Lawrence's draft, though Kenyon augmented the draft, adding the passage about *Boone* v. *Eyre*, for example.

[76] 8 T.R. 366 (1799).

[77] 8 T.R. at 370.

[78] Ibid., at 372.

[79] Ibid., at 373.

[80] Ibid., at 373–74. In his discussion, Justice Lawrence quoted from the declaration and the plea in *Boone*. It is likely that Lawrence had before him Justice Ashurst's copy of the *Boone* Demurrer Book. The collection of paper books that eventually became the Dampier Manuscripts at Lincoln's Inn covers four justices: Ashurst, Buller, Lawrence and Dampier. Although there was overlap, these four justices served successively on King's Bench (in the order just given), and the paper books were probably passed along and accumulated from one justice to the next.

do not know that it would have been holden sufficient'.[81] And in *Campbell* v. *Jones*, 'the substantial part of the consideration was the right of using the method of bleaching described in the patent', whereas the failure to instruct 'might be compensated in damages'.[82]

Justice Lawrence's copy of the Demurrer Book is among the Dampier Manuscripts.[83] There, in notes on the backside of the first page, Lawrence sketched out his thoughts about *Boone* and *Campbell*. He wrote:

> In Boone, a want of title to a negro did not make the whole consideration as to him fail, for he might still go on with the plantation. So was teaching Jones, for notwithstanding that, he might use the patent which of itself must be presumed a sufficient instruction. But here the want of title to the place where the business was to be carried on might make it impossible to carry it on & if so it goes to the whole consideration, as if in Boone there had been no title to the plantation.

Finally, Justice Grose's opinion in *Glazebrook* is of special interest due to its treatment of *Kingston* v. *Preston*. Grose was the prevailing counsel in *Kingston*, and having now become a justice on King's Bench, he seized the opportunity to catapult *Kingston* into prominence. Grose referred to the early confusion in the books and older cases on the issue of dependency or independency of covenants, and then observed that on this subject, 'the case of *Kingston* v. *Preston* was the first strong authority', and 'nothing indeed could exhibit the doctrine which ought to prevail in these instances in a stronger point of view than the circumstances of that case'.[84] He then recited the facts, described the plaintiff's attempt there as seeking 'possession of the whole stock in trade of the defendant to a great amount, without giving him any security at all, to his inevitable ruin', and stated that 'the absurdity and injustice of the thing struck the Court so forcibly, that they said it could never have been the intention of the parties'.[85]

As indicated previously, the full text of the declaration and pleas in *Kingston* presents quite a different picture to that given by Justice Grose in *Glazebrook*. Justice Grose's final sentence in his opinion was: 'How far the determination in *Boone* v. *Eyre* militates against the principles I have laid down, may be a matter of doubt; but the intention of the parties is, or is assumed to be, the governing principle of all the late determinations'.[86] This remark is a little curious, since *Kingston* and *Boone* are ordinarily viewed as congenial, connected parts of the rules governing breach of constructively conditional promises in bilateral contracts, as indeed

---

[81] Ibid., at 374.

[82] Ibid.

[83] Lincoln's Inn Library, MSS Dampier, Lawrence Paper Book 299.

[84] 8 T.R. at 371.

[85] Ibid.

[86] Ibid., at 372.

Justice Le Blanc demonstrated in his opinion in *Glazebrook*. Le Blanc viewed the case then before the court as falling within the rule laid down in *Kingston* – 'that no person shall call upon another to perform his part of a contract until he himself has performed all that he has stipulated to do as the consideration of the other's promises'.[87] He later noted that *Boone* was consistent, since there, 'the *substantial part* of the agreement' had been conveyed by the plaintiff.[88]

The difficult question in each case, of course, is how to decide whether the plaintiff's alleged failure to perform 'goes to the whole of the consideration', or in other words, was a condition precedent to the defendant's obligation to perform. Chief Justice Ellenborough demonstrated a clear understanding on the principles in *Havelock* v. *Geddes* (1809), involving a claimed breach of a promise to make a ship staunch and watertight before releasing her on a charter-party.[89] There, Lord Ellenborough observed, 'if this were a condition precedent, the neglect of putting in a single nail for a single moment after the ship ought to have been made tight, staunch, &c., would be a breach of the condition, and a defence to the whole of the plaintiff's demand'.[90] The defendants had accepted the ship, used her for several months, and then refused to pay anything, arguing that there had been a failure of a condition precedent. Citing the rule of *Boone* v. *Eyre*, Lord Ellenborough stated: 'Had the plaintiff's neglect here precluded the defendants from making any use of the vessel, it would have gone to the whole consideration, and might have been insisted upon as an entire bar; because the consideration for the defendants to pay the freight would then have failed in toto; but as the defendants have had some use of the vessel, notwithstanding the plaintiff's neglect, the plaintiff's covenant is to be considered as going to a part only; the consideration has not wholly failed; and the covenant cannot be looked upon as having raised a condition precedent, but merely gives the defendants a right, under a counter-action, to such damages as they can prove they have sustained from the neglect'.[91]

My last example of the usefulness of manuscript casenotes involves the decision in *Hawkes* v. *Saunders*.[92] This story is in print already,[93] and I return to it briefly in order to illustrate some of the unpredictabilities of the late eighteenth-century process of judicial decision-making. The *Hawkes* case involved a simple fact situation – a suit by a legatee against the executor of an estate on the executor's personal promise that the

---

[87] Ibid., at 374.
[88] Ibid. (emphasis added).
[89] 10 East. 555 (1809).
[90] Ibid., at 563.
[91] Ibid., at 564.
[92] 1 Cowp. 289 (1782).
[93] See Oldham, *The Mansfield Manuscripts and the Growth of English Law*, pp. 228–29.

legacy would be paid. Comparable facts had been presented in the case of *Rann* v. *Hughes*,[94] in which the House of Lords took the opportunity to overrule Lord Mansfield's evident attempt in an earlier case to scrap the doctrine of consideration.[95] In *Rann*, the executor's personal promise was not enforced because it was deemed unsupported by consideration. Thus when the *Hawkes* case came along, any reasonable student of prior cases might have supposed that *Rann* would be controlling. This was what Justice Buller thought, and he came to Westminster Hall on the day when the court's opinion in *Hawkes* was to be announced with a long draft of his opinion written out – an opinion based on quasi-contract theory, grounded in *Moses* v. *Macferlan*.[96] Lord Mansfield spoke first, however, and must have stunned Buller by casually distinguishing *Rann* (because *there*, the estate had no assets when the executor made his promise, whereas *here*, the estate was solvent at the time of the promise), and by deciding *Hawkes* on traditional consideration theory. Consequently, Buller must have quietly shelved his handwritten opinion and improvised verbally a different opinion agreeing with Lord Mansfield. This interpretation of what happened is the more likely because Buller, a very smart judge, is reported by Cowper to have applied the doctrine of consideration to the facts of the case in a way that is flatly incorrect.[97]

A manuscript report of the 1697 case of *Slater* v. *May*[98] confirms that Chief Justice Holt did indeed refer to 'the inconveniences of these scambling reports' which 'will make us appear to posterity as a parcel of blockheads'.[99] Some of us try on occasion to do a measure of 'unscambling', though at times it seems as daunting as *unscrambling* an egg.

What I have attempted in this essay is to tell a cautionary tale, and to entreat us to attend to the question of textuality. We know that the law that has governed us for centuries has been the law reflected in the printed word. Yet, not infrequently, unprinted sources can give us a clearer understanding of facts, context, legal interpretation or behavioural

94 4 Bro. P.C. 27, 7 T.R. 350 (1778).

95 *Pillans* v. *Van Mierop*, 3 Burr. 1663 (1765).

96 2 Burr. 1005 (1760). See generally, Oldham, *The Mansfield Manuscripts and the Growth of English Law*, pp. 169–75.

97 Ibid., pp. 229–30, n. 112. The full text of Buller's original handwritten draft of his opinion in *Hawkes* is given at J. Oldham, 'Reinterpretations of Eighteenth-Century English Contract Theory', *Georgetown Law Journal* 76 (1988), pp. 1984–91.

98 2 Ld. Raym. 210 (and other reports not containing the language being referred to).

99 Harvard Law School, MS 2136, fol. 134. Holt's remark is often misrepresented as referring to 'scrambling reports'. (I have done so myself: see, J. Oldham, *The Mansfield Manuscripts and the Growth of English Law*, p. 102; see also, C.G. Moran, *The Heralds of the Law* (London, 1948), p. 10.) The error is ironic, given the definition of 'scambling' – 'clumsily or carelessly executed; slipshod, slovenly; makeshift' – *Oxford English Dictionary* (compact edn, Oxford, 1971).

dynamics. This is an obvious facet to the social historian; perhaps it should be more so to the legal historian, especially as technology allows us to gain access to manuscripts on a worldwide basis.

The popular marketplace now offers computers that are programmed to read handwriting. It is probably not fanciful to imagine a day not too distant when computers can be programmed not only to read law French or fifteenth-century Latin court hand, but also to translate the reading into any language of choice. This may generate a new discipline that will study the margin for error in computer-read text, but never mind. When this not-so-improbable world arrives, the unprinted voices from the past may become almost as accessible and important as the printed word, at least in some eras. This will in turn present us with a new array of unanticipated interpretative challenges, but will this not be a champagne problem?

Appendix 1

Kingston v *Preston*

Lincoln's Inn Library, MSS Dampier, Ashurst Paper Book 17

[Caption and Ashurst's summary, on cover:]
Kingston v. *Preston*   Demurrer Book
                               Judgment for Defendant
Set down to be argued on Tuesday, the 4th May 1773
Impey for Whitchurch, Agent for Defendant
Entered (?) 1st May 1773

A covenanted to serve B for a year & ¹/₄ & in consideration of the premises & the several covenants to be performed by A, B covenanted at the end of the year & the ¹/₄ to yield up & surrender his business to him, & at the end of that time A covenanted to procure good & sufficient security to be given to B for the payment of the ££ – to be paid monthly in satisfaction of the stock in trade. A cannot maintain Covenant against B for not surrendering the business without having first procured the security for the stock.

[Ashurst's notes of arguments of counsel, backside of Demurrer Book (underscoring by Ashurst)]

Buller for Plaintiff:

The 3[d] & 7th pleas [are] bad. 2 grounds.
1st, the import [is] that Plaintiff has not performed <u>his</u> [covenant], which [is] no excuse to Defendant. [These are] mutual covenants.
2 Mod. 309. Reciprocal covenants of money to be paid.
3 Lev. 41.
1 Ld. Raym. 124. Covenant in consideration of money to be paid.
Saund. 319. A to give so much for A's land.
Str. 537. To transfer so much stock & defendant to accept & pay.
Str. 712. In consideration of _____ covenanted to transfer.
These cases go further than the present. Here it is in <u>consideration of the premises.</u> This is a covenant to do an act at a particular time. Hilary 8 Geo. III, covenant to compleat a house by 3rd December, covenant to pay part 2 December, rest 7(?) December. Held, the covenants were mutual – the covenant being to do an act before a particular day.

2nd point:
The subject matter of the Plaintiff's covenant could not be performed till Defendant had performed his.
   To deliver up his trade & <u>thereupon</u> to enter into articles, &c. Before the articles, Defendant ought to do two acts – to name a partner & yield up his trade. When delivered up, the articles [were] to be entered into.

Grose, contra, for Defendant:

The question [is] on the mutuality & independence of the covenants.
In the cases cited, the court have considered the covenants as <u>independent.</u> [It is] always laid down that where the covenants are dependent or the one precedent to the other, performance must be averred.

The giving up the trade [was] not to be done till Plaintiff had given security. Consider the intention of the articles [of agreement].

Defendant [is] a mercer. [He] had a very large stock. [He] had in view the taking his nephew into partnership & securing the payment for his stock. Defendant [was] worth nothing. His covenant [was] worth nothing. <u>After the execution of articles [of partnership]</u> Defendant covenants to let them come into the shop. And Plaintiff, <u>before the delivery</u> of the articles is to give security.
[It would be] absurd to say that though the Plaintiff stipulates previously to give security, the Law should say Defendant shall do the act & trust to his personal security.

[Edited Text of Demurrer Book (underscoring by Ashurst):]
Hilary Term in the thirteenth year of the Reign of King George the third.

[Declaration:]

London. Be it remembered that in Michaelmas Term last past before our Lord the King at Westminster came John Kingston by William Sleigh his Attorney and brought in the Court [of King's Bench] his Bill against Richard Preston, being in the custody of the Marshall of the Marshalsea of our Lord the King ... of a plea of Debt and there are pledges for the prosecution, to wit, John Doe and Richard Roe, which said Bill follows in these words, to wit:

London (to wit), John Kingston complains of Richard Preston ... of a plea that he render to him one thousand pounds of lawful money of Great Britain which he oweth to and unjustly detaineth from him, For **That Whereas**, by certain Articles of Agreement made upon the twenty fourth day of March [1770] at London aforesaid (to wit) in the parish of Saint Mary Le Bow in the Ward of Cheap between the said Richard Preston ... of the parish of Saint Clement Danes in the County of Middlesex, Silk Mercer, of the one part, and the said John Kingston ... of the parish of Saint Paul, Covent Garden, in the said County of Middlesex, Silk Mercer, of the other part, which said Articles of Agreement ... the said John Kingston now brings here into Court .... The said John Kingston for the considerations therein mentioned did covenant, promise and agree to and with the said Richard Preston ... that he the said John Kingston should and would become a Covenant Servant and Assistant to and diligently and well and faithfully serve, abide and continue with the said Richard Preston ... from the date of the said Articles of Agreement for and during ... the full end and term of one year and one quarter ... as his and their Covenant Servant and Assistant in the trade and business of Silk Mercer, which the said Richard Preston then used, and should and would during the said term well, truly, honestly and faithfully discharge his duty as such Covenant Servant and Assistant, and according to the utmost of his power, skill, knowledge and ability, apply, employ, and exercise himself in and about the trade and business of the said Richard Preston and do and perform all such service and business matters and things whatsoever as should or might necessarily or in any wise relate to, touch or concern the said trade or business to and for the utmost gain, profit, benefit and advantage of the said Richard Preston ..., that he the said John Kingston possibly could, and should in all things lawful touching the same, follow and obey the orders and directions of the said Richard Preston ..., and their secrets relating thereto inviolably keep and should not nor would absent himself from the said business during the said term without the leave or consent of the said Richard Preston ... nor embezle, secrete, or purloin or cause, procure ... any of the monies, silks, goods, wares or merchandizes of the said Richard Preston .... **And Further** that he the said John Kingston should and would during the said term keep just, true and faithful accounts in the books of the said Richard Preston of all goods bought and sold, monies received and paid, and of all other matters and things whatsoever relating to the said trade and business of the said Richard Preston as should come to his the said John Kingston's knowledge or be committed to his care, management or disposal during the said term .... [and account for the same when asked, and at the end of the said term]. **And Further,** that he the said John Kingston should and would at his own proper costs and charges find and provide for himself board and lodging and all other necessaries out of the said Richard Preston's dwelling house during the said term. And in consideration of the premises and of the said service and the several matters and things to be done and performed by the said John Kingston as aforesaid, he, the said Richard Preston ... did covenant, promise and agree to and with the said John Kingston by the said Articles of Agreement, that he, the said Richard Preston ..., should and would at the end and expiration of the said term of one year and one quarter ... well and truly pay or cause to be paid unto the said John Kingston or his assigns the sum of two hundred pounds of lawful money of Great Britain. And the said Richard Preston in further consideration of the premises and of the several covenants thereinafter as well as thereinbefore contained ... to be done and performed did ... by the said Articles of Agreement further covenant, promise and agree to and with the said John Kingston ... that at the end and expiration of the said term of one year and one quarter of a year from the date thereof, he the said Richard Preston should and would quit and leave off his said trade and business of a Silk Mercer and yield up and surrender the same unto the said John Kingston and John Preston (the nephew of him the said Richard Preston) or unto the said John Kingston and some other person to be nominated by him the said Richard Preston in the stead of his the said nephew in case his said nephew should happen to be dead or he the said Richard Preston should not then approve of him for that purpose, together with all the stock which should be then remaining in his the said trade at a fair valuation and appraisement to be made and settled by and between them the said Richard Preston and John Kingston jointly, and in case it should happen that they should differ therein that then some one indifferent person should be by them jointly nominated to settle and adjust all matters in difference between them relating thereto, who should settle and adjust the same accordingly, and whose determination should be final, binding and conclusive. **And Further** that Articles of Copartnership should thereupon be entered into and executed by and between the said John Kingston and the said John Preston or by and between the said John Kingston and such other person so to be nominated by him the said Richard Preston as aforesaid as copartner with the said John Kingston ... for the term of fourteen years ... (**Subject** to such covenants, conditions, provisos, and agreements as are usually inserted in such kind of Articles), **And** that he the said Richard Preston ... should and would from and immediately after the execution of the said Articles permit and suffer the said John Kingston and the said John Preston [or his substitute] to carry on the said

trade and business in copartnership together in his the said Richard Preston's shop
in his dwelling house in Holywell Street . . . in which the same was then carried
on, for and during the residue of his the said Richard Preston's term which
should be then to come and unexpired in his said dwelling house, free from the
payment of any rent or taxes whatsoever. **And** the said John Kingston in further
consideration of the several covenants therein contained on the part and behalf of
the said Richard Preston . . . to be kept, done and performed, **Did** . . . covenant,
promise, and agree to and with the said Richard Preston . . . by the said Articles
of Agreement that at the end and expiration of the said term of one year and
one quarter . . ., said John Kingston should and would jointly with the said
John Preston [or his substitute] take and accept his the said Richard Preston's
trade and business and carry on the same jointly with the said John Preston [or
his substitute] in the said trade as aforesaid in his the said Richard Preston's said
shop in his said dwelling house in Holywell Street aforesaid in which the same
was then carried on, for and during the residue of his the said Richard Preston's
term which should be then to come and unexpired in his said dwelling house.
And also that he the said John Kingston should and would jointly with the said
John Preston [or his substitute] at the end of the said term of one year and one
quarter . . . also take and accept from the said Richard Preston all his then stock
in his the said trade and business at such valuation and appraisement as aforesaid
to be made and settled as aforesaid. **And Further** that he the said John Kingston
should and would at the end and expiration of the said term of one year and
one quarter . . . enter into and execute Articles of Copartnership for carrying on
the said trade and business jointly with the said John Preston [or his substitute]
as his the said John Kingston's copartner in the said trade for the said term
of fourteen years from thence next ensuing . . . . **And Further** that he the said
John Kingston should and would at and before the ensealing and delivery of the
said Articles cause and procure good and sufficient security to be given unto the
said Richard Preston . . . to be approved of by the said Richard Preston . . . for
the payment of two hundred and fifty pounds . . . in satisfaction and lieu of and
as and for one moiety of the monthly produce of the said stock unto the said
John Preston . . . monthly and every month until the value of the said stock
should be reduced to the sum of four thousand pounds . . . and that then the
said John Kingston . . . should and would cause and procure to be given unto
the said Richard Preston . . . good and sufficient security to be approved of by
the said Richard Preston . . . for payment of the said sum of two thousand
pounds . . . (one moiety of the said four thousand pounds), payable at such time
or times and in such manner and proportions with lawful interest for the same
as he the said Richard Preston . . . should think proper. **And also** that he the
said John Kingston and he the said John Preston [or his substitute] should and
would yearly and every year during the residue of the said Richard Preston's term
which . . . should be to come and unexpired in his said dwelling house well and
truly pay or cause to be paid unto the said Richard Preston . . . the sum of three
hundred pounds . . . by four even and equal quarterly payments by and out of the
profits and gain of the said trade and business by way of good will and as and for
a recompense and compensation for his the said Richard Preston's relinquishing
and given up unto them the said stock in trade and business and for their being
permitted to carry on the same in his the said Richard Preston's shop in his said
dwelling house for and during the residue of his said term therein free from
the payment of rent or taxes. **And** that he the said John Kingston and the said
John Preston [or his substitute] should and would at or before the ensealing and
delivery of the said Articles, execute and as their act and deed deliver one bond
or obligation bearing even date therewith unto the said Richard Preston . . . in
the penalty of three thousand pounds . . . to be thereunder written for the

payment of the said three hundred pounds per annum during the term aforesaid and in manner aforesaid unto the said Richard Preston .... **And Lastly** they the said Richard Preston and John Kingston (the parties to the said Articles of Agreement) did ... severally, mutually and reciprocally covenant, promise and agree to and with each other ... that they the said Richard Preston and John Kingston ... should and would forfeit and pay the one unto the other of them ... the sum of five hundred pounds ... in case of the nonperformance of all or any or either of the said several covenants, articles, clauses, and agreements therein before contained on either of their parts ... to be observed, kept, done and performed. And for the true and just observance and performance of all and every of the said covenants, articles, clauses and agreements therein before contained, each of the said parties to the said Articles did bind himself ... to the other of them ... in the penal sum of one thousand pounds ... firmly by the said Articles of Agreement, as in and by the said Articles of Agreement more fully appears.

And the said John Kingston in fact saith that in pursuance of the said Articles of Agreement, he ..., on the twenty-fourth day of March [1770] at London ... entered into the service of the said Richard Preston as his Covenant Servant and Assistant in the trade and business of a Silk Mercer ... until and upon the twenty-ninth day of June [1771]. And [although he, John Kingston, did so honestly and faithfully to the utmost of his power, perform all things that he possibly could do for the profit of Richard Preston, following all orders, keeping all secrets, being scrupulously honest, keeping all necessary accounts, and paying over to Richard Preston from time to time (as requested) all monies received on account, also accounting for same at the end of the year and a quarter, and observed all other terms of the Articles of Agreement], and at the end and expiration of the said term of one year and one quarter ... was ready and willing to take and accept and did then and there offer to take and accept jointly with the said John Preston [or his substitute] said trade and business and to carry on the same ... [and to accept the stock in trade, evaluated as laid out in the Articles], and ... was ready and willing to enter into and execute and did then and there offer to enter into and execute Articles of Copartnership ... and was also ready and willing and did then and there offer at or before the ensealing and delivery of the said Articles to cause and procure good and sufficient security to be given unto the said Richard Preston ... to be approved of by the said Richard Preston for the payment of two hundred and fifty pounds ... in satisfaction and lieu of and as and for one moiety of the monthly produce of the said stock unto the said John [Richard] Preston ... until the value of the said stock should be reduced to the sum of four thousand pounds .... **Nevertheless** the said Richard Preston at the end and expiration of the said term of one year and one quarter ... did not quit and leave off his said trade and business of a Silk Mercer and yield up and surrender the same unto the said John Kingston and Johh Preston (nephew to the said Richard Preston) [or his substitute] together with all the stock which was then remaining in his said trade at a fair valuation and appraisement to be made and settled by and between them [as aforesaid] ... but wholly neglected & refused so to do, contrary to the form and effect of his said covenant in that behalf made as aforesaid, whereby an action hath accrued to the said John Kingston to demand and have of the said Richard Preston the said one thousand pounds above demanded. Nevertheless the said Richard Preston (although often requested to do so) hath not paid the said one thousand pounds or any part thereof to the said John Kingston, but hath entirely refused, and still refuses, to pay the same to him. For the damage of the said John Kingston of five hundred pounds, & thereof he bringeth suit, &ca

Plea:

And now this day . . . the said John by his said Attorney, as the said Richard by John Impey, his Attorney, do come before our Lord the King at Westminster and the said Richard defends the wrong and injury . . . and says

1st, that the said John ought not to have or maintain his aforesaid action . . . because he says that the said John did not offer to take and accept jointly with the said John Preston [or his substitute] . . . the said Richard Preston's said trade & business, together with the . . . stock in trade at such valuation & appraisement as in the said Articles of Agreement mentioned as the said John hath above in his said Declaration alledged, and of this the said Richard Preston puts himself upon the country, &ca. And the said John doth so likewise.

2. And for further plea . . . the said Richard by leave of the Court . . . says that the said John ought not to have or maintain his said action thereof against him because he says that the said John did not offer to enter into and execute such Articles of Copartnership as the said John hath above in his said Declaration alledged, and of this the said Richard puts himself upon the country, &ca. And the said John doth so likewise.

3. And for further plea . . . the said Richard by like leave of the Court . . . says that the said John ought not to have or maintain his said action thereof against him because he says that the said John did not <u>offer to cause & procure such good and sufficient security to be given unto the said Richard Preston as the said John hath above in his said Declaration alledged,</u> and of this the said Richard puts himself upon the country, &ca.

4. And the said Richard for further plea . . . by like leave of the Court . . . says that the said John ought not to have or maintain his aforesaid action thereof against him because protesting that the said John Kingston did not offer to take and accept the said Richard Preston's said trade and business together with the said Richard Preston's stock in trade [nor did offer to enter into the Articles or to obtain the security] as in his said Declaration above alledged. For plea in this behalf, the said Richard says that he . . . on the last day of the said term of one year and one quarter . . . and until the extreme part of that day [on 24 June 1771] was in his said shop in his said dwelling house in Holywell Street aforesaid ready to quit and leave off his said trade and business and to yield up and surrender the same unto the said John Kingston and to some other person to be then and there nominated by him the said Richard Preston together with all the stock then remaining in his said trade at a fair valuation and appraisement to be made and settled according to the form and effect of the said Articles, but that the said John Kingston did not on any part of that day either by himself or by any other person attend at the said shop to take and accept the said trade and business together with the said stock. And this the said Richard Preston is ready to verify, wherefore he prays judgment if the said John Kingston ought to have or maintain his aforesaid action thereof against him, &ca.

5. And the said Richard for further plea in this behalf by like leave of the Court . . . says that the said John ought not to have or maintain his aforesaid action thereof against him because protesting that the said John Kingston did not offer to take and accept the said Richard Preston's said trade and business together with the said Richard Preston's said stock in trade [nor did offer to execute the Articles or obtain security] as the said John hath in his said Declaration above alledged. For plea in this behalf the said Richard says that he the said Richard at

the end and expiration of the said term of one year and one quarter . . . and for a reasonable space of time, to wit for the space of three days then next following, was in his said shop in his said dwelling house in Holywell Street aforesaid ready to quit and leave off his said trade and business and to yield up and surrender the same unto the said John Kingston and to some other person to be then and there nominated by him the said Richard Preston [together with the stock, evaluated as laid out in the Agreement], but that the said John Kingston did not at the end and expiration of the said term of one year and one quarter of a year or in any reasonable space of time then next following either by himself or by any other person or persons on his behalf attend at the said shop to take and accept the said trade and business together with the said stock. And this the said Richard Preston is ready to verify, wherefore he prays judgment if the said John Kingston ought to have or maintain his aforesaid action thereof against him, &ca.

6. And the said Richard for further plea in this behalf by leave of the Court . . . says that he the said Richard at the end and expiration of the said term of one year and a quarter . . . to wit on [24 June 1771] at London aforesaid in the parish and ward aforesaid in pursuance of the said Articles did nominate one William Preston, brother of the said Richard, to be copartner with the said John Kingston in the stead of the said John Preston, nephew to the said Richard, in his the said Richard's trade and business, and then and there gave notice thereof to the said John Kingston and which said William Preston was then and there ready and willing to become copartner with the said John Kingston accordingly, and that he the said Richard then & there was ready and willing to quit and leave off and always hath been ready to quit and leave off his said trade and business and to yield up and surrender the same unto the said John Kingston and the said William Preston, brother of the said Richard, being the person so nominated by the said Richard, as aforesaid, together with all the stock which was then remaining [evaluated as aforesaid], but the said John Kingston then and there refused and always hath refused to become copartner with the said William Preston . . . . And this the said Richard is ready to verify, wherefore he prays judgment if the said John Kingston ought to have or maintain his said action thereof against him, &ca.

7. And the said Richard for further plea in this behalf by leave of the Court . . . says that the said John Kingston ought not to have or maintain his said action against the said Richard because protesting that the said Richard always after the making of the said Articles was ready and willing to do, perform, and fulfill all things in the said Articles contained on his part . . ., the said Richard says that the said John Kingston hath not at any time hitherto caused or procured good and sufficient security to be given unto the said Richard Preston for the payment of two hundred and fifty pounds . . . in satisfaction and in lieu of and as and for one moiety of the monthly produce of the said stock unto the said Richard Preston . . . monthly and every month until the value of the said stock should be reduced to the sum of four thousand pounds . . . . And this the said Richard is ready to verify, wherefore he prays judgment if the said John ought to have or maintain his said action against him the said Richard, &ca.

Bartholomew Lucas

Replication & Demurrer:

And now the said John as to the said plea of the said Richard by him thirdly above pleaded in bar says that he the said John by reason of anything therein alledged ought not to be barred from having or maintaining his said action thereof against him because he says that the said plea thirdly above pleaded in bar and the matter therein contained are not sufficient in law to bar or preclude him the said John from having or maintaining his said action against the said Richard, to which said plea in manner and form as the same is above made he the said John is under no necessity nor is he in any wise bound by the law of the land to answer. And this he is ready to verify, wherefore for want of a sufficient plea in this behalf the said John prays judgment and his debt together with his damage by him sustained by reason of the detaining of the said debt, to be adjudged to him, &ca.

And the said John as to the said plea of the said Richard by him fourthly above pleaded in bar says that he the said John by reason of any thing therein alledged ought not to be barred from having or maintaining his said action thereof against him because he says that he the said Richard at the end and expiration of the said term of one year and one quarter . . . was not ready to quit and leave off his said trade and business and to yield up and surrender the same unto the said John and to some other person . . . together with all the stock then remaining in his said trade at a fair valuation . . ., and this he prays may be inquired of by the country and the said Richard doth the like, &ca.

And the said John as to the said plea of the said Richard by him fifthly above pleaded in bar says that he the said John by reason of any thing therein alledged ought not to be barred . . . because he says that he the said Richard at the end and expiration of the said term of one year and one quarter . . . and for a reasonable space of time then next following was not ready to quit and leave off his said trade and business and to yield up and surrender the same . . . [or to give up the stock], & this he prays may be inquired of by the country, and the said Richard doth the like, &ca.

And the said John as to the said plea of the said Richard by him sixthly above pleaded in bar says that he the said John by reason of any thing therein alledged ought not to be barred . . . because . . . the said John Kingston did not refuse to become a copartner with the said William Preston in manner and form as the said Richard hath in his said plea by him sixthly above pleaded in bar alledged & this he prays may be inquired of by the country, and the said Richard doth the like, &ca.

And the said John as to the said plea of the said Richard by him lastly above pleaded in bar says that he the said John by any thing therein contained ought not to be barred . . . because he says that the same plea and the matter therein contained are not sufficient in Law to bar or preclude him the said John from having or maintaining his said action against the said Richard . . . nor is he in any wise obliged by the law of the land to answer, and this he is ready to verify, wherefore for want of a sufficient plea in this behalf the said John prays judgment and his debt together with his damages by reason of the detaining of the said debt in the said Declaration mentioned to be adjudged to him, &ca.

Francis Buller

Joinder:

And the said Richard saith that the said plea of him the said Richard thirdly above pleaded in bar and the matter in the same contained are sufficient in law to bar the said John from having his said action thereof maintained against the said Richard ... and because the said John hath not answered the said plea nor hitherto in any manner denied the same the said Richard as before prays judgment . . . .

And the said Richard says that the said plea by him ... lastly above pleaded in bar and the matter therein contained are sufficient in law to bar the said John from having his said action thereof maintained against him ... and because the said John hath not answered the said plea nor hitherto in any manner denied the same the said Richard as before prays judgment . . . . And because the Court [of King's Bench] now here will advise amongst themselves what judgment to give in the premises whereof the said parties have put themselves upon the judgment of the Court here before they give judgment thereon a day is therefore given to the said parties to come before our Lord the King at Westminster ... for that the Court of our said Lord the King now here is not yet advised thereof. And as well to try the several issues aforesaid above joined on occasion of the premises whereof the said parties have put themselves upon the judgment of the Court in case judgment shall be therein given for the said John. Let a Jury come before our Lord the King at Westminster . . . .

Appendix 2

Boone v. *Eyre*

Lincoln's Inn Library, MSS Dampier,
Ashurst Paper Book 41

Demurrer, 23 April 1777.

[Ashurst's notes on the backside of the first page of the Demurrer Book (underscoring by Ashurst)]

Buller for Plaintiff:

Question whether defendant can dispute the title of plaintiff. The Plea [is] bad. If it relates to all the Negroes, it is denying the deed. But it goes to that which was not conveyed – viz., all, in the Declaration, whereas seven are said to be dead.

But the deed don't import he was seized or possessed of them, for it states they are in mortgage. [It] don't say [he] had no right, subject, &c.

Further, the Plea [is] bad because the land is conveyed. Shall he keep that & pay nothing because plaintiff had not title to the Negroes? Supposing that were true, the words performing, &ca can't amount to condition precedent.

One covenant can't be pleaded against another. This [is] not a case in which the damages are not equal. 3 Lev. 41, *Cole* v *Chadwick*. So here the damages on the respective covenants are not equal. Plaintiff might not have title to one – yet [that would be] no reason why [defendant] should have all the rest for nothing. Ergo [plaintiff] must have recourse to the covenant.

Baldwin for defendant:

The question [is] whether this [is] a covenant precedent or mutual. If mutual I agree [it] can't be set off.

Defendant purchases an Estate & all the Negroes. [He is] to pay 160£ per annum – this to arise from the profits of the plantation.

The Negroes had been removed.
These covenants [are] considered as precedent:
3 Leonard 219, Brocas's Case
1 Ld. Raymond 662. Thorp v. Thorp

Cur:

Whether precedent or subsequent must depend on the nature of the case.

This in its nature must be considered as mutual & the part[ies] take mutual remedies.

Judgment for plaintiff

[Declaration (edited) (underscoring by Ashurst)]

Hilary Term 1777. Roll 1455. Lee.

Middlesex (to wit) Be it remembered that on Thursday next after 8 days of St Hilary in this same term ... comes John Boone by John Santer his Attorney and brings in the Court [of King's Bench] of a plea of covenant broken and there are pledges for the prosecution .... John Boone complains against Francis Eyre, Esquire, being in the Custody of the Marshall of the Marshalsea for [the King] ... whereas by a certain Indenture made on the 28th day of February ... 1775 at Westminster ... between the said John Boone and Diana his wife of the one part and the said Francis Eyre by the name and description of Francis Eyre of Surry Street Westminster ... of the other part ... that whereas the said John Boone being seized & possessed of a plantation or estate in the parish of St John in the Island of Dominica called Capuchin with the Negroes, Cattle and Appurtanences, the great part thereof was subject to a Mortgage or Mortgages of £11,500 to Thomas and Rowland Hunt of London, Merchants, and also to an annuity of £160 sterling, payable to Ezekial Lewis for his life, contracted and agreed with the said Francis Eyre for the sale thereof to him by an agreement in writing dated the 18th day of April then last, whereby the said John Boone agreed to sell the said Francis Eyre the said plantation, 112 Negroes, stock & other particulars & all other his the said John Boone's estate in Dominica in consideration of £500 sterling and of £160 sterling a year payable half yearly in London for the life of the said John Boone and Diana his wife and the survivor of them and to convey the same forthwith to the said Francis Eyre free of all incumbrances except a debt of £11,500 sterling to the said Messrs Thomas and Rowland Hunt and an annuity of £160 sterling a year to the said Ezekial Lewis then of Cambridge in New England with general warranty of all the premises except of Negroes said to be dead, instead whereof one Negroe in New York and another, in Mary Gallant, were to be conveyed against all persons and all usual common covenants in the plantation deed, and at the signing thereof the said John Boone received of the said Francis Eyre in case £167 in part of the said £500. And whereas the said John Boone had been paid by the said Francis Eyre the said sum of £500 & also £80 as for the first half year's annuity. It was witnessed that for & in consideration of the said £500 before the sealing and delivery thereof well and truly paid to the said John Boone and Diana his wife in manner therein after mentioned, the said John Boone and Diana his wife and each of them did give, grant, bargain, sell, alien, remise, release, ratify & confirm unto the said Francis Eyre in his actual possession then being by virtue of a bargain & sale thereof to him for one whole year made by Indenture bearing date next before the day of the date of the said Indenture & by force of the Statute for transferring of uses into possession, and to his heirs and assignees, all that and those the plantation & estate of the said John Boone in the parish of St John, formerly called the Quarter of Grandance in the said Island of Dominica consisting of several lots or pieces of land erected into a plantation called Capuchin, with the appurtenances, and all and every other lots, pieces or parcels of land of or belonging to the said John Boone or to any person or persons in trust for him in the said parish of St John or elsewhere in the said island of Dominica, together with the water mill, boiling house, curing house, & all other houses, messuages, tenements, erections, and buildings whatsoever to the said lands and premises belonging or thereon or on any part thereof erected and built & all the coppers, still, worms, worm tubs, cisterns, coolers, saddles, carts, wagons, horses, mules, asses, oxen, bulls, cows, sheep & stock of every kind, plantation utensils of every kind, household furniture & chattels of every kind in upon or about the said lands and house & appurtenances whatsoever to the said plantation, lands, buildings and premises with the appurtenances belonging or appertaining. And also all deeds, plans, evidence and writings whatsoever to the said lands, premises or any part thereof belonging. And also all and singular the following Negroes, that is to say, George a Driver, Caesar a Driver, Marshall Gill, Valentine Barnes, Bristol George a Boiler, Ebonezer[?] George, Jack Lawley, Andrew Kingstone, Caesar Thomas [etc. – scores of names listed, including women and children – e.g. after a number of men are named, 'Negroe Women and children[:] Venus and 3 children, Phillis & 2 children, June, Sarah and her child Billy, Moll Rose and 1 child [etc.].] ... together with the said Negroe called Pompey at New York and the said Negroe called Antonia at Mary Gallant and all other the Negroes and slaves of the said John Boone and Diana his wife and the reversion and reversions, remainder and remainders yearly & other rents, issues, services, and profits of all and singular the said lands, buildings, Negroes and the issue of the females above mentioned and every part and parcel thereof with the appurtenances, and also all the estate, right, title in use, trust, possession, equity, and power of redemption under the said mortgages, to Thomas & Rowland Hunt or any other person or persons or otherwise howsoever claim and demand whatsoever of the said John Boone and Diana his wife and each of them of into and out of the said lands, plantations, Negroes, cattle & premises therein beforementioned or intended to be thereby sold and released into and to the use of the said Francis Eyre, his heirs and assignees ... subject nevertheless ... to [the £160 annuity to Boone & wife on terms specified] .... And the said John Boone did ... covenant, promise, grant and agree to and with the said Francis Eyre ... in manner & form following, that is to say, that he the said John Boone then had in himself full power, true title and good and lawful authority to bargain, sell and release the said plantation, Negroes & premises, with the appurtenances, unto the said Francis Eyre ... and that it should & might be lawful to & for the said Francis Eyre ... into & upon the said plantations, Negroes & premises peaceably & quietly to enter, have, hold, use, occupy, possess & enjoy & to take & receive the rents, issues, produce & profits thereof ... & also the crop of the then last year ... without the lawful let, suit, trouble, denial, eviction, or interruption of or by the said John Boone ... and that free and clear and freely and clearly acquitted, exonerated, and discharged or otherwise by the said John Boone ... well & sufficiently saved, defended, kept harmless, and indemnified of from and against all former & other gifts, grants, bargains, sales, leases [etc.] ... whatsoever, save & except the said annuity of £160 a year to the said Ezekial Lewis & a sum of £11,500 due to the said Thomas & Rowland Hunt ... [and Boone will do anything else needed to make all this happen]. And the said Francis Eyre did ... covenant, promise, grant & agree to & with the said John Boone & Diana his wife, that he the said John Boone well, truly & faithfully doing, fulfilling & performing all & singular the covenants, clauses, recitals & agreements in the said Indenture contained, that he the said Francis Eyre ... should & would well & truly pay or cause to be paid in London unto the said John Boone ... from thenceforth & by half yearly payments during all the natural life of him the said John Boone the annuity or clear yearly rent of £160 .... And although the said John Boone hath well & truly performed, kept & fulfilled all and singular the covenants & agreements in the said Indenture contained on his part ... yet protesting that the said Francis Eyre hath not performed, kept & fulfilled any of the said covenants & agreements in the said Indenture contained on his part ... the said John Boone in fact says that £240 of the said annuity of £160 a year payable to the said John Boone as aforesaid for one year & the half of another year ended on the 28th of August ... 1776 on that day & year were & still are unpaid to the said John Boone ... which said sum of £240 the said Francis Eyre ought to have paid but hath not yet paid to the said John Boone according to the form & effect of the said covenant in that behalf made with the said John Boone in the said Indenture set forth. And so the said John Boone says that the said Francis Eyre although often requested hath not kept the said covenants so by him made with the said John Boone aforesaid, but hath broken the same and to keep the same with the said John, he the said Francis Eyre hath hitherto wholly refused and still doth refuse, to the damage of the said John Boone of £500 & thereof he brings suit, &ca.

Plea:

And the said Francis by Brook Allen Bridges, his Attorney, comes and defends the wrong and injury when &ca. And saith that the said John ought not to have or maintain his aforesaid action against him because he says that he the said John at the time of the making of the said Indenture in the said Declaration mentioned was not seized, possessed of or intitled unto the said Negroes in the said Declaration mentioned & so the said Francis says that he the said John had not then in himself full power, true title, and good and lawful authority to bargain, sell & release the said Negroes in the said Declaration mentioned unto the said Francis in manner & form as the said John hath above alledged, and this he is ready to verify. Wherefore he prays judgment if the said John ought to have or maintain his aforesaid action thereof against him, &ca.

Mr Baldwin

Demurrer:

And the said John as to the said Plea of the said Francis by him above pleaded in bar says that the said Plea and the matters therein contained are not sufficient in law to bar or preclude him the said John from having or maintaining his said action thereof against the said Francis to which said Plea in manner and form as the same is above pleaded he the said John is under no necessity nor is he bound by the laws of the land in any manner to answer. Wherefore, for want of a sufficient plea in this behalf the said John prays judgment and his damages by reason of the premises to be adjudged to him, &ca.

Francis Buller

Joinder:

And the said Francis says that the Plea aforesaid in manner and form aforesaid by him the said Francis above pleased & the matter in the same contained are good & sufficient in law to bar the said John from having his action aforesaid against him the said Francis, which said Plea and the matter therein contained he the said Francis is ready to verify and prove as the Court shall award. And because the said John hath not answered the said plea nor hitherto in any manner denied the same, he the said Francis as before prays judgment and that the said John may be barred from having his said action against him &c. But because the Court [of King's Bench] is not yet advised what judgment to give of & concerning the premises, a day is therefore given to the parties aforesaid to come before our Lord the King at Westminster . . . to hear judgment thereon for that the Court [of King's Bench] is not yet advised thereof.

10

Words, Words, Words: Making Sense of Legal Judgments, 1875–1940

Steve Hedley

This essay is about changes in the style of legal judgments over the period 1875–1940. It might prevent some misconceptions if I state immediately that this is not naturally how I would describe my current researches, which are really about contract law and the judges who produced it. I am attempting to integrate the history of contract law with the history of the people who actually produced it, the judges, the lawyers and the academics. Obviously, law reports come into this. So the subject here is the changes that took place in the contents of the law reports over the period (say) 1875–1940. In other words, what counted as a good legal justification over that period, and how it changed within that period, and why. I am not confining myself today to contract cases here by any means, though I am sure a bias for private law over public law, and for common law over statute, will quickly become apparent.

First, what are the changes? Length. Judgments in the law reports got longer and longer over the period I am considering. The reports of course contain other things as well, such as the head-note, but the bulk of the reports consists of the judgments, and it is the judgments that are getting longer. Take the first volume per year of the Queen's Bench reports throughout the period, and count how many pages the first twenty cases took. You have a clear upward trend – something like a four-fold increase in the size of the average report from 1875 to 1940. Note that there is no similar trend in sentence length. The inter-war judges did not use more complex language than their predecessors to justify their decisions. They just used more of it.

So the reports were longer. Yet when you start looking at the sorts of reasons given by the judges, you notice a strange opposing trend. The range of possible arguments and possible materials to justify decisions gets narrower.

References to civilian sources became fewer and fewer: you cannot write a serious history of the development of private law in the nineteenth century without referring to the civilians at great length, whereas it becomes easy to ignore their increasingly minimal influence as this century progresses.[1]

More generally, reference to textbooks of any provenance became less and less common. A rule seems to spring up that it is wrong to cite a textbook if the author is still living – which ensures of course that in a rapidly moving legal system the only textbooks you can cite are usually out of date. (In parentheses, it is actually very difficult to work out what the position was here. It is commonly asserted that there was a rule that live authors may not be cited, sometimes on the ground that dead text writers cannot change their minds. But it is not merely a case of a rule being more honoured in the breach than the observance, but rather of there being good reason to doubt whether there was ever such a rule at all.)[2] Be that as it may, there are fewer and fewer citations from textbooks as time draws on; a notable fact, given the positive explosion of legal publishing. It seems to have been decided that more means worse.

Appeals to custom become fewer and fewer. Of course, this development is not quite what it seems; as Arthurs has shown,[3] the disappearance of custom is only apparent: local and special jurisdictions disappear *as courts* but reappear as arbitration; commercial customs drop out of sight *as custom* but reappear in standard forms. So from one point of view the change is simply at the verbal level. But that is precisely the level I am concerned with here. Custom as such is no longer acknowledged as a significant source of law.[4]

Citation of foreign cases also drops considerably. References to US cases are not uncommon in the 1870s and 1880s but are rare thereafter.[5] How genuine the English courts ever really were in trying to achieve empire-wide consistent application of the law is a matter of opinion, but at the strictly verbal level we can say that they at least claimed to be promoting this in the mid Victorian period, but not afterwards.

---

[1] On civilian influences in (for example) contract see P. Hamburger, 'The development of the nineteenth-century consensus theory of contract' *Law and History Review*, 7 (1989), p. 241.

[2] Much of the evidence for the lack of authority accorded to textbooks is very indirect; for example H. Cecil, *Just within the Law* (London, 1975) pp. 50–51. For a clear example of someone who evidently knew of no such rule, but presumably would have done had it existed, see F. Pearson, *Memories of a KC's Clerk* (London, 1935), pp. 62–63.

[3] H. Arthurs, *Without the Law* (Toronto, 1985), especially ch. 3.

[4] On the relation between custom and standard forms see R. Ferguson, 'The Adjudication of Commercial Disputes and the Legal System in Modern England' *British Journal of Law and Society*, 7 (1980), p. 141. The view that standard terms *are* law in all but name is of course highly relevant here; see W.D. Slawson, 'The New Meaning of Contract: The Transformation of Contract Law by Standard Forms', *University of Pittsburgh Law Review*, 46 (1984), p. 21.

[5] This may or may not have had something to do with the arrival (in 1865) and retirement (in 1882) of Judah P. Benjamin, on whom see E. Evans, *Judah P. Benjamin: The Jewish Confederate* (New York, 1989).

Appeals to what we would now think of, anachronistically, as other academic disciplines vanish by the turn of the century. Bramwell and others in the mid nineteenth century were happy to quote Adam Smith in support of their arguments. Yet there was never any question of their successors quoting Keynes: the very idea is ridiculous. Law and economics were by then separate subjects, and for that matter they remain so in the UK, *deo volente*.[6] The criminal lawyers tell a parallel story of the initial acceptance of some criminological ideas early in the nineteenth century, but these insights then being written in stone, and not discarded until long after everyone but the lawyers had rejected them; perhaps the most notable example is the continued use of the archaic M'Naghten rules for insanity, even today.

So, in these various respects, the definition of what constituted a good legal argument narrowed but the length of judgments got longer. What happened was that more and more appeal was made to domestic precedents, and to them alone. The nature of those references also changed.[7] If we compare the authority of domestic precedent as at (say) 1800 and 1950, various points stand out. The very much greater extent to which the later judges say they are *bound* by precedent, and the correspondingly greater apparent freedom of the earlier judges. Moreover, the reasons given for saying that an earlier precedent is binding change. When in the earlier period a precedent is said to be binding it may be for a number of reasons, together or singly: the eminence of the court which decided it; the harm done by not following it (as where it is said that many legal instruments had already been framed on the assumption that it was the law); or simply the reason of the thing – it was not at all uncommon to regard a decision as binding or not depending largely on whether it seemed to be correct. And it was often the *number* of precedents that was important. A succession of precedents, none of which in itself would have been regarded as a binding reason for decision, became unanswerable by sheer weight of numbers. The precedents, it has been said, hunted in packs.

Contrast this with the rigidity of the later jurisprudence, as exemplified in the ruling in *Young* v. *Bristol Aeroplane Co.*[8] Here the stress is on the single binding decision, and the enquiry is simply into the status of the court which laid down the earlier precedent: the decisions of the court

---

[6] Cf P.S. Atiyah, *The Rise and Fall of Freedom of Contract* (Oxford, 1979), especially pp. 293–94, 363–65, 373–74, 606–9, 617, 679–703.

[7] For another approach see J. Evans, 'Changes in the Doctrine of Precedent during the Nineteenth Century', in Goldstein (ed.), *Precedent in Law* (Oxford, 1987). Once due allowance has been made for Evans' rather different methods and topics of interest, I do not think that there is any incompatibility between Evans' conclusions and mine.

[8] [1944] KB 718.

of appeal bind it for the future, except in the rare cases where following this rule is impossible, or would entail ignoring an even higher authority – statute, or the House of Lords. The alleged need for certainty is no longer confined to the need for security of transactions to be preserved, but is used in a broad way to justify the entire notion of precedent.

The important point about the later view is perhaps not so much its detail – though its abstract and mechanical character is significant – but the point that the Court of Appeal were in a position to insist on it. So practice no longer varies from judge to judge. A new area of law emerges, which can then be discussed. So perhaps the point about Robert Wright's discussion of Precedent is not so much that he was, as a law lord writing in an academic journal, putting forward controversial views, as that there was at last a doctrine for people to have views about.[9] A clean slate to write on.

There are other, less tangible aspects of style, which cannot be tackled simply by counting references, but nonetheless can be shown with reasonable certainty to have changed. Various ways of putting it can be imagined. For Stevens, who seems to prefer elaborate judgments as some kind of guarantee that the case has been properly debated, the short Victorian judgments indicate bigotry: so he is scathing in his criticism of (for example) Lord Halsbury's terse judgments, his apparent lack of doubt over anything, and his expressed contempt for anyone who *did* have doubts.[10] Milsom, whose preferences as to judgments are otherwise, put it this way: in the later period, 'Longer judgments cite more cases to settle smaller questions less clearly. Sometimes indeed the reader . . . finishes without knowing quite what has been settled, sure only that the intention was not to be "wrong" in the sense of being inconsistent with the numerous authorities discussed . . .'[11] Atiyah sees it as a move from a morality that stressed general tendencies (so leaving the judges free to pontificate in general terms without much reference to the facts), to a more situational morality, which necessarily required a full investigation.[12]

The Victorian style was very brusque. If Lord Cockburn CJ thought a plaintiff's claim could be answered simply by saying 'I have never heard of such an action as this', then that is all he would say, and that is what appears in the law reports; never mind that the judges below had said something different.[13] Moreover, there is a decided absence of doubt in these judicial

<hr />

[9] 'Precedents', *Cambridge Law Journal*, 9 (1940), p. 118.

[10] R. Stevens, *Law and Politics* (Chapel Hill, NC, 1978), pp. 120–21.

[11] 'The Past and Future of Judge-Made Law', in *Studies in the History of the Common Law* (London, 1985), pp. 217–18.

[12] P.S. Atiyah, *From Principles to Pragmatism* (Oxford, 1978).

[13] For example *Giles* v. *Walker* (1890), 24 QBD 656, where his full judgment reads: 'I have never heard of such an action as this. There can be no duty as between adjoining occupiers to cut the thistles, which are the natural growth of the soil. The appeal must be allowed.'

pronouncements. The motto that George Jessel MR supposedly took for his own – 'I am often wrong, but never in doubt' – could equally have been claimed by many of his contemporaries. It is perhaps very hard to accept that we do not know, and never will know, precisely what lay behind that unnatural certainty.

It seems clear to me however that we would be making a mistake if we did not look, as well as within legal culture, also outside it. It is not just the judges who were dogmatic. Houghton's famous work *The Victorian Frame of Mind* was of course not particularly concerned with lawyers, but much of what he says on dogmatism could easily be applied to the law reports.[14] It is not so much, Houghton argues, that the Victorians believed in the existence of universal truths, true at all times and in all cultures. They did; but then we too believe in truth. Where the Victorians were different was in believing that they had *found* truth. And yet it was only because the grounds for this confidence were ebbing away, because irreconcilable differences of view were beginning to appear, that the opportunity to dogmatise arose. 'What a magnificent opportunity for the ego to assert itself', Houghton comments, 'when nothing is settled and everyone is arguing and no one else seems smart enough to come up with the answers – except me . . .'[15]

As a final point about the less tangible aspects of style, we might consider the use of what we might loosely (and inaccurately) call non-legal arguments. Care is needed in definitions here. There is no principle, and there never has been, that what passes for a legal argument has to be totally different from what passes for a good reason in other spheres of life; merely because an argument appeals to morality or to practical convenience does not rule it out as a possible legal argument. And, on the other side of the coin, not even the wildest of the Victorian moralistic judges quite denied that law and morals were separate, in theory at least.

Nonetheless, with all those caveats, I would argue that, overall, the difference between Victorian legal reasoning on the one hand, and Victorian reasoning on practical issues with a moral element on the other, was considerably narrower than the same gap at a later date. Law and morals, as they shifted, drew apart. Victorian judgments have what reads today as a very moralistic tone, a willingness to condemn by reference to standards the judge feels no need to justify. It is only rarely that the judges met a counter-view they felt compelled to reason with: as for example in the notorious case *in re Besant*; though even there Jessel's rejection of Besant's atheistic and feminist views was based not so much on precedent as on his repeated claim that, 'as a man of the world', he

---

[14] W.D. Houghton, *The Victorian Frame of Mind, 1830–1870* (New Haven, 1957), especially ch. 6.

[15] *Ibid.*, pp. 138–39.

knew better than she what was good for her children.[16] The inter-war judges have none of this certainty; their justification is precedent, and if the reasonableness of the precedent is challenged they tend to retort that reasonableness did not come into it. Precedent bound because it proceeded from a higher authority, not because it was reasonable.

So that is an overall picture of the shift in the *type* of reasons given; and this overall picture has surprising features. The judges have more and more to say for themselves, but rather than providing an opportunity for diversity it seems to have been the occasion for the imposition of uniformity. At a time when there was a positive explosion of knowledge in other domains, the lawyers themselves become more and more narrow. If the main way lawyers develop new ideas is by stealing them from other people, and so the most creative and innovative legal developments should occur when there is a rich new seam of ideas to plagiarise – a view which Simpson has cogently argued[17] – why is it that the very opposite occurred, at what was potentially the time for great innovation indeed?

In considering this question, I want to digress somewhat into the whys and wherefores of intellectual history, and distinguish first between two different possible types of explanation for the development of some intellectual system or discipline. In describing and explaining the development of an intellectual system, we can distinguish between an 'internal' point of view which seeks to share the point of view of those within the discipline, and an 'external' point of view which does not.

For many systems this is obvious: anyone who writes the history of a religion, for example, will have to decide whether they are going to treat the tenets of that religion as unproblematical or not; the choice here can hardly be evaded. Or again, in studying the rise of a particular political creed, either we treat it as evident and uncomplicated that it gained adherents, or we treat this as quite baffling, and in need of explanation. So equally in writing the history of law, the historian cannot but notice judges justifying their behaviour by reference to this law or that, and the legal historian cannot but take a view on whether to treat these references as unproblematical, or to regard them as part of the problem to be solved.

We see immediately that the writer of an 'internal' history will be attracted to very different explanations from those which convince the 'external' historian. 'Internal' historians of law are inclined to trace the development of law in a smooth and reasonable progression from less enlightened views to the wisdom of the current position, whereas 'external' historians are less convinced of the wisdom of the modern position, and in

---

[16] *In re Besant* (1879), 11 ChD 508.

[17] A.W.B. Simpson, 'Innovation in Nineteenth-Century Contract Law', *Law Quarterly Review*, 91 (1975), p. 247.

any event cannot see how events in one century can be influenced by what happens afterwards. 'Internal' historians try to absorb the assumptions of their subjects, and use them to explain why their subjects' behaviour was perfectly reasonable; 'external' historians start with the behaviour, and use it to show the strange assumptions their subjects must have been making.

So 'internal' and 'external' viewpoints often lead to very different explanations for the same phenomena. Further, the phenomena themselves often look different. If we compare anthropological work on the magical practices of the Azande tribe with accounts that might have been produced by the magicians themselves, we immediately see that not simply are the accounts different, but it is problematical even to say that they describe the same thing. An account of magic that leaves out the central assumption that it actually works is so different from an 'internal' account that assumes magic *does* work that we may doubt that it is really describing the same thing. The very subject-matter is different: the 'internal' historian is studying magic, whereas the 'external' historian is studying ritual beliefs and practices. Or again, an 'internal' history of injury actions against employers in the nineteenth century would discuss the development of legal principle; an 'external' history would talk about how many people actually received compensation, and would no more be surprised that far fewer people received compensation than you might have assumed from the tort books than Evans-Pritchard was surprised at the disparity between the Azande magicians' claims and their actual results.[18] The 'external' historian expects nothing else.

So the accounts given by 'internal' and 'external' historians may be very different. And whenever these different schools meet head on, there are the most ferocious quarrels, for each is ignoring what the other thinks of as central. You see this whenever practising scientists dispute the history of science with the philosophers of science. How can you write a coherent history of science, the scientists ask, if you leave out the most important point, namely that the process produces truth? To which the philosophers retort, Why should we be expected to regard your current version of science as truth, when you scientists were telling us a different truth a few decades ago and will no doubt be telling a different one again in a few decades time? What is wrong with simply asking questions about the process itself? One might, indeed, imagine similar exchanges of insults if the Azande magicians ever caught up with Evans-Pritchard: of course you will misunderstand the point of magical practices if you dogmatically assume that magic does not work, the magicians would say. We can imagine the retort of the anthropologist to that.

There are many examples of such squabbles amongst legal historians, too. Take the rather heated dispute over whether the judiciary were biased

---

[18] Evans-Pritchard, *Witchcraft Oracles and Magic among the Azande* (Oxford, 1980).

against the nascent trade unions. From an 'external' point of view it is all rather obvious. Given the judges' backgrounds, it would be very surprising if they did *not* have a low opinion of the average trade unionist. Both general voting patterns, and the fact that trade unions lost almost every important case they were ever involved in, lead rapidly to an unsurprising conclusion. To the more 'internal' historians, however, this is problematical indeed. To them, it amounts to accusing the judges of bias, to which they indignantly retort that there is no evidence to that effect. The simple and obvious point about the judges' politics has no place in the 'internal' scheme, and is accordingly rejected.

I have said that this contrast between 'internal' and 'external' approaches is by no means confined to law. But which approach is used very much depends on the subject-matter. It is very hard indeed for anyone from our culture to write an 'internal' history of practices we find superstitious or otherwise unreasonable. Again, there are some practices which make no sense from an 'external' point of view. Despite some bold attempts,[19] there really is not anything much to say about pure mathematics except from an 'internal' point of view. If you do not accept that the mathematicians really are doing what they say they are doing, the whole business is a meaningless ritual with pencils and blackboards and strange diagrams.

Yet many fields of endeavour can be made sense of from both perspectives. So far as law is concerned, both belief and non-belief in the integrity and self-sufficiency of the legal system are commonplace. The 'internal point of view' is familiar enough amongst jurisprudes after Hart's arguments in its favour;[20] and his inability to imagine what a believable 'external point of view' could look like is par for the course in this area. My object here is not, indeed, to argue for or against an 'external' point of view of law; that is a far harder question than the one I am posing. My point is rather that the particular development I am describing, namely the shifting and narrowing of the types of reasons given in legal judgments, makes no sense at all from an 'internal' perspective, and that explanations must be sought through an 'external' viewpoint.

So, returning to law alone: 'Why not an 'internal' history of the narrowing of legal argument?' you might ask. There is no reason against, in principle.

---

[19] For example E. Livingston, *The Ethnomethodological Foundations of Mathematics* (London, 1986).

[20] On Hart's famous 'internal point of view' see H. Hart, *The Concept of Law* (Oxford, 1961), ch. 4. Those more familiar with the philosophies of law and of science will realise that very little of what I have said is inspired by Hart, and rather a lot by Bloor, *Knowledge and Social Imagery* (2nd edn Chicago, 1991), ch. 4 and Latour, *Science in Action* (Milton Keynes, 1987), not to mention Maine's famous reference to a 'double and inconsistent set of ideas' about law in *Ancient Law* (London, 1861), pp. 80–81, a view which seems remarkably like Latour's.

There is no reason why the judges of a particular jurisdiction should not all get together, collectively declare that they had been insufficiently long-winded in the past, and resolve to use more words in future. For that matter, some of them might have met secretly: 'Look chaps, I know it's a bore but the word is that that we're just not saying enough when we give judgment! Buck your ideas up!' Or perhaps – and we are really going into the realms of fantasy here – perhaps persistent academic complaints at poorly-reasoned judgments might have been taken to heart by the judges, and incorporated into changes in judicial technique. It is not impossible.

None of these suggestions are, in fact, impossible ones. It is just that there is not any substantial evidence that it happened that way. There is no evidence of any widespread dissatisfaction with judicial technique generally. There are complaints enough at individual decisions, of course. You can find the occasional judge who hated Roman law and did his best to make counsel look silly if they cited it;[21] the decline of the more ancient and obscure citations might be blamed on Lord Macnaghten's gentle mockery in *Van Grutten* v. *Foxwell*,[22] which was neither the first nor the last occasion when *Shelley*'s case became a butt for humour; or for that matter the decline of citations from textbooks might have been premised on the view that the academics who wrote them must have been failed barristers.[23] But while there are examples of all of these attitudes being taken, in each case these seem merely to have been personal and idiosyncratic views. As for the increasing prolixity, and the changes in the doctrine of precedent, these seem not to have been noticed by anyone until very late in the day, and those who did notice them did so with regret.[24]

So the 'internal' point of view provides no explanation, and we are thrown back on the 'external' point of view, on trying to explain what is going on by changes to background assumptions. I will cover five general and overlapping heads: changes in what law was; changes in what facts were; changes in who judges were; changes in what Parliament was; and changes in accountability.

1. Law

There have always been some lawyers ready to claim that under all the rubble of the centuries there is order and rationality, that the disorder

---

[21] For example Reginald Brett (Viscount Esher): see Witt, *Life in the Law*, p. 107. Compare also 'The proud parent who did his best for Alfred', in 'O' (=Theo Mathew), *Forensic Fables* (London, 1961), p. 155.

[22] [1897] AC 658.

[23] For Lord Alverstone quoted to this effect (if at third hand) see *Holmes–Laski letters*, p. 1439 (13 May 1933).

[24] For example R. Wright, 'Precedents', *Cambridge Law Journal* 9 (1940), pp. 118, 127 ('It may be that the true moral is that judgments should be shorter'.)

is only apparent. It is indeed only relatively late that this can sensibly be regarded as anything other than a bluff.[25] Before the middle of the nineteenth century anyone seeking elucidation of the alleged general principles of the law would probably have been referred to the many legal maxims; yet these maxims were themselves very haphazard; most attempts to order them in any other way than alphabetically soon collapsed under the weight of their own contradictions.

So anyone learning their law before, say, 1850 would have to come to terms with its unsystematic character. The more systematic texts we are used to today began to be written rather earlier than that, but were not yet the norm. University teaching of law hardly existed. The most obvious, and commonest, way of learning the law was by following a lawyer around and seeing what he did, which while arcane and ritualistic was at least fairly concrete.

The young John Duke Coleridge, then twenty-four and eagerly following in his father's footsteps as a barrister, wrote to him in 1844: '. . . I think the legal studies get on fairly. I am terribly ignorant and I feel quite in a maze when cases and deeds are put before me as yet . . . Only the worst of it is, that it is all *rudis indigestaque moles*, and for aught I can see, is like to remain so. How did you *systematise* your law? . . .'[26] The latin tag *rudis indigestaque moles* is highly suggestive: it is a quote from Ovid, describing the confused state of matter before the creation of the world:

> Chaos, a raw and undivided mass
> Naught but a lifeless bulk, with warring seeds
> Of ill-joined elements compressed together
> . . . all objects were at odds, since in one mass
> Cold essence fought with hot, and moist with dry
> And hard with soft and light with things of weight.[27]

Or so the common law seemed to the young Coleridge.

Three decades on, with a little more experience of the common law, Coleridge, now attorney-general, at least knew the answer to the question which had troubled him, namely: 'How do you systematise your law?' The answer was, of course, that you do not. And that is precisely why, he told the House of Commons, it would be a mistake to institute a series of public lectures on the common law with a view to training barristers. Lectures are

[25] See A.W.B. Simpson, 'The Legal Treatise and Legal Theory', in E. Ives and A. Manchester (eds), *Law, Litigants and the Legal Profession* (London, 1983); idem, 'The Rise and Fall of the Legal Treatise: Legal Principles and the Forms of Legal Literature', *University of Chicago Law Review* 48 (1981), p. 632.

[26] John Duke Coleridge to John Taylor Coleridge 8 December 1844; quoted E. Coleridge (ed.), *Life and Correspondence of Lord Coleridge* (London, 1904), i, p. 163.

[27] Ovid, *Metamorphoses* (1962) (translated by A. Melville), book 1.

systematic treatments of their subject-matter, he explained, whereas the common law is irredeemably *un*systematic; the very idea of such lectures was therefore, he said, 'pure delusion . . . [A] knowledge of English law can only be obtained by practice'.[28] It would perhaps be unfair to say that he was *proud* of the lack of system; he claimed, after all, to be in favour of codifying the law, and there is some evidence that he meant it. But what was true was that he was perfectly at home in an unstructured system; and, as a judge, he felt free to be correspondingly anarchic and eclectic in his reasoning.

The change brought about by the prevalence of systematic treatises in the modern style, and the use of these treatise not simply as reference books but as the means of initiation into the mysteries of the law, must have been profound, and was, I argue, one major factor in the increasing technicality of post-Victorian judges. The common law always held out the promise that it could resolve particular cases by reference to past precedents; yet inevitably, the precedents could never do this without being supplemented by all sorts of other considerations. Systematising the law does not get around this problem entirely, but it does make the goal of working from the precedents alone somewhat more attainable. It makes it possible to begin thinking of avoiding uncertain and questionable grounds such as foreign precedents, or conclusions of common sense which (however confident you are of them personally) are at root mere matters of opinion. The move to a narrow and more technical conception of law is thus a direct if unintended consequence of attempts to expound the law more clearly.

The role of the academics in this is obscure. The treatise-writers of the Oxford Law Faculty – Anson, Pollock, Dicey, and others – were as bullish as one might have expected about the mess English law was in before the clever men of Oxford got to work on it; Pollock, for example, describing the former state of the law as being merely 'case law tempered by Fisher's Digests'.[29] But if the consequences are as I have described, then these changes were for the most part *unintended* consequences. Reading Pollock's own irascible commentaries on recent cases, or his private fulminations against those who tried to treat law as if it were a branch of geometry, it seems a little harsh to lay the increasing narrowness of legal argument at his door.

---

[28] *House of Commons Debates*, series 3, 209, cols 1243–44 (1 March 1872), quoted in R. Cocks, *Foundations of the Modern Bar* (London, 1983), p. 179. Coleridge was prepared to make exceptions for 'the law of real property, mercantile law, and the comparatively modern law of easements, the first two of which are highly scientific, and the last named is more or less scientific . . .'

[29] Quoted by Lord Wright MR, 'In Memoriam: Sir Frederick Pollock', *Law Quarterly Review* 54 (1937), pp. 151, 153.

It may be, in fact, that the influence of the academics lay not so much in their textbooks, or in any respect the bar had for their views – any such respect is a little hard to find – but in the mere fact that they were there at all. Just as in the earlier years of the nineteenth century the solicitors and attorneys had begun to chip away at the exalted status of the bar by ensuring that they, too, were increasingly *learned* professions, so the existence of a class of legal academics poked further holes in the bar's pretentions to be the sole custodians of the law. Law is no longer simply the private knowledge of a secretive guild of barristers. To know whether an argument sounds like a good one, it is no longer enough just to try on a few friends in the mess and see what they make of it; law becomes more bookish, less attuned to the culture of the Bar, rather more public property. Of course, the backlash comes in Bar humour: jokes, the point of which is that you can have an excellent knowledge of law-in-the-books and yet still be incapable of winning the simplest of cases,[30] if indeed you can find your way to the right court in the first place.[31] The real point is quietly admitted: a wedge has been driven between law and the practice of the bar, and they are now distinct.

2. Facts

The mirror-image question is about the facts, to which this law is applied. Of course, our whole way of teaching law today encourages us to treat facts as unproblematical: apart from small, optional courses on evidence and procedure, English and Welsh universities tend to teach law as if facts were givens. Yet obviously matters are different if facts are found by a jury, who may never discuss their findings publicly, and who are assumed by polite fiction to be following the judge's direction on the law. The idea that law was being applied to facts was at the earlier period theoretical only; the change consisted of its becoming actual.

The decline of the civil jury, then, is the flip-side of the increasingly complex law. It is necessary to emphasise this, if only because growing complexity of law does not necessarily and always lead to more lengthy judgments; as Goutal points out,[32] similar pressures in France over the same period did not have that effect at all. Victorian judges could afford to be brief and cutting in their reasoning; they did not usually have to take

[30] For example G. Alexander, *The Temple of the Nineties* (London, 1938) pp. 188–89.

[31] For example 'The Emeritus Professor of International Law and the Police Court Brief', 'O' (=Theo Mathew), *Forensic Fables*, pp. 147–49.

[32] J. Goutal, 'Characteristics of Judicial Style in France, Britain and the USA', *American Journal of Comparative Law*, 24 (1976), pp. 43, 62; and note the comments of Lawson, 'Comparative Judicial Style', *American Journal of Comparative Law*, 25 (1977), pp. 364, 367.

the really hard decisions. The common law could afford its reputation for harshness and simplicity, because it left the complexities to the jury. When the judges themselves have to handle these issues, it is hardly surprising that more careful enquiries are needed, and that the issues suddenly seem tremendously complicated. They always were, of course. It was all just hidden away.

So, on the professional side, we have three interlinked developments which together lead to a more complex set of facts for the law to get to work on, and so inevitably a more complex final legal product. There is the virtual disappearance of the civil jury; the growing length of trials; and a general softening of advocacy, so that the argument in court is less heated, and more directed at detailed factual enquiries. The decline of the jury was a slow process which is not, indeed, over.[33] The lengthening of trials and the softening of rhetoric are barely perceptible processes, except over a long period;[34] there was the occasional small explosion, such as the Court of Appeal's disciplining of Marshall Hall for carrying on in the rumbustious Victorian style, a dressing-down that almost ruined Hall's practice.[35]

3. Judges

My third factor here concerns the way the judges saw themselves and were seen by the bar. A judge is seen as a very important sort of a figure, doing a valued job. But what sort of a figure, and what sort of a job? Barristers, it seems, cannot help gossiping about the judges it is their job to convince. A history of this is hard to write – gossip does not improve with age – but two main conclusions can be drawn.

The first is that there is simply less and less interest, as time goes on, in individual judges and their foibles. As bench and bar grow in size, as lawyers become more specialised, as the number of judges that *all* lawyers could name goes down, it becomes more convincing to see the judges as occupying rather minor roles within the system of legal rules; and to see their personal idiosyncrasies as irritating departures from the norm, rather than as evidence of the independence of spirit that a great

[33] For a general survey see A.W.B. Simpson, 'The Survival of the Common Law System', in *Then and Now: Commemorating 175 years of London Bookselling and Publishing* (London, 1974), pp. 66–68.

[34] Both are commonplaces of legal memoirs. See for example C. Humphreys, *Both Sides of the Circle* (London, 1978), pp. 79–80. It should not be thought that it was only before judges sitting alone that the rhetoric grew calmer: on jury trials see P. Hastings, *Cases in Court* (London, 1953), pp. xi–xii, 232–35, 275–76, 331–32.

[35] See E. Marjoribanks, *The Life of Sir Edward Marshall Hall KC.* (London, 1929), ch. 7.

judge is entitled and bound to display. Originality becomes a vice rather than a virtue.

The second is that judges increasingly claim their status not as being important officers of state with the affairs of the nation in their charge, but as highly skilled specialists at the peak of their profession. This subtle change is well observed by Stevens,[36] who notes the continued ambiguity over whether the law lords were to be seen as members of the upper chamber of Parliament, or as simply distinguished lawyers who by historical accident had ended up at entirely the wrong place; and charting the eventual triumph of the 'professional' model.

For that matter, anyone with a tolerable knowledge of geography could guess what was going on simply from the titles. The early law lords were free to pick styles which emphasised their aristocratic pretentions, their country seats in the far hinterland many miles from London: Baron Wensleydale, say, or Earl Selborne. Yet by the turn of the century, it is becoming rather obvious where they really live. So we have Viscount Reading or Lord Esher. These people are obviously commuters. Esher is only one stop down the commuter line from Surbiton in fact. So after a while it becomes the almost universal practice to retain the name by which they had been known professionally: Lord Atkin, say, or Lord Wright.

These changes, I need hardly say, were by no means distinct from changes taking place at the same time at the bar. A good book to note here is Ray Cocks' *Foundations of the Modern Bar*,[37] by placing the changes in the attitudes of the bench alongside analogous changes at the bar. So just as legal argument narrowed and became more technical, so the qualities the bar lauded in famous advocates and judges were no longer those of the cultivated dilettante but of the narrow legal specialist. Just as the common law became more bookish and orientated towards precedent, so too bar ethics came to be written down. Just as law became less and less the preserve of the bar and more public property, so barristers became less and less subject to the opinion of the bar mess and more subject to general and abstract rules of discipline. The causation here was doubtless mutual.

4. Parliament

My fourth heading is that of the rise of an activist Parliament. In this respect the legal philosopher Austin was very far-sighted. If your legal system is headed by a sovereign, said Austin, who can change any law at all, then that sovereign controls the whole legal system. The question is not

---

[36] Stevens, *Law and Politics* (Chapel Hill, 1978).
[37] R. Cocks, *Foundations of the Modern Bar* (London, 1983).

whether the sovereign personally wrote all the existing laws. It is the ability to change them that gives responsibility, and any law *un*changed continues with the sovereign's authority.

As late as 1960 Hart was still denying this. Is it not rather silly, says Hart, to say that a complex body of law is 'impliedly authorised' by the sovereign? Surely this is a legal fiction? Is not the truth that the laws continue *despite* the sovereign's ability to change them, not *because* of them?[38] And if you envisage a 'sovereign' as a person with a crown sitting on a throne, this is of course quite true. If however your 'sovereign' is the colossus that is the modern state, controlling and consuming a respectable proportion of GDP, the case is somewhat altered. For most of this century, Austin's description is perfectly fair. Any bits of the common law still extant remain so at the sufferance of the state. They are there because a decision not to abolish them was made at some point, perhaps at several points.

From this it follows that the state is responsible for its own laws in a way it was not in (say) 1800, and the judiciary does *not* feel responsible. The Victorian judges consistently, and sometimes even passionately, sought to demonstrate that what they were doing was right, reasonable and in full accord with the dictates of public policy; whereas the norm later was to show rigorously that, right or wrong, it was the *law* that was being applied, and not some arbitrary whim of a judge. A century ago, the great judicial fear was to be seen to be acting unreasonably; later, it was to be seen to be making law.

Interestingly, it was the *judges* who, by the end of the period, expressed most concern about arbitrary judicial whims, who suggested that signs of individuality from their own colleagues threatened to bring down the arch of civilisation. 'Underneath our wigs and gowns', they bleated pathetically, 'we are actually very dangerous people.' This was quite contrary to the Victorian practice, where it was the Bar who openly worried about the judges, and insisted that the collective opinion of the bar was an important aspect of civil liberties because it provided 'a check on the judges'.

There are various landmarks in the inter-war period. An interesting incident showing the changes in values is the attempt in the early 1920s to stop Edward Carson from complaining about the terms of settlement over Ireland, by making him a law lord. It did not work, of course. Carson knew of no convention that law lords should not make controversial speeches – why should not a member of the upper house make political speeches? – and the government's initiative in having this debated in the House of Lords rapidly revealed that most of the other law lords had not heard of it, either. Yet the evident opinion of the lay peers that this was conduct unbecoming a judge had its effect. The convention was established in defiance of the lawyers' opinions.[39]

---

[38] H. Hart, *The Concept of Law* (Oxford, 1961), pp. 62–64.
[39] On this controversy see S. Shetreet, *Judges on Trial* (Amsterdam, 1976), pp. 257–58.

It is in relations between the judges and Labour that the change became most obvious. It was of course a very unstable situation: the electorate had moved several steps to the left while the judges, with the rest of the professional classes, had stayed pretty much where they were. It was apparent from the start that relations would be somewhat frayed. The ambiguous position of the lord chancellor came to the fore. Traditionally this person must be a prominent lawyer-politician of the ruling party. Yet there was no person that could fill that job-description when the party was Labour. In the end Labour settled first for a prominent lawyer-politician from another party – Viscount Haldane thus having the dubious distinction of being both the last Liberal lord chancellor *and* the first Labour one – and then for Viscount Sankey, who while arguably a Labour supporter was an undistinguished lawyer, and no sort of politician at all: he was the first example of that strange if harmless breed, the non-political Lord Chancellor.[40]

5. Accountability

My final factor is the rise of effective means of appeal. It was noted right from the time of the Judicature Acts that one important effect of the greater availability of appeal was to alter the atmosphere of first-instance hearings. Coleridge complained in 1889 (in a private letter to Lindley) that it reduced the lower courts to 'note-takers and hearers of dress rehearsals for the court of appeal', which he thought made them 'hasty and slovenly.'[41] Yet the long-run effect was, I would argue, rather the reverse: to make the first-instance judges *more* careful, *more* determined to render their judgments appeal-proof.

Counsel were fully aware of the tactical possibilities left open by appeals. G.D. Roberts gives various examples. One case is where a trial judge decides against him on a point of evidence. Roberts is sure the judge is making a mistake and considers what to do. His decision is to remonstrate with the judge further. Wrong move. This time the judge agrees with him, and retracts the earlier ruling. Roberts thus loses what would have been a plain ground for overturning his client's eventual conviction. 'Fifteen months', wails Roberts, 'and all because I did not know how to keep my mouth shut.'[42] Or again, he narrates the cautionary tale of

[40] On Sankey's chancellorship see R. Heuston, *Lives of the Lord Chancellors, 1885–1940* (Oxford, 1964), pp. 499–538. For leftish criticism of the legal system in this period, see for example *Justice in England; By a Barrister* (London, 1938).

[41] 22 September 1889; reprinted in *Life and Correspondence of Lord Coleridge* volume ii p. 362.

[42] G.D. Roberts, *Law and Life* (London, 1964), pp. 28–29.

a prosecution colleague of his, who casually made a racist remark about Jewish moneylenders while questioning a witness. This was not farsighted. The appeal was important enough to be heard by the Lord Chief Justice, Rufus Isaacs, himself, who saw this particular remark in the transcript, and in open court demanded an explanation. Counsel is reduced to mumbling that he never meant to suggest that Jewish moneylenders are any more dishonest than Christian ones. Eventually the Lord Chief Justice allows him to resume his argument, which is somewhat subdued, and fails to convince the court.[43]

So the effect of appeal on that generation of advocates was profound; and by the time they became judges themselves, there was the further factor of a more aggressive style of appeal hearing, typified by Scrutton LJ.[44] A particularly nasty example occurred in 1932, on the hearing of an appeal from McCardie J. in an action for enticement.[45] McCardie had talked at some length on recent changes in the status of women, arguing that they made many of the presuppositions of the law of enticement rather dubious, and that a particular 200-year-old case he did not want to follow had lost whatever relevance it might once have had.

The response of Scrutton in the Court of Appeal was positively incandescent: 'I think that the less sociological knowledge that is brought into the discussion of these questions the better . . . I think these things are better left out of legal questions.' He also opined that bachelor judges like McCardie should keep their opinions of married life to themselves, and was also gratuitously critical of an earlier judgment where McCardie had officially pronounced – quite properly – on what was the proper underclothing for respectable women. These remarks provoked a fierce reply from McCardie himself, who announced that he would no longer co-operate with the appeal process in any case until assured that Scrutton was not involved. It was only with considerable difficulty that Lord Hanworth managed to get the two to patch up their dispute.

While an extreme case, this illustrates the pressure the Court of Appeal could bring to bear. It also illustrates the *type* of effect that this pressure brought about. If McCardie had struck with the 200-year-old precedent, he would have been safe; if he had found some technical way of distinguishing

---

[43] *Ibid.*, pp. 34–35. See also pp. 66–67, where Roberts successfully overturns a murder conviction for misdirection. He had not complained of the misdirection at trial because he had not noticed it: '[The defendants] probably never realised that they owed their lives to my negligence!'

[44] See for example G. Alexander, *The Temple of the Nineties* (London, 1938), pp. 140–41.

[45] For a detailed, if partisan, account of the incident, see G. Pollock, *Mr Justice McCardie* (London, 1934), chs xix-xx. The report at (1932) 48 *TLR* 428 is presumably close to what Scrutton actually said; it contains the remark about 'sociology', though not the more insulting remarks. The official law reports version has been heavily edited, and contains none of this: [1932] KB 497.

it, he might have had a chance. His mistake was to say what he was doing, and why. The drive towards even more careful adherence to the precedents, in the face of whatever other arguments might be available, was thus reinforced through the appeal process. This was enhanced still further through legal specialism: the higher up the judicial tree you went, the less likely you were to be an expert on the precise matter under consideration. Adherence to precedent became the only technique available, the technique of last resort by a court that did not otherwise have the understanding to do anything at all.

Of course, as we know the legal system did not grind to a halt in 1940. Plainly the reports could not continue to grow; the economics of law publishing forbade them. Neither did the doctrine of precedent become yet narrower; after the *Bristol Aeroplane* case in 1944, it had sunk to its lowest point, and there was nowhere for it to go but up.

11

Planning Law and Precedent:
A Study in Twentieth-Century Law Reporting

Raymond Cocks

Planning law has done much to determine the appearance of twentieth century Britain. It has been the chief instrument for preserving the countryside through imposing restrictions on farmers seeking to convert their land to non-agricultural uses.[1] It has been the most important of the means adopted for controlling the precise location of new factories and houses.[2] It has even been used with a view to regulating standards of design.[3] Of necessity, such a body of law has had to be wide-ranging and detailed, and it is not surprising that precedent in this area has developed distinctive qualities of its own in the course of its brief history.

Planning law was created by the Housing, Town Planning, etc., Act (1909),[4] and since that date it has given rise to two distinctive bodies of reports. There have been numerous decisions by inspectors appointed by successive Secretaries of State; and there have been many decisions by courts such as the Divisional Court, the Court of Appeal and the House of Lords. The decisions of the inspectorate merit immediate attention. They serve as a reminder that the historical analysis of precedent cannot be approached entirely through conventional legal reasoning of the sort that is found in the courts and which provides the source for law reports. The decisions of the inspectorate have to be viewed 'in their own right' and they provide a challenge to a legal historian who is used to the 'established' sources.

Inspectors have been appointed by Secretaries of State to hear inquiries and appeals relating to many issues. For example they hear appeals from those who have been refused permission for development when they

---

[1] See, for example, P. Hall et al. *The Containment of Urban England*, vols i and ii (London, 1973).

[2] See, for example, M. Grant, *Urban Planning Law* (London, 1982).

[3] See, for example, J.B. Cullingworth, *Town and Country Planning in Britain* (10 edn, London, 1988) particularly at pp. 208–12.

[4] (9 Edw. 7, c. 44). For a discussion of the early years see, for example, E. Reade, *British Town and Country Planning* (Milton Keynes, 1987) ch. 2.

have applied to local authority planning committees.[5] In such a context the Inspector may be deciding on the fate of a major scheme for the provision of hundreds of houses; or he may be dealing with the right of a householder to use his property for the breeding of dogs. The decisions are often full of the details of life in particular areas and the problems arising out of individual circumstances. Frequently, Inspectors have to balance the need for economic progress against the possibility of environmental damage. Many of the cases go to the heart of popular debates about social justice and the preservation of amenities.

Of course, this raises numerous issues in the history of modern constitutional law. There is a major study to be written on how politicians and others came to think that decisions of this type were unsuited to both the courts and civil servants. We need an explanation as to why it was that tribunals came to be seen as the most desirable method for making planning decisions.[6]

For present purposes, the central issue is the distinctive quality of the decisions produced by these Inspectors. It is just because the written decisions of the Inspectors frequently refer in such detail to local social and geographical facts that their decisions appear to be unlike law reports. In technical terms they do not make for conventional precedents because it is very rare for them to be in any way binding. In general they do not bind the courts or Inspectors in other cases. They are not even mentioned in discussions of precedent in student books on the 'English Legal System'; nor are they found in leading academic studies of precedent.[7]

Yet it is necessary for the historian of precedent to consider them because they are used again and again by practitioners when giving advice to clients contemplating appeals. As a matter of historical reality they are influential because they are regarded as being influential. Despite the fact that they are not binding they are seen as being useful in providing guidance as to how Inspectors are likely to react to different types of case. At one time selections of them were published by departments of government. Now Sweet and Maxwell produce a bi-monthly series of reports.[8] One agency offers ready access to over 30,000 recent decisions.[9] Professional realities render technical doctrines of precedent irrelevant.

[5] The Planning Inspectorate is considered by M. Grant, *Urban Planning Law*, at pp. 44–46.

[6] See ibid., p. 44: Planning Inspectors are the quasi-judicial arm of the Department, and consider references at pp. 44–46 to further studies. Of course, this is part of a broad debate about the use of tribunals in the modern system of justice.

[7] For example, there is no reference to them in R. Cross and J.W. Harris, *Precedent in English Law* (4th edn, Oxford, 1991). But tribunals are mentioned at p. 124.

[8] 'Planning Appeal Decisions'.

[9] 'Compass': see *Planning*, 1029, 30 July, 1993, p. 2.

Appeals to Inspectors: Precedents and Social Life

In discussions of law reporting it is common for legal historians to comment on the extent to which the reports under analysis reveal significant information relating to procedure and little – sometimes nothing – about the facts of the case. Here, the reverse may be so. The report appears to consist almost entirely of a summary of those facts which are seen to be most relevant to the case in hand. Of course, the assessment of what is relevant will often be a matter of law, but these legal issues may be assumed by the parties involved, or else spelled out with brevity.

Consider, for example, the Bulletin of Selected Appeals for September, 1947. Appeal 1/6 stated that:

The appellants were the owners of a factory used for heavy industry consisting of a number of buildings of different size and design, which had been erected over a period of years on land situated at the rear of a terrace of small houses in a predominantly residential neighbourhood. In addition they were using some houses in or adjoining this terrace for industrial purposes as offices and stores. The neighbourhood in general was one which had seen better days, many of the houses now being occupied by more than one family.

The appellants applied for permission to erect a new two-storey building with a three-ton crane on one of two alternative sites, each of which would involve the demolition of two adjoining houses, with the object of meeting their manufacturing needs by increasing the number of their employees and of improving working conditions. Permission for both applications was refused by the Council on the ground that the industrial use of the proposed building would be out of conformity with the intended zoning of the area for residential purposes, and would be likely to affect adversely the amenities of the surrounding property.

The appeals were dismissed 'on the ground that the intrusion of a heavy industry into an area surrounded by dwelling-houses and, except in the immediate vicinity, entirely residential, was contrary to the interests of the community, and that further haphazard expansion by means of the conversion of adjoining houses would increase the detrimental effect on the neighbourhood without satisfactorily meeting the requirements of a modern factory'.

These observations provide a picture of social and economic tensions in post-war Britain.[10] The report reveals a concern for 'balance'. The industrialist has put forward a proposal which would enhance local prospects for employment and, in a tiny way, assist the country's economy at a time of acute difficulty. But, against this, there is a concern for

---

[10] For a discussion of such tensions see K. Middlemas, *Politics in Industrial Society* (London, 1979), ch. 14; and P. Hennessy, *Never Again: Britain 1945–1951* (1992); particularly ch. 4, 'Building Jerusalem'.

amenities. There were young families in the area, and a residential context was hardly appropriate for such a heavy installation.

The last sentence of the decision points towards an attempt at the reconciliation of economic and social considerations with the suggestion that the particular proposal would not meet the requirements of a modern factory. This, surely, was a reflection of the concerns of a government which was engaged in a programme of radical nationalisation, but which at the same time was anxious not to appear hostile to businessmen.[11] The tone of the decision, as well as the precise use of words such as 'modern', reveals that the report of the case is in part a reflection of current concerns and in part a recommendation to those involved in giving advice in future cases which might be found to be similar.

Examples such as this could be given many times over. Taken as a whole the reports of decisions by Inspectors do much to reveal changes in the economic and social life of England. Because of the range and extent of their interference with modern life it might be argued that the cases show that planning law had come to assume a number of roles previously regulated by other bodies of law. For example, the late E.P. Thompson wrote of the changing role of eighteenth-century criminal law in English society.[12] It was used in new ways to regulate the access of non-property owners to open spaces; it restricted the ways in which they could earn a living; it prevented them from acquiring food in what were taken to be traditional ways. Generally, it did an increasing amount to regulate the everyday life of communities. In a similar style, planning law has become the twentieth-century instrument for regulating access to resources such as open spaces and the location of work-places. Its influence upon everyday life has been powerful and intricate, and it is inevitable that the decisions arising out of this invasive role have reflected social tensions. It is a vivid example of a particular type of law report providing a picture of the society which produced it.

In drawing attention to this form of reporting the present paper invites more than the study of the constitutional issues mentioned above. It also suggests the further comparative study of similar types of decisions in other areas of law. There are a significant number of other examples of decisions made by those who have not been judges but who have sat in what might be called a semi-administrative capacity. Obvious examples include, in the nineteenth century, the Guardians of the Poor or much of the work of those who sat at quarter sessions. At a later date there is the work of tribunals charged with hearing disputes about labour law or tax law or social security law.

---

[11] Ibid.

[12] For instance, (to give the most general example possible) in *Whigs and Hunters: The Origin of the Black Act* (Harmondsworth, 1977).

If non-court decisions of this type have any distinctive quality it lies in the immediacy and strength of the pictures they reveal of social life. For the most part unencumbered by procedural issues and lengthy references to previous decisions, they take the reader directly to the details of the everyday problems of individuals and communities.

The Law Reports

There are now some thousands of law reports relating to planning issues. Many involve appeals from Inspectors to the courts, with appellants seeking to persuade judges that an Inspector had misdirected himself on the law. Some arise out of attempts to challenge the decisions of local government committees. In many ways the reports reflect the numerous changes there have been in planning legislation since it was first created in the Housing, Town Planning, etc., Act, 1909. In particular, there are contrasts between the sort of issues which faced the courts in the years before 1947 and those which subsequently arose out of attempts to interpret a major, reforming Act of that year.[13] But it will be argued here that the law reports were not, as it were, some mere foot-note to changes on the statute book. Precedent had a significant dimension of its own.

In the early years there were notably few reports on the sections of the new legislation.[14] In part this may have been because the arrangements for enforcing the terms of the new schemes were minimal; it was as if they were expected to work through a process of negotiation and agreement. In one of the few cases which came to court the defendant to the proceedings had been responsible for placing two petrol pumps in a position which put the pumps in conflict with the local scheme.[15] After conviction in the magistrate's court he appealed to the divisional court where the conviction was upheld but a fine of only four shillings was imposed. A court which was, surely, sympathetic to the rights of a property owner made no reference to grand issues of principle arising out of the new powers of the state. It sought what might be called a practical solution to a minor dispute. The major issues were not made explicit.

[13] The Town and Country Planning Act (1947) (10 and 11 Geo. 6, c. 51). For a commentary on the Act see H.A. Hill, *The Complete Law of Town and Country Planning* (4th edn, London, 1949).

[14] For an analysis of these reports see S.D. Mordey, 'Major Aspects of the Development of Statutory Town Planning, 1909–1932', vols i and ii (unpublished LL.M. thesis, University of Birmingham, 1979), at p. 263–293.

[15] *Mackenzie* v. *Abbott* (1926) 7. S.J. 358; 24 L.G.R. 44. The case is discussed ibid., pp. 277–79. The pumps were beyond the building line. The court consisted of Lord Hewart CJ, Shearman and Roche JJ.

There was more judicial activity in respect of the provisions which fixed the amount of compensation which was available to landowners who had the value of their property reduced by the new type of scheme. It was only to be expected that this would give rise to disputes because the restrictions on the right to compensation were extensive and complicated. But, again, the response of the courts was – with one exception – to concentrate upon points of legislative detail and not to discuss the 'rights of the citizen'. The exception was a judgment of Scrutton J. who took a view which advanced the social purposes of the legislation at the expense of the property-owner in question.[16] It stands alone as an indication of what might have been produced; it shows that there could have been a contentious and substantial body of case law.

In contrast, the case law relating to planning which did develop during these years was on what might be called the frontier of the subject. In some respects this took forms which look strange today but which were less surprising to contemporaries. For example, the licensing committees of local authorities decided on the distribution of public houses by the indirect means of controlling who might be given a licence to run such a place. At the time they had such high social status that they felt able to assert that they, and not any novel form of planning authority, had the final say in the distribution of licensed premises.[17] They won in a decision at the level of the magistrate's but thereafter the matter was left unresolved, with (presumably) attempts to reach mutual agreement on the part of the committees. Eventually, the legislation of 1947 decided the issue by giving the planning authority the right to decide on the location of what might become a public house.[18]

Of greater legal significance were decisions arising out of uncertainty as to the relationship between planning law and property law. Town planning schemes imposed burdens on the land affected by them. The

[16] *Ellis* v *Ruislip-Northwood UDC* (1920), 1 KB 343, 83 JP 273, 35 TLR, 17 LGR 607. Amongst other issues this case involved the notoriously difficult provisions of section 59 (2) of the Housing, Town Planning, etc., Act, 1909 (9 Edw. 7, c. 44). Scrutton LJ was sufficiently adventurous to attempt a definition of 'amenity': 'the word 'amenity' is obviously used very loosely; it is, I think, novel in an Act of Parliament, and appears to mean 'pleasant circumstances or features, advantages'. In considering Mr Ellis' failure to obtain compensation Scrutton LJ observed (at p. 370) that 'Parliament appears to have sacrificed the individual to the welfare of the area possibly thinking that the increased value of the rest of the land would compensate him for the fetter imposed on part of the land. However, its motives are not for me; it is only my duty to interpret and apply its enactments'. Mordey, The Development of Statutory Town Planning, discusses the case at pp. 263–70.

[17] Ibid., p. 279–82.

[18] For discussion of the issues in 1929 to 1932 see JP 93, p. 630; 94, p. 105; 174 LT 269. See, too, references in the preface to T.J. Sophian, *Town and Country Planning Legislation, 1933–1945* (1945).

case of *Re Forsey and Hollebone's Contract* produced a decision of the court of Appeal which caused alarm to conveyancers.[19] The property was in Eastbourne and it was subject to a resolution of the borough council by which it was incorporated within a town planning scheme. The resolution was registered as a land charge despite the fact that steps had not been taken to implement the scheme and it had not been approved by the minister. The timing of events was such that neither of the parties in the case knew of the resolution at the date of the contract. In response, the buyer took out a summons asking for a declaration that good title had not been shown to the property. The details of the argument are not in point for present purposes. What was significant in this context was the extent to which it became clear that planning law occupied an as yet uncertain place in property law. There was no clear understanding as to what place a mere resolution of a council had in land law. By itself it was akin to a statement of intent to do things which would change rights over the land. The notion of *potential* interests was complicated and unsettling. Obviously, this sort of uncertainty was likely to puzzle property lawyers attempting to be sure about which interests would bind buyers and which would not. The practical result of the case was that buyers had to carry out various searches at an earlier stage than had previously been the case. After repeated demands for reform Parliament changed the law in 1969, but for the whole of the mid-twentieth century the new planning provisions had had a disruptive impact upon this area of property law.[20]

There were similar problems in respect of issues relating to what we would now call administrative law. In particular, there was interest in whether *certiorari* was available in respect of decisions on the part of planning committees. It had been assumed that it would not be available because the decisions of local authorities were usually perceived as being of an executive nature: it was expected that, if questioned by the courts, they would be subject to *mandamus*. However, in *R. v. Hendon Rural District Council ex parte Chorley* (1933), the court held that in respect of two decisions the Hendon Rural District Council's Committee for Plans and Highways had been exercising a judicial discretion.[21] The court took account of

[19] [1927] 2 Ch. 379; (1927) WN 248; 97 LT Ch. 4; 138 LT 26; 25 LGR 442; 71 SJ 823; 91 JP 182. Discussed in Mordey, 'The Development of Statutory Town Planning', pp. 282–90.

[20] For more recent discussion of the case see D.G. Barnsley, *Barnsley's Conveyancing Law and Practice* (3rd edn, London, 1988), pp. 189, 199, 352. The provision reversing the controversial decision is the Law of Property Act 1969, section 24(1).

[21] [1933] 2 KB. 696, 31 Section 332, 97 JP 210, 49 TLR 48, 148 LI 535, 102 LJKB 658. It is discussed in Mordey, 'The Development of Statutory Town Planning, 1909–1932', pp. 291–93. Lord Hewart CJ, Avory J and Humphreys J were chiefly influenced by the reasoning in *Rex v. Electricity Commissioners, Ex parte London Electricity Joint Committee Co.* [1924] 1 KB 171.

the fact that the resolution was advertised, objections were invited and considered, and the decision conferred legal rights and affected legal rights. This case, and a few others of these years, created a considerable potential for planning disputes in the courts but, as Mordey emphasises in his helpful and detailed study of the cases, it was only much later that this potential was to be realised.[22]

With so little case law relating directly to the new provisions for planning it is not surprising that when the reader turns to the early practitioners' guides he even finds references to cases arising out of different subjects. At times, planning issues were interpreted by reference to the past interpretations given to words in statutes which had nothing to do with planning law. For example, the significance of such cases can be seen in part of the commentary by Ivor Jennings on the Town and Country Planning Act of 1932.[23] To a large extent, he was concerned with giving an exposition of the various sections of planning legislation which had been passed by Parliament. But in explaining these sections he was, in places, driven to refer to cases decided in different contexts. He provided a detailed analysis of cases arising under previous Acts concerned with public health and highways and proceeded to show how in some respects they may provide guidance on the interpretation of the words 'a person aggrieved'. For instance, he used the older cases to suggest that an ordinary rate-payer is not 'a person aggrieved'.[24] Sometimes cases relating to other Acts were used by him to provide guidance on an issue which was clearly of major importance. In various sections Parliament had stated that 'The validity of a provision shall not be called in question'. This clear attempt to prevent the intervention of the courts into some aspects of the new law led Jennings to look at cases under housing legislation. For example, in *R*. v. *Minister of Health, ex parte Davis* (1929) and *Minister of Health* v. *The King, ex parte Yaffe* (1931) it had been stated that such words in housing legislation had prevented proceedings by prohibition or *certiorari*.[25] Arguments such as these went to the heart of the new legislation yet the author was not using planning cases to resolve them.

In looking at these years as a whole the reports of planning cases seem almost to suggest that planning law was not seen as a distinct subject suited to the full development of its own case law. The majority of reports used

---

[22] Mordey, 'The Development of Statutory Town Planning', at, for example, p. 263. From an early date, some had foreseen the potential. 'The era of State control of building operations is now in its inception. It will be for the next generation to judge of its results': E. Jenks, *Stephen's Commentaries on the Laws of England*, (17th edn, London, 1922), i, *Public Law*, p. 594.

[23] I. Jennings, *The Law Relating to Town and Country Planning* (London, 1933).

[24] Ibid., p. 70 n. 2.

[25] Ibid., p. 71 n. 4. The references to the respective cases are: [1929] 1 KB 619; 27 LGR 677; and [1931] AC 494; 29 LGR 305.

by the lawyers either relate to attempts to incorporate planning law in a satisfactory manner into other subjects which already existed (such as land law or housing law), or they are decisions under other areas of legislation. It was as if planning law by itself did not 'breathe'. The law reports reveal that the subject was of little interest to the legal minds of the day. There is something paradoxical about the fact that the cases which were used are to be found in a great variety of series of reports. They may be found in *Appeal cases*, the *All England Law Reports*, the *Weekly Law Reports*, the *Chancery Reports*, the *Justice of the Peace*, the *Local Government Reports*, the *Solicitors Journal* and elsewhere. At first sight this would suggest that there was widespread interest in the new subject of planning law in its own right. In fact, when the cases are looked at, it becomes clear the lawyers for the most part saw planning law as an intrusion into other areas of law rather than as a subject which could be understood in its own terms. Before a substantial body of cases concerned exclusively with planning law could emerge there would need to be changes in the law.

An Identity for Modern Planning Law Reports

The Town and Country Planning Act of 1947 introduced radical reforms.[26] Planning law was now of relevance to most landowners who sought to carry out most forms of development. In practice, a landowner would have to obtain permission from a local planning authority before carrying out substantial building or arranging for any significant change in the use of the land. Given the extent to which people have always become emotionally involved with the fate of their property, and the greatly increased scope of th law's range, it was safe to predict that an increased volume of case law was only a matter of time.

This new area of law was of interest to publishers. In particular it attracted the attention of the legal publishers Sweet and Maxwell. John Burke and Peter Allsop have pointed out that Sweet and Maxwell were faced with something of a crisis in the years immediately following the Second World War.[27] For example, as a result of enemy action, the whole of the sheet stock, the manuscript copy and the paper stock of the *Encyclopedia of the Laws of England* had been destroyed and publication had to be suspended.[28] There was also concern at the way in which other major

---

[26] For a contemporary guide to the Act see H.A. Hill, *The Complete Law of Town and Country Planning* (4th ed, London, 1949).

[27] *Then and Now, 1799–1974: Commemorating 175 Years of Law Bookselling and Publishing.* (no editor given) (London, 1974), section on 'Law Publishing Today' by John Burke and Peter Allsop, pp. 137–51.

[28] Founded by Sir Frederick Pollock, the chief work was done by A.W. Renton as editor (1897–1903); there was a third edition, edited by E.A. Jelf (1938–1940).

works such as Mew's *Digest of English Case Law*[29] and Chitty's *Statutes of Practical Utility*[30] had been losing ground to more modern competitors. There was a view that some new departure was called for.

The first initiative was *Current Law* published in 1947.[31] This was designed to provide up-to-date information on changes in the law: it gave 'all the law from every source'. It was an instantaneous success and encouraged further novelties. In the words of Allsop and Burke 'the second breakthrough came in 1948'. The Town and Country Planning Act of 1947 came into force on 1 July 1948 when the

> legal profession and the owners and managers of property were in a state of some uncertainty as to its effects. At exactly the right moment there appeared the *Journal of Planning Law*. Its team of experts in all aspects of planning law, headed by Mr (now Sir) Desmond Heap, proceeded to lead its bemused public, month by month, through the maze of the new legislation. The *Journal* had an even more immediate success than *Current Law* and confirmed in the minds of the profession the impression of liveliness at Sweet and Maxwell.[32]

The significance of this for the reporting of planning law was not at first apparent. In the early editions of the new *Journal* there was an emphasis on articles which gave practitioners the chance to come to terms with the principles of what was in many respects a new subject. However, it was not very long before the courts began to hear cases involving the new law and, for obvious reasons, these were reported in the *Journal*.[33] For the first time planning law cases were being reported in a journal devoted exclusively to the subject. In this sort of context there is nothing surprising in the fact that the emphasis was more and more on what might be called pure issues of planning law. There was much more planning law to give rise to litigation, and there was a journal designed to respond to the disputes with commentaries and analysis. It was as if, in the legal world, planning law and its precedents had achieved an identity which previously had been lacking. They were no longer seen merely in terms of the problems they presented to other subjects.

In the words of Allsop and Burke: 'On the sound military principle of reinforcing success planning law was reinforced by the publication in

---

[29] The first edition of this *Digest* appeared in 1884. Between the two world wars most of the work on the *Digest* and its *Supplements* was done by Aubrey J. Spencer.

[30] Originally produced in 1829 by Joseph Chitty, there was an edition of 1913 produced by V.M. Lely.

[31] John Burke was the general editor of *Current Law*.

[32] *Then and Now, 1799–1974*, p. 139. The managing editor was John Burke, and the editorial board was D. Heap, H. Potter, E.J. Rimmer and E.C. Strathon.

[33] For example, the *Journal* for June 1951 contained 'Notes of Cases', 'Lands Tribunal Decisions' and 'Notes of Planning Decisions'.

1950 of the *Planning and Compensation Reports* (subsequently to widen its scope and become *Property and Compensation Reports*).'[34] The combination of the new *Journal* and this new series of reports pointed to the assured position of planning law in the post-war legal world. Their success reveals a strong and sustained interest in the subject on the part of lawyers. In this instance a change in the volume and style of law reporting may be seen as a response to changes in the nature of professional work.

Going beyond this, it may be possible to suggest that the method of producing law reports could do something to influence professional practice and, perhaps, even to change the law. In the case of planning law after the legislation of 1947, the change in reporting pointed not just towards an increase in planning work on the part of the profession but also towards the enhanced role of the printed page in the development of the subject's doctrines. It was now possible for problems to be considered in full, and for principles and concepts which would otherwise have remained undeveloped to be made explicit. Fully to justify this argument would require writing the history of post-war planning law. But at least it is possible to point to particular developments which appear to reveal a positive role for the new methods of reporting for planning. For example, the notion of the 'planning unit' was not to be found in statute law until the mid 1980s. Before that time it may be seen as the product of post-war judicial creativity, and, just because of this, it may also be seen as the product of the intellectual and professional opportunities afforded by a particular method of law reporting which provided the 'platform' for discussion in court.[35] In other words, it is suggested that in the context of planning the methods of reporting did something to determine the substance of the law. At the least, it may be argued that they made it easier for planning law to be considered independently of other subjects.

[34] *Then and Now, 1799–1974*, p. 140.
[35] See M. Grant, *Urban Planning Law*, particularly at pp. 167–71.